Selected Addresses of Clarence Steves C.S.B.

Text is set in *Palatino* typeface with
title and headings in *Desdemona* type.

Paperback: ISBN: 978-0-9645803-7-4
Kindle: ISBN: 978-1-68007-014-9

First edition
Third Issue

Published
by

Healing
Unlimited
(800) 962-1464
heal@ChristianScience.org
http://www.ChristianScience.org

Printed in the United States of America
and other countries.

Addresses

About the Author

Clarence Steves was a Christian Science teacher from 1948 through 1962. He came in to Christian Science through a healing following World War I. He served in the navy in World War I, was severely wounded and spent a number of years in a Veterans Hospital. There a hospital nurse offered him a copy of Science and Health with Key to the Scriptures by Mary Baker Eddy. He devoured it. The passage that awoke him and brought his healing was 228: 3-6, particularly "...that nothing inharmonious can enter being, for Life *is* God." He had Primary Class with Judge Clifford P. Smith and entered the full-time practice. He was a member of the Normal Class of 1946, and became a teacher.

His wife was also a *Journal* listed practitioner, and they taught and practiced in Washington, D.C. He had prepared his address on *Love* for his 1963 Association, but passed on in March, 1963. His last address was read by his wife and two students at the 1963 Association meeting.

Mr. Steves was most fondly remembered for his lack of personal sense, which enabled him to state the Truth so clearly. Absence of personal sense is a main theme expressed throughout his addresses, and he himself was a living example of what he taught.

The Scientific Statement Of Being
Association Address of 1952

by

Clarence Steves

When Mary Baker Eddy was healed through reading the Bible story of the palsied man, she knew she had touched the current of spiritual healing so evident in the life of Jesus. Now let us read an account of this healing:

And they come unto him, bringing one sick of the palsy, which was borne of four.

When they could not come nigh unto him for the press, they uncovered the roof where he was: and when they had broken it up, they let down the bed wherein the sick of the palsy lay.

When Jesus saw their faith, he said unto the sick of the palsy, Son, thy sins be forgiven thee.

But there were certain of the scribes sitting there, and reasoning in their hearts,

Why doth this man thus speak blasphemies? Who can forgive sins but God only?

And immediately when Jesus perceived in his spirit that they so reasoned within themselves, he said unto them, Why reason ye these things in your hearts?

Whether is it easier to say to the sick of the palsy, Thy sins be forgiven thee; or to say, Arise, and take up thy bed, and walk?

But that ye may know that the Son of man hath power on earth to forgive sins, (he saith to the sick of the palsy,)

I say unto thee, Arise, and take up thy bed, and go thy way into thine house.

And immediately he arose, took up the bed, and went forth

before them all; insomuch that they were all amazed, and glorified God, saying, We never saw it in this fashion.

Was it simply the reading of this healing that healed her? It had been read many times before but without any healing effect. Was it the words which healed? Was it what Jesus said? Or was it that she discerned that there was principle behind the healing? That it was not Jesus who healed the man; that it was not the words he spoke which had any healing in or of themselves; but it was the Christ-understanding present as the identity of the Master which had healed? In *The Life of Mary Baker Eddy* by Sybil Wilbur, on page 130, we read:

"It was to me a revelation of Truth," she has written. "The lost chord of Truth, healing as of old. I caught this consciously from the Divine Harmony. The miracles recorded in the Bible which had before seemed to me supernatural, grew divinely natural and apprehensible. Adoringly I discerned the principle of His holy heroism and Christian example. . ."

A spiritual experience so deep was granted her that she realized eternity in a moment, infinitude in limitation, life in the presence of death. She could not utter words of prayer; her spirit realized. She knew God face to face; she "touched and handled things unseen." In that moment all pain evanesced into bliss, all discord in her physical body melted into harmony, all sorrow was translated into rapture. She recognized this state as her rightful condition as a child of God. Love invaded her, life lifted her, truth irradiated her. God said to her, "Daughter, arise!."'

Many years later, the Discoverer of the Science saw the law behind the healings of Jesus. In the Christian Science textbook, *Science and Health with Key to the Scriptures*, she could write: "The starting point of divine Science is that God, Spirit, is All-in-all, and that there is no other might nor Mind, — that God is Love, and therefore He is divine Principle."

The formation of this Principle was beginning to take shape, but it was to come forward clearly and distinctly only when this woman, working in the realm of divine metaphysics, discarded the human mind as a factor in the healing work.

This intrepid Discoverer had outlived Quimby and his personal magnetism, and had seen that it was the personality of this man, rather than divine law, which seemed to heal the sick. This wise Leader saw that this revelation could not stand on personalities for it would then be lost to the ages. Witchcraft had but recently been wiped out in New England. Here was a woman daring to rise above the religious atmosphere of her surroundings and investigate spiritual law and spiritual healing.

As the investigation went on, she learned valuable lessons from her efforts to explain the principle aspects of this spiritual law to the human mind. As each one appeared, the clear-sighted Discoverer saw the incorrectness of the position, corrected her course, and sailed further away from matter and the human mind.

Mrs. Glover, as she was then known, had tried for months to persuade those who were more akin to her in social and intellectual heritage to accept the truth she had to impart. Some loved her, but were impervious to her doctrine. A Unitarian clergyman of Lynn and his wife were friendly, but they feared for their faith when she spoke to them of God as Principle. But a Mr. Hiram Crafts appeared on the scene, and she guided him and taught him daily. Soon he was able to demonstrate and set up an office for practice. But Mrs. Crafts was filled with dissatisfaction and suspicion by her doubting relatives. Soon Hiram Crafts withdrew. But fortunately before this took place, a certain work had been accomplished which could not be undone. One experience taught her that not only could she herself heal, but she could impart the understanding of the *modus operandi* to another. She could detach the work from herself,

Step 3:

and separate it from her personality. What remained was to give the discovery its scientific statement.

Another experience showed her the obstructionism of superstition. Still another experience with a student uncovered personal mesmerism and spiritualism.

There appeared a Mr. Tuttle. He was the exemplification of superstition, and could only accept what Mrs. Glover was teaching if it had the coloring of his ignorance of divine light. He fell away because the light became too bright. Then came a Mr. Stanley. He was the dogmatic Baptist and argued for what he believed to be correct theological teaching. Mrs. Glover endeavored to lift him above his misconception of God; but it was no use because he only wanted to verify a position which he had taken, and our Leader saw this would only delay the full revelation. She was groping in the dark herself. Her constant prayer was for light. Let there be light. She was on the way of spiritual healing and nothing could thwart this woman. Let them laugh, let them scoff, let them put her out of their homes. She knew she could not turn back, because this was the quest for Truth, and Truth would sustain her until she could see the fullness of its appearing.

Next came a Mr. Wright, a student of psychology, mixed with personal mesmerism. At first he had fine success in practicing what he thought was the Truth as given by Mrs. Glover. Then even he began to question himself — was it understanding or was it mesmerism which was healing? He even questioned to see if spiritualism or mediumship was entering in. But his intellectual self-sufficiency claimed him, and he separated himself from the fountain of pure water. Here Mrs. Glover, the searcher, was able to see that mesmerism and spiritualism were not factors in this work. It had begun to dawn that there is but one divine Mind because there is but one God, and this God is Principle, and there is no personal mind to mesmerize or to be mesmerized.

As yet, Mrs. Glover had not named the discovery Christian Science, the Science of Mind itself. She was still groping in the dark, discarding that which was no longer needed and holding on to that which was seen to be of God. A little later in the discovery, Mrs. Glover could write telling of the falsities of spiritualism and denounce it, for in the First Edition we find the chapter "Imposition and Demonstration," and in later editions it is entitled "Christian Science versus Spiritualism." Mrs. Glover definitely and clearly saw, as each of us must see in our revelation of the Scientific Statement of Being, that there is no mediumship between God and man. It was beginning to appear to her more brilliantly that the human mind was not a factor in the healing work. Actually, it was the absence of the human concept which permitted the Christ to appear in the same brightness as it appeared hundreds of years before and was called 'Christ Jesus.' Later we find in the textbook: "Let us rid ourselves of the belief that man is separated from God, and obey only the divine Principle, Life and Love. Here is the great point of departure for all true spiritual growth." But what is the great point of departure for all true spiritual growth? To rid ourself of any belief in separation, of 'twoness.'

Do you see, these were not persons appearing, but states of consciousness which had to appear to Mrs. Glover in order that she might see the errors of the human mind which would attempt to defeat this revelation, and divert her from the straight and narrow path? *Seeing through phases of m.m. only*

Now appears a Mr. Kennedy who *seemed* to be a scientific worker. Mrs. Glover worked long and faithfully with him, and he seemed able to demonstrate the teaching. Mrs. Glover felt he knew and saw something of what she saw. But it was from this experience that the Discoverer of Christian Science found the great gulf existing between the Science of Mind and mental science so-called. When Mrs. Glover endeavored to show Mr. Kennedy the gulf between

Christian Science and so-called mental science, he turned from her, and it was then she saw he had been using mental suggestion, a form of personal mesmerism, which up to that moment had fooled her. She saw she must separate Christian Science from the magnetic healer. In 1872, Mrs. Glover made a clean break with mesmerism, magnetism, manipulation, spiritualism, and any attempt to use mental science so-called to change one form of matter into another form of matter. It was nine years after her discovery before the First Edition appeared. From 1866 to 1875, Mrs. Glover was separating the tares from the wheat, always praying to find the way of the Master.

In the Wilbur book, we read: "It was at Red Rock one evening when she felt her ego slip away from her, and divine Science lifted her to the consciousness of spiritual being above the waves of time."

Here she experienced eternity in a moment, for in her willingness to let this personal sense of ego slip away, the Ego that is divine made itself evident. We call this revelation. Revelation is never personal. It is the willingness to let the old go for the new, which renders thought receptive to the advanced idea. Our Leader was humble enough to let the personal sense of ego go, and find the divine Ego to be the one universal Ego forever identifying itself as the All. She wrote in *Retrospection and Introspection*: "Limitations are put off in proportion as the fleshly nature disappears and man is found in the reflection of Spirit. This great fact leads into profound depths. The material human concept grew beautifully less as I floated into more spiritual latitudes and purer realms of thought. From that hour personal corporeality became less to me than it is to people who fail to appreciate individual character. I endeavored to lift thought above physical personality, or selfhood in matter — to man's spiritual individuality in God — in the true Mind, where sensible evil is lost in supersensible good. This is the only way whereby the false personality is laid off."

Do you see, students, that every honest seeker for Truth must free himself of all these phases of the human mind? Free himself from the satanic suggestion of being a person with a private mind knowing something of the divine Mind, and attempting through human will to demonstrate this Science or to project it on something and change it? Our Leader had found the Way — the Christ Way. She permitted the ego to go to the Father, and stay with and as the Father. In *Message of 1902*, we find "for the ego or I goest to the Father, whereby man *is* Godlike." And again in *Miscellaneous Writings*, "The 'I' does go unto the Father, the ego does arise to spiritual recognition of being, and is exalted, . . . God understood."

The human mind with its superstition, egotism, intellectuality, spiritualism, and mental gymnastics, was seen not to be the factor. The gulf was being fixed. It was becoming more evident that this is Mind Science, or the Science of the Christ.

In these first years, she must teach whosoever would come. The humble and the meek would come, even as the fishermen in Jesus' time came to hear the Nazarene.

In the Wilbur book, we read:

> It is not possible to draw a picture of those first classes in Mind Science that will appeal to a sense of the beautiful. The students who were drawn together were workers; their hands were stained with the leather and tools of the day's occupation; their narrow lives had been cramped mentally and physically. Their thoughts were often no more elevated than their bodies were beautiful. At night, then, these first classes met, and it was in the heat of July and August. In the barely furnished upper chamber a lamp was burning which added somewhat to the heat. . . . Insects buzzed at the windows. . . . Yet that quiet was permeated by the voice of a teacher at whose words the hearts of those workmen burned within them. 'The light which never was on land or sea' was made to shine there

in that humble upper chamber.

The response was a spiritual thrill which vibrated through consciousness to the circumferences of the world's horizon. . . and that moment of exquisite tenderness, evoked in the humble upper chamber, seems destined to swell into an eon, where time melts into eternity; for it was in such a moment that the understanding of divine consciousness was imparted. . . The shoe worker from his dingy bench, his foul smelling glues and leathers, the whir and clamor of machinery, saw the walls of his limitation melt, and experienced the inrush of being where the lilies of annunciation spring.

It is necessary at this point to see that the ideas which constitute Christian Science have been forever in the Mind that is divine. Only Mind can evolve or create ideas, and the Mind which conceives the idea, maintains the idea. Mrs. Glover did not originate the ideas which were being taught. Mind is the origin, source, cause. Mind is the one divine Mind, and man is Mind's means of self-expression. Reasoning from the standpoint of the one divine Mind, God, as the only Cause, and man as creation, the only effect, we can exercise our God-given dominion over frustrating human-limiting conditions.

Mary Baker Glover had seen through the human mind — from its claim of birth to death; she was lifting the curtain on man as never born and never dying — coexistent with His creator. The human mind, being enmity to God, cannot entertain divine ideas. The personal sense of mind cannot be enlightened. No such thing can occur. The term *human mind* or *mortal mind* designates the error, or belief, in a mind apart from God. Error therefore is incapable of receiving enlightenment. Error is capable only of extinction. The human mind cannot receive infinite ideas from the infinite divine Mind. The divine idea of the infinite Mind is the functioning presence of this Mind itself. If there is a point of contact between the human mind and the divine Mind, it would be the point of extinction or expulsion. We cannot arrive at the infallibility of the Scientific Statement of Being if we believe the human mind is becoming better enlightened, etc. What appears as the enlightenment of this mortal mind is the dispelling of the belief that being is human, and the Scientific Statement of Being is becoming one's own identification.

Mrs. Glover was not trying to enlighten students. She was endeavoring to show them that their present mind is divine. Of course, she was not as yet entirely free of former teachings, but she did see that the human mind was not a factor in Christian Science. It had to be the divine Mind present and dispelling the suggestion of a limited, finite personal mind. As this occurred, the light began to break.

After nine years, the book was finished in that little attic room. There was no light in this room but the sun, no air but through the skylight in the roof. No one but Mrs. Glover entered that room until the book was finished. She had to forsake forever the world belief in a personal mind. Here was the gulf appearing which would wipe out forever the mental science which was trying to counterfeit the divine appearing.

Do you ever feel utterly cast down, forsaken, misunderstood? Then visit this little room. Sit quietly in the old-fashioned haircloth rocker and be very still and hear the pen of Mrs. Glover recording the revelation. See the pages of this precious book fall to the floor. And then read in the Tomlinson book: "It was divine Mind expressing itself. I never could have written such a book."

In Julia Johnston's book *Mary Baker Eddy: Her Mission and Triumph*, we find: "During these momentous days, Mrs. Glover was also teaching classes, imparting to seekers rare gleanings from the Bible. She was looking out from celestial heights, not up to them. It was difficult to persuade her pupils that their outlook could be from the same standpoint. She strove to inspire them to understand her words, and to love and live what she taught."

It was in this little attic room that Mrs. Glover says for three years she sought the Science of Mind healing. She "searched the Scriptures and read little else, kept aloof from society and devoted time and energies to discovering a positive rule. The search was sweet, calm, and buoyant with hope, not selfish nor depressing." *(Science and Health)* And is this not our experience also? The search is sweet, calm and buoyant, never depressing, never selfish. From the standpoint of infinite Mind's allness and oneness was there a little room, without comfort? Or was this the way the restricted senses were depicting one of the most glorious experiences to ever come to earth? To our Leader, it was not depressing nor limiting. It was glorious, freeing, and with a sense of reality. She was looking out from celestial heights, not up to them. It was here that the child was born whose name is Wonderful. It was here that the great verities of being were recorded. "The three great verities of Spirit, omnipotence, omnipresence, omniscience, — Spirit possessing all power, filling all space, constituting all Science, — contradict forever the belief that matter can be actual. These eternal verities reveal primeval existence as the radiant reality of God's creation, in which all that He has made is pronounced by His wisdom good."

Do we see here that these three verities constitute our very identity or being? Man is the conscious identity, or being, these verities eternal and just at hand. It is only through radical reliance that scientific healing power can be realized. And this radical reliance must mean that we are not permitted to have any mind but God, and this God-Mind is being our Mind yesterday, today and forever. Of course, this is radical reliance, radical meaning *rooted, grounded*. Therefore we are rooted in the one source.

Thou shalt have no Mind but Me. This Me is Spirit. I will not give My glory to another. Therefore we are not another, but the radiance of the eternal noon. Therefore, there should be but one fact before the thought —namely, spiritual existence. This right reasoning is the controlling power in every incident. It is the governing factor. The Scientific Statement of Being does not permit us to have any other fact before thought — namely, infinite Mind without any possibility of an opposing mind. To have this factor before consciousness is the fast that the Ego has chosen. To afflict the personal sense of ego, to deprive it, to hold it as something seen or felt, is no fast at all. In Isaiah, we read:

> Is it such a fast that I have chosen? a day for a man to afflict his soul? is it to bow down his head as a bulrush, and to spread sack-cloth and ashes under him? wilt thou call this a fast, and an acceptable day to the Lord?
>
> Is not this the fast that I have chosen? to loose the bands of wickedness, to undo the heavy burdens, and to let the oppressed go free, and that ye break every yoke?
>
> Is it not to deal thy bread to the hungry, and that thou bring the poor that are cast out to the house? when thou seest the naked that thou cover him; and that thou hide not thyself from thine own flesh?
>
> Then shall thy light break forth as the morning, and thine health shall spring forth speedily; and thy righteousness shall go before thee; the glory of the Lord shall be thy rereward.
>
> Then shalt thou call, and the Lord shall answer; thou shalt cry, and he shall say, Here I am. If thou take away from the midst of thee the yoke, the putting forth of the finger, and speaking vanity;
>
> And if thou draw out thy soul to the hungry, and satisfy the afflicted soul; then shall thy light rise in obscurity, and thy darkness be as the noon day:
>
> Then shalt thou delight thyself in the Lord: and I will

cause thee to ride upon the high places of the earth, and
feed thee with the heritage of Jacob thy father: for the mouth
of the Lord hath spoken it.

Then along came the student who seemed to understand what the discovery would mean to the world.
His name was Asa Eddy, and the marriage between Mrs.
Glover and Mr. Eddy took place. From this union, we
now have the name Mary Baker Eddy, the Discoverer and
Founder of this great light — that there is but *one* universal Mind holding within itself all identity, and man, not
a person at all, but man, the functioning presence of this
Light itself. What revelation!

As you know, under the name of Mrs. Glover, there
appeared in 1870 a book, *The Science of Man.* In this, we
find the original version of the Scientific Statement of Being.
This small book became Recapitulation in later editions. It
may be helpful to see that the Leader wrote this statement
of true being before the textbook appeared. So great is this
statement that it has revolutionized the world and is up-
setting all that is not right. Matter has lost its solidity and
is seen to be nothing more than moving particles; heaven
has been moved farther back due to the astronauts having
invaded space or what is called 'up there'; theology is losing
its hell and brimstone and finding heaven and hell as states
and stages of consciousness; medicine is losing its drugging
and more and more delving into what is called the mental
nature of things. And so it is the leaven which the woman
planted, which is leavening the whole. It is upon this statement that the whole of the revelation of Christian Science
rests. It is the basis of what is called healing, regeneration,
evangelization. It is the Nay, Nay of the Master and the
Yea, Yea of the Christ. What does this statement of true
being really indicate? Let us ponder it here and now, and
feel its majestic power, the grandeur of its outlook, and feel
without any limitation Mind's infinitude, Mind's oneness

of infinity felt universally and specifically, and feel it here and now directly.

This Scientific Statement of Being is found in *Science and Health*:

> *There is no life, truth, intelligence, nor substance in matter. All is infinite Mind and its infinite manifestation, for God is All-in-all. Spirit is immortal Truth; matter is mortal error. Spirit is the real and eternal; matter is the unreal and temporal. Spirit is God, and man is His image and likeness. Therefore man is not material; he is spiritual.*

Mrs. Eddy also states: "Man's privilege at this supreme moment is to prove the words of our Master: 'If a man keep my saying, he shall never see death'. To divest thought of false trusts and material evidences in order that the spiritual facts of being may appear, — this is the great attainment by means of which we shall sweep away the false and give place to the true. Thus we may establish in truth the temple, or body, 'whose builder and maker is God'."

Do you see, if there is no truth in matter, then it must be the essence of evil? Is this not the reason we find in *Unity of Good*: "This abortive ego, this fable of error, is laid bare in Christian Science. Human theories call, or miscall, this evil a child of God. . . Bruise the head of this serpent, as Truth and 'the woman' are doing in Christian Science, and it stings your heel, rears its crest proudly, and goes on saying, *'Am I not myself? Am I not mind and matter, person and thing?'* We should answer, 'Yes! you are indeed yourself, and need most of all to be rid of this self, for it is very far from God's likeness.'

"In the walk to Emmaus, Jesus was known to his friends by the words, which made their hearts burn within them, and by the breaking of bread. The divine Spirit, which identified Jesus thus centuries ago, has spoken through the inspired Word and will speak through it in every age and clime. It is revealed to the receptive heart, and is again seen casting out evil and healing the sick.

The Master said plainly that physique was not Spirit, and after his resurrection he proved to the physical senses that his body was not changed until he himself ascended, — or, in other words, there is no other source of life. Organization, corporeality, is not life nor does it sustain life nor maintain life."

So the symphony of the Scientific Statement of Being continues like a melodic chord. There is no truth in matter. Matter is seen to be the subjective experience of mortal mind. Matter is a misstatement of Mind. Matter is objectified error. Matter is but the suppositional objectification of mortal mind. Today many students are neglecting this important point. Christian Science does not heal matter. Christian Science is purely metaphysical. Therefore matter must be reduced to mortal mind, and then it can be handled successfully and scientifically in Christian Science, and our cases can be met more readily and permanently. This abortive evil ego must be dispelled. There is no Truth in matter; then why look to that which is error to tell us the truth concerning identity? It cannot tell the truth, for there is no truth in it.

There is no intelligence in matter. Intelligence is the primal quality of Mind. Intelligence is present as Mind's primal self-expression. Man is the witnessing. Then, because there is no intelligence in matter, it cannot even *seem* to think. What is called thinking is not going on in or of the head, but is present as mortal mind suppositional activity — its consolidation of mortal material mentality. Mrs. Eddy writes of brain "which is but a mortal consolidation of material mentality and its suppositional activities."

There is no substance in matter. Substance is spiritual consciousness. Substance is incapable of objectification. There are no objects of sense in substance. Substance is primal consciousness. Consciousness includes within itself all identity. Substance is the knowing of Mind itself. What the infinite Mind knows, is substance.

Then we do not die out of matter; we are scientifically delivered from it. Seeing the nothingness of personality, the abortive evil ego, and willing to take off our shoes because we stand on holy ground, then we are never reluctant to let the old go for the new. We are not afraid of absorption.

We find the following in the textbook: "Beholding the infinite tasks of truth, we pause, wait on God. Then we push onward, until boundless thought walks enraptured, and conception unconfined is winged to reach the divine glory."

"Error is false, mortal belief; it is illusion, without spiritual identity or foundation, and it has no real existence. The supposition that life, substance, and intelligence are *in* matter, or *of* it, is an error. Matter is neither a thing nor a person, but merely the objective supposition of Spirit's opposite. The five material senses testify to truth and error as united in a mind both good and evil. Their false evidence will finally yield to Truth, — to the recognition of Spirit and of the spiritual creation."

"The time has come for a finite conception of the infinite and of a material body as the seat of Mind to give place to a diviner sense of intelligence and its manifestations, — to the better understanding that Science gives of the Supreme Being, or divine Principle, and idea."

Matter grows larger under the physicists' microscope, but it disappears under the microscope of Spirit. Why? Because Spirit's allness denies the possibility of matter. Again from the textbook: "Mind, not matter, is causation. A material body only expresses a material and mortal mind. A mortal man possesses this body, and he makes it harmonious or discordant according to the images of thought impressed upon it."

"When will it be understood that matter has neither intelligence, life, nor sensation, and that the opposite belief is the prolific source of all suffering? God created all through

Mind, and made all perfect and eternal. Where then is the necessity for recreation or procreation?"

"What is left of matter? Nothing, and that is just what I call it," our Leader writes. All that is present is the I AM, called God, being the I AM that is man, and the one I saying I AM that I AM.

This statement of being has to give up the spectral at every point. The symphony breaks forth into its grand rhapsody: "All is infinite Mind and its infinite manifestation, for God is All-in-all." In this infinitude of Mind, all being is found harmonious and eternal. The great verity of divine Science becomes more evident: Without the Word of God was not anything made that was made. All is God saying I AM that I AM. There is no lesser ego here to say 'I'. Only the Ego that is divine, incorporeal, infinite and eternal is present saying I AM, and constituting the identity man.

After Mrs. Eddy discovered the Science of being, it took her years to assimilate this discovery and to be able to write it in a form that could be appreciable to the human concept. "My discovery, that erring, mortal, misnamed *mind* produces all the organism and action of the mortal body, set my thoughts to work in new channels, and led up to my demonstration of the proposition that Mind is All and matter is naught as the leading factor in Mind-science." The discovery waited for her full comprehension and acknowledgment.

The Christian Science textbook is the recording of the divine revelation of the oneness of Principle and idea. This is the good news or gospel to be preached in all the world — the oneness of all being. Accepting this revelation as the truth of being brings the Scientific Statement of Being into absolute focus. The personal sense of ego fades into its nothingness, and the Ego that is divine, begins to supply all intelligence. Let us be willing to give up the ghost here today — the ghostly sense of being person or personal — and let us experience the Holy Ghost as identity itself. Let us live this Scientific Statement of Being and have the transfiguration and walk the earth as some Holy thing, and experience the Christ identity.

Does this book exist as an object in sense or as an idea in Soul? Is not the textbook the way the Christ-Mind is appearing at the moment? The textbook is Divine Science brought to human comprehension, and named Christian Science. When Mary Baker Eddy interpreted the revelation — the Science of being — into English words, she named it Christian Science, because it was the Science of the teachings of the Master Christian, and it is Christian, benevolent. The fact that our Leader used English words in order to clothe the divine idea, is the reduction she speaks of: "Divine metaphysics is now reduced to a system, to a term comprehensible by and adapted to the thought of the age in which we live. This system enables the learner to demonstrate the divine Principle, upon which Jesus' healing was based, and the sacred rules for its present application to the cure of disease." "Since then her highest creed has been divine Science, which, reduced to human apprehension, she has named Christian Science."

Divine Science is the Science of divinity. It is the correct understanding of Divine Science that brings forth human words which appear in our textbook. As students of Christian Science, we translate these words back into divine revelation because as metaphysicians, we exchange the objects of sense for the ideas of Soul. We appear to call this 'study,' but let us not be fooled — this is a human metaphysical process that one has to go through before fully understanding the Christ Science operating from the standpoint of the Scientific Statement of Being. Man is the Science of being in identification. Man is actually *now* the Son of God, or Mind's knowing. We may not study to become the Son, but rather to acknowledge from the standpoint of all, "all is infinite Mind and its infinite manifestation," that we are not human beings, personal concepts. In other words, "There is no life, truth, intelligence nor substance in matter." It is giving up the spectral at all points which permits the full appearing of the Son. This must not be misinterpreted that we do not need to study the textbook; but from the correct metaphysical viewpoint, it will appear that we love the book more and more.

If your study is difficult, it must be because you are trying to understand Christian Science from the standpoint of personal sense, trying to use it to change something or to bring something into being which does not exist. If we run into the suggestion that study is difficult, let us go into the closet and shut the door on the satanic suggestion that we are persons trying to understand our divinity. The more we know that we do not go anywhere to find our sonship, makes the books more available, makes them better understood. This is the same way we deny that man is a sinner, but see man as the spotlessness of being itself. This appears to make that sinning concept less sinful until the concept disappears for lack of identification. We study spontaneously. Man is the spontaneity of being.

Every chapter amplifies the Scientific Statement of Being that all, absolutely *all*, without a single exception, is God, Mind, saying, "I AM ALL," and "Dwelling in Light I see only the brightness of My own glory. . . A knowledge of aught beside Myself is impossible." (*Unity of Good*)

The Scientific Statement of Being is the vantage point from which we live and look out on the universe. This statement of indivisible being permits us to see the nothingness of the mortal illusion of division and finiteness. It gives us the simplicity of being, because the oneness and allness of the divine Mind is seen to be the present Mind of all. If this were not true, Jesus could not have taught the peasant folk and fishermen on the hillsides. Nor could Mary Baker Glover have taught those shoe workers fresh from their benches. Both Jesus and Mrs. Glover kept the singleness of eye, and it is now our work to see the simplicity of the Christ.

It is the Scientific Statement of Being that shows us this Way. This scientific statement is the deep, absolute fact. No one says this statement is too absolute. And yet, we can find nothing more absolute than this statement of reality.

A friend once said, "To practice Christian Science, to live our Science, we must let the divine Mind, the only Mind there is, be our present Mind. We must know out from the immutable facts of Principle. This is simply being what we are, being man — that is, Mind's self-expressing idea, the functioning of Mind itself."

This unbroken scientific fact maintained as conscious identity, erases the mortal error, the illusion, and it disappears because it cannot maintain itself in the face of reality. Man is Mind's wondrous, glorious enjoyment of its own immortal wisdom and self-containment.

The acceptance of the Scientific Statement of Being as present identification, gives one the glorious feeling and the complete release from the need of thinking. To see that the infinitude of Mind, the one self-conscious being, is the Mind of all, is to immediately preclude the possibility of any lesser mind, called mortal, carnal, or human mind.

Mortal mind is seen not to be an entity, or to have identity. It is seen to be the name for that which occupies no space, has no substance, no intelligence, and certainly no truth. Hence it must be a lie, or mortal error. Spirit is immortal Truth, matter is mortal error. Mortal error and malpractice are one.

Now the music comes to a gentle, slow movement. Spirit is the real and eternal; Spirit is tangible, solid; Spirit is substantially real and eternal, always the same, not subject to change or time lapse in which to become eternal, not an eternal continuation of time, but the eternal noon, the evergreen of Soul. The gentleness of it all, *now*, eternal *now*, never a moment to elapse in order to experience now. There is not a split second in which there can be a lapse from or return to the eternal now. Then quietly we hear: Matter is unreal and temporal. It needs no emphasis; there is no contention. It is Truth uttering its own verities. "Dwelling in Light I can see only the brightness of My own glory." It is Soul feeling its grand symphony, and what Soul feels in all its grandeur is the beloved Son.

Now the sound begins to increase, and with lawful certainty, with lawful assurance and conviction we hear *therefore*; but 'therefore' coming from the Christ needs no clashing symbols; that 'therefore' is not arguing with anything, not contending with what is called another; rather is it stately Science pausing not, but moving before us, a pillar of cloud by day and of fire by night, leading to divine heights; and from the divine heights of revelation, from the mount of Transfiguration, comes the sweet sound of the Christ: Man is not material, personal, finite, limited, frustrated, decrepit, but from the celestial heights the sweetest music ever heard: *He is spiritual.* The music fades away; all the instruments which brought forth the symphony are quiet; the Scientific Statement of Being is the identification of all — no argument, no contention, no Michael, only the Gabriel of the Father's presence left to impart the presence of Love that never loses sight of its own loveliness.

Then the voice from harmony cries: Go and take the Scientific Statement of Being, take it, and eat it and it shall make thy belly bitter — the first sentence which says there is no identity or belief of being personal — but eat the statement and it shall be sweet as honey in thy mouth; when it is seen there is nothing personal; only divine, infinite Mind to experience its allness. This appreciation has eaten the Christian Science of Being. Therefore it is now conscious identity as found in Science and nothing is left to have to digest or to have bitter feelings. Nothing is left out, but all is included, and this law of inclusiveness includes all from a blade of grass to a star as distinct and eternal; and we find All is infinite Mind and its infinite man, its universal man, its indivisible man or individuality, and he heard the Father say: "Son, all that I have is thine."

And as Ezra sang: "All the people gathered themselves together as one man and sang: Stand up and bless the Lord your God for ever and ever; and blessed be thy glorious name, which is exalted above all blessing and praise. Thou, even thou, art Lord alone; thou hast made heaven, the heaven of heavens, with all their host, the earth, and all things that are therein, the seas, and all that is therein, and thou preservest them all; and the host of heaven worshippeth thee." And now we no longer sing the Song, but find identity to *be* the Song. Man is the singing of the Song. As Jesus said: "It is your Father's good pleasure to give you the kingdom."

Mental malpractice is based upon the assumption that there is life, truth, intelligence and substance in matter. Roman Catholicism claims to take the textbook and reverse the statements therein, asserting that there is life in matter. In fact, their religious beliefs are predicated upon the assumption of life in matter. If there is no life in matter, then what happens to the belief of indwelling soul that must be prayed out of hell? This is one of the greatest advertising gimmicks in the world. It brings in more revenue than all the quack medicine, patent medicine, and the rest of that ilk. Christian Science is seen to be Romanism's greatest foe because Christian Science lays the ax at the root of their tree. Where and how can Romanism stand without the fear of its followers over the belief in death and the belief in heaven and hell as places to go?

The Scientific Statement of Being wipes out the whole mass of errors, and the earth should open up and swallow the whole mass. Students of Christian Science should never be afraid of the supposed power of Roman Catholicism. But because of the teaching of the Scientific Statement of Being, we have divine authority. If we are acting from the standpoint of person with a knowledge of Christian Science, then we are on the level of the belief. By accepting the infinitude of Mind as one's present Mind, one annuls any claim of aggressive mental suggestion; and this gives the student the dominion promised in the Bible, because the student is not person, but is the activity of the Christ Mind itself.

Malpractice is always based on the denial of the

Scientific Statement of Being. It is a claim of reversion, perversion. Understanding the Scientific Statement of Being and living this Christ understanding, is a law to the malpractice produced by the denial of the Scientific Statement of Being.

Continuing with the music of the spheres, Mrs. Eddy says: "God is Mind, and God is infinite, hence all is Mind. On this statement rests the Science of being." And the marginal note is "Scientific Ultimatum." Then if we are to have any restfulness, it must be upon this scientific ultimatum. Every Christian Science treatment should be scientific in its ultimatum. All is Mind, and this Mind is infinite, precluding the possibility of finiteness.

With this Scientific Statement of Being, we have a spiritual ultimatum to give to the world. One of the weaknesses we sometimes allow, is to permit this sense of false appeasement to come in. Mrs. Eddy says that Christian Science is revolutionary. In *Miscellaneous Writings*, she tells us, "Science is absolute and final. It is revolutionary in its very nature; for it upsets all that is not upright."

We have great respect for our President and Statesmen when they stand up to the ultimatums of dictators, and we must support this righteous government with the spiritual ultimatum that "there is no life, truth, intelligence nor substance in matter." Let the notes all blend in one — All is infinite Mind, etc. In this there is no possibility of false appeasement. It is radical by its very nature. If our conception of Christian Science is that it is to make the human situation more pleasant and more comfortable, is this not a form of appeasement? The radicalness demanded by this revelation is that there is no substance in objectivity, no identity in objectivity. The understanding of this spiritual ultimatum will have the appearance conform more nearly to the knowing. But let us not be fooled. It is not the betterment of the concept; it is the fuller appearing of the Scientific Statement of Being. If we as students of this revelation understand that it is the truth of being *now*, we will never be tempted to change the seeming into the being.

When Mrs. Eddy gave her scientific ultimatum to the world, the denial of matter as substance, she threw the gauntlet down to every science so-called and dared them to pick it up and prove her discovery false. When our Leader threw down this glove, this spiritual scientific ultimatum, she said to theology: "Your basis is as wrong as Ptolomy. There is no personal soul. All Soul is divine, and man is Soul's own self-identification. There is no fallen man." The glove was thrown to chemistry and physics, and she said: "There is no substance matter. Atomic power is Mind; man is not chemical, man is not statistical, man is the harmony, the music of the spheres." To astronomy, she said: "Man includes his universe and looks out from the stars." To medicine: "There is no matter-pill, no matter surgery. It is all Mind and Mind's one and divine manifestation." To psycho-this and psycho-that she said: "Brain is not mind. Mind is divine, incorporeal, and man, as divine idea, functions as Mind itself."

This glove, this scientific ultimatum, All is Mind and Mind is infinite, is not the "lavender-kid zeal" which our Leader decries; but the gauntlet is the gauntlet of David, the sling and stone of the fearless man facing the Goliath, putting off the armor of the world because he had not proved it. David knew the power of Truth. Let us read from *Miscellaneous Writings*: "What will you do about it? Will you be equally in earnest for the truth? Will you doff your lavender-kid zeal, and become real and consecrated warriors? Will you give yourselves wholly and irrevocably to the great work of establishing the truth, the gospel, and the Science which are necessary to the salvation of the world from error, sin, disease, and death? Answer at once and practically, and answer aright!"

Yes, we answer aright and rest on the scientific ultimatum of the Scientific Statement of Being. This restfulness knows no false appeasement. Appeasement: to make still as to appease the tumult of the ocean! Christian Science enters into no false peace, where there is no peace. Christian Science is revolutionary and upsets all that is not upright. Upsets entrenched tradition, upsets the Puritanism that would hold the movement as a moral issue. Science produces morality, but human morality cannot produce Science. The Scientific Statement of Being is the glove thrown down with the ultimatum — God is All, there is no evil! God is Spirit, there is no matter. God is Love, there is no fear and nothing to fear! Let us see today that man is God's glorious ultimatum: Be ye perfect because I AM perfect! What a marvelous ultimatum! Let there be light and there is light! Let there be man and there is man — man the effect of infinite Mind's knowing.

The Scientific Statement of Being shows us that our world, church, home, employment, etc., are all transpiring as consciousness. This must be so because all is infinite Mind infinitely manifesting itself as All. Nothing is being experienced objectively. As we see "there is no life, truth, intelligence nor substance in matter," which means objectivity, then we can see that what we seem to be experiencing negatively is not outside, but is actually aggressive mental suggestion claiming to be our mind and claiming to be our own experience. Malpractice says the experience is going on out there. Is it? Where does healing take place? Out there? Is the patient out there, or is it aggressive mental suggestion, suggesting that out there is a sick child? But where is the sick child but here as suggestion? To see that it isn't going on at all is the Christ way. It is here only as suggestion and not as condition out there, and this understanding is the law to malpractice whether asleep or awake.

Then is not the remedy at hand, the Scientific Statement of Being? If this statement is understood, it is the law to every situation. We are not dealing with persons. We are either dealing with the one universal consciousness, God-man, Principle-idea, or we are dealing with the one claim of absence of mind called mortal mind. When we hear of some catastrophe out there — a major disaster, a world crisis, an impending financial failure in a company, something wrong with the church organization, all appearing beyond our control — do we see the impossibility and leave the basis of belief of life in matter, and unite with the one Mind in order to bring out God's unerring direction? If we do not do this immediately, we are admitting the possibility of the suggestion as one's own experience.

Students who seem to be having a health problem, or a financial problem, or one of human relationships, frequently say, "But how could I have such an experience? I never thought of such a thing!" No, perhaps they did not think of this specific experience. But did they deny its possibility from the standpoint of the Scientific Statement of Being when they perhaps heard of a similar situation? On TV, from a newspaper, or it might have come to them through gossip. Do you see the impersonal nature of every false suggestion? The first sentence of the Scientific Statement of Being shows us the impersonal nature of existence. It also shows that there is no believer to have personality, because without a believer, a belief is nothing. As long as we permit belief to hang around as person, or part of person, or in person, we cannot handle it. Christian Science is purely metaphysical. The only way suggestion can be handled scientifically is to let the I return to the Father's house, the consciousness of the infinitude of Mind. Then the impersonal Christ leaves nothing unlike the risen Christ.

This Scientific Statement of Being gives the student the quiet assurance that whatever appears at the door of consciousness, which is erroneous, can be rejected instantly. Don't hold your foot in the door by believing that a person out there is in difficulty, or someone out there is calling for help. Shut the door and give Goliath no man to fight with. There is no sick man, no sinner. It is hypnotic suggestion here. In the textbook, Mrs. Eddy says, "If mortals claimed no other Mind and accepted no other, sin would be un-known. We can have but one Mind, if that one is infinite."

If we are ill, seem to lack, have fear, or lust, is it not because we have accepted a mind apart from God? A belief in two minds? We may not consciously have done this. We claim our Mind to be Christ, but then turn around and have a personal mind through which to experience lust, hate, fear, gossip. If we do not assume the attitude of the one omnipresent, omnipotent Mind and see through the belief with accurate, scientific knowing, we can never act as the Son of God. The Son of God is the Father-Mind in opera-tion, or expression, God in action. Mortal mind claims to be the mind of mortals. Are we mortals?

Did not the Scientific Statement of Being bury the per-sonal sense of man?

Science and Health defines burial as "Corporeality and physical sense put out of sight and hearing; annihilation. Submergence in Spirit; immortality brought to light."

An early lecturer once said: "We are either acknowl-edging God, Mind, in all our ways, or we are consenting to, or unconsciously accepting the prevailing beliefs of the world. Then we say, 'O Lord, how long?' The answer comes back, 'As long as you deny My omnipresence.'" To whine and complain if something or somebody were doing something to us, unbidden and unbeknown to us, only adds to the confusion; for after all, we are merely the victims of our own ignorant and limited sense of God. There is a ten-dency among Christian Scientists to talk and act as if there is another mind, and then to look upon the one Mind as a lovely ideal to be attained later.

Is this not the duality we are warned against? We cannot have two minds. Since Mind is one and Mind is infinite, then there is no mind to malpractice or to suggest malpractice. Malpractice is belief. If someone is malprac-ticing on what is called 'me,' they are not malpracticing on what I am nor what I know myself to be. Therefore, they are malpracticing on their own belief and will suffer accordingly, whether it is done ignorantly or maliciously.

We must not ignore malpractice. We must see that there is no personality, and no mind to malpractice with or be malpracticed upon. Malpractice is nothing and nobody, and must be reduced to this status in order for one to be the law to it, and to be obedient to the teachings of our textbook. We must look through malpractice and see it for what it is *not*, and not for what it claims to be.

Fear is the basic claim to be healed in malpractice. If we are afraid or feel fear, handle malpractice or animal magnetism. Never handle it as your own fear. It is not anyone's fear. It is fear without person or place. There is no mind to fear with and no mind to fear. Mind is divine Love, and in this Mind all being is found. God hath not given us the spirit of fear. Handle fear in every case, because fear is giving reality to evil, or to the claim of suggestion. Fearlessness looks the claim in the face and sees its nothingness, even when it claims to be in the body or on the body. It is malpractice, not condition. Infinity is, and man is what infinity is being.

The Scientific Statement of Being wipes out any suggestion that Christian Science is mental science. It leaves only the Science of Christ. Christian Science is not mental; it is *spiritually* mental; or *divinely* mental; but it is never merely mental. There is a great gulf between Christian Science and all else. Other systems take the human into consideration. Christian Science knows the human is not a factor.

One of the most deadening things happening within our movement today is that many students are mental scientists and not wholly Christian Scientists. The mental scientist is always watching his thoughts; the Christian Scientist is always knowing there is *one* Mind present to express itself. This relieves us from the heavy burden of thinking correctly or correcting our thought. Man has no Mind but God. Man's Mind is divine now. Man is the functioning presence of the Christ Mind. Man cannot think. Man is reflection. Reflection does nothing of itself. Reflection has no life, intelligence, substance, or truth of its own. Reflection is God being; God's reflection of Himself is termed *man*. When Mind looks into the mirror of Divine Science, what does Mind see? Why, His own emanation, His own infinitude of being; and this emanation, this conscious identity, is termed man. Man is not an object separate from divine Mind. Rather is man the directness of Mind's expression. Mind knows, and knows that it knows. Man is the reflection of this knowing, flowing knowing, and never dammed up and called personality.

Every Association is based on the textbook. Each Association is to lift us out of the belief of being persons, even temporarily, and permits us to experience the Ascension where the eternal Christ is being lived as present identity.

Each Association is a clearer, more definite sense that we are dealing with Divine Science. In studying the concordances, we find some imperative demands made by our Leader under the heading "Divine Science" such as:

"God and man in divine Science, or the logic of Truth, are coexistent and eternal, and the nature of God must be seen in man, who is His eternal image and likeness." (*Message for 1901*)

"In divine Science, God is recognized as the only power, presence, and glory." (*No and Yes*)

"This comforter I understand to be divine Science." (*Science and Health*)

Study the textbook definitely, practically. Read the textbook as your own autobiography. What is true of divine Mind, is true of the divine idea, man. There are not two of us. The Scientific Statement of Being does not permit us to live as fallen children of God, Spirit. Man does not exist as physique, but as divine idea. Therefore, man has never lived as a mortal, because man as divine idea is the functioning presence of the Mind that is divine

— the one universal Ego forever self-identifying. Man exists in the now of radiant reality. Man has not one quality underived from Deity. So man is the spotless purity of the divine Mind in being.

In the textbook, we find two cardinal points which were the foundation of Jesus' words. Jesus "best understood the nothingness of material life and intelligence and the mighty actuality of all-inclusive God, good." These were the two cardinal points of Mind-healing, or Christian Science, which armed him with Love. These two cardinal points elucidate the Scientific Statement of Being — "the nothingness of material life and intelligence and the mighty actuality of all-inclusive God, good."

From the standpoint of these two cardinal points and from the Scientific Statement of Being, Life and intelligence are purely spiritual. This Life is infinite consciousness or divine manifestation, and knows only its own infinitude, grandeur, harmony, spotless purity and blissful being. Divine Mind is self-sustained, self-expressed, self-existent; and from this allness and oneness there is no possibility of a finite mind to know or to be known. There is no truth in matter; therefore there is no truth in what is called a mortal past with its frustrations, limitations, lack of companionship, etc. The only experience man is having now, or ever has had, is the joy of spiritual dominion. Because there is no truth in matter, we must refuse to permit thought to ruminate in past history. To accept the mighty actuality of divine Mind, is to see that the unpleasant mortal experiences never went on. We must be willing to let go of the pride, or condemnation of personal sense. Let us be done with injustices, hurt feelings, mistakes, and experience the mighty actuality of all-inclusive God, good.

To really understand the Scientific Statement of Being, would be to prove that error, mortal mind, or matter, has no intelligence with which to deceive us; and we can see, here and now, it has no intelligence, no presence, no mind with which to act, speak, see or know. Error claiming to be active, is called animal magnetism. See that it cannot influence us, govern us, because we acknowledge no US but Principle and idea. The divine US and this Christ knowing, wipes out the lie appearing as many.

We cannot begin our work from the basis that we are mortals now. The realization that Life, Truth, and Love are ever-present and ever-operative, acts as a law of completeness, satisfaction, joy and abundance to every phase of experience. Mrs. Eddy says it this way: "The substance, Life, intelligence, Truth and Love, which constitute Deity, are reflected by His creation; and when we subordinate the false testimony of the corporeal senses to the facts of Science, we shall see this true likeness and reflection everywhere." (*Science and Health*)

We must always have the same starting point: God, Spirit, is All-in-all. Never start out with a patient, another or yourself. In the degree that we claim and affirm the truth of the Scientific Statement of Being — that man does not exist as personality, but exists wholly and completely as divine idea, the functioning presence of the Mind which is infinite — we assimilate more and more the divine characteristics, and they appear more as our experience here and now. Again, in the textbook, our Leader says: "The relations of God and man, divine Principle and idea, are indestructible in Science; and Science knows no lapse from nor return to harmony, but holds the divine order or spiritual law, in which God and all that He creates are perfect and eternal, to have remained unchanged in its eternal history."

Christian Science teaches the forever oneness of Principle and idea. Infinite Mind and its infinite manifestation are not two, but one. Man is God-being. Never forget this for a moment. The Mind that is divine is the Mind that is man — divine reflection. No matter what the difficulty, no matter how long it has claimed to be us, or a part of us, it has never touched, marred, or scarred our identity. It is our work today to demonstrate that personality, the three-dimensional sense of self, has never left any impression on individuality. Man is divine expression and cannot be impressed. A most aggressive suggestion is that we were once healthy, active, young, satisfied, but now it is not so, or made evident. Handle this here and now. These suggestions have never been a part of experience. Man has never been anywhere but in the Mind that is divine, hid with Christ forever in the Father's holy plan.

In *Science and Health*, we read, "Matter is an error of statement." Then in this Scientific Statement of Being, we have the true statement. There is no ego in matter because matter is mortal error, and matter is error of statement. Again, in the writings, we find: "Matter is a misstatement of Mind." Then one cannot look to a misstatement or mortal error for the ego. The Ego must be found in the infinitude of Mind and as the infinitude of Mind itself, or Mind scientifically stating itself.

Matter is not something to be discarded, changed or moved. Matter is misstatement, or a false sense being entertained. Again from *Miscellaneous Writings*, we read, "Let us open our affections to the Principle that moves all in harmony, — from the falling of a sparrow to the rolling of a world." And Christ Jesus said, "Are not two sparrows sold for a farthing? And one of them shall not fall on the ground without your Father."

Does this not show us that what is appearing as the sparrow falling to the ground is nothing more than a misstatement or false sense of some tremendous spiritual fact? Surely it must. The least is as important as the imperishable verity of the infinity of being. "All from the rolling of worlds in the most subtle ether, to a potato-patch is Mind." (*Miscellaneous Writings*) Again we are reminded that the infinity of being includes within itself *all*. Nothing is unimportant, because all is the Ego saying, I AM that I AM.

Let us ask, "What is the kingdom of heaven?" and then Mrs. Eddy answers: "The abode of Spirit, the realm of the real. No matter is there, no night is there, nothing that worketh or maketh a lie. Is this kingdom afar off? No, it is ever present here. The first to declare against this kingdom is matter." (*Miscellaneous Writings*) But if we keep matter as substance, then Christian Science cannot heal it, and we leave the heaven of Spirit's presence and are plunged into hell — the hell of trying to demonstrate over matter. But keeping matter as a misstatement of Mind, as mortal error, it can be healed instantly, and this is to experience heaven, the heaven of functioning as Mind's infinity. Many cases evade healing because the student has become a matter-physician rather than a metaphysician. Then in order to correct a misstatement, we must translate matter back into Mind. "It is the language of Soul instead of the senses; it translates matter into its original language, which is Mind, and gives the spiritual instead of the material significance." (*Christian Healing*)

Jesus was tempted to change matter-stone into matter-bread, but he knew it was "the Spirit which quickeneth, the flesh profiteth nothing." Jesus said to this suggestion, "Get thee behind me." He rebuked the personal sense of self and the personal sense that would try to produce a better form of matter.

Some believe that dying is the way out of matter. Yet, if matter is a false sense or deflection, then we cannot die out of a mistake; we can only correct it by living. Then does not a "lie unwittingly confirms the Truth?" Of course it does, and "by reversal, errors serve as waymarks to the one Mind." This deflection rightly viewed, serves to suggest the proper reflection. So we are not dealing with a substance called matter. According to the Scientific Statement of Being, we are dealing with mortal error. Now, the only place mortal error can be corrected is in and as consciousness. The moment the Christ Truth is entertained — at that moment the objects of sense yield to the ideas of Soul. This is metaphysical practice, is it not? Then if we translate the negative into the positive, we are experiencing the kingdom of Spirit, or Truth. What is it that seems to keep us from experiencing the kingdom here and now without any time lapse? Is it not that we are accepting the satanic suggestion that we are temporarily involved in personal sense, and that somehow this personal sense is connected with identity? Are we sure that we are willing to live the Scientific Statement of Being?

If we were sitting in a rocket and had a button in our hand, and all we had to do was to press it, and immediately there would be no record of personal nature — where personal sense ceased and where the grandeur and bliss of loving unselfishly, and the infinitude of being experienced as conscious identity, where we would never know anyone in personal depict, would we push the button? Or would we say with the allegory in *Miscellaneous Writings*:

> *And the Stranger saith unto him, "Wilt thou climb the mountain, and take nothing of thine own with thee?"*
>
> *He answered, "I will."*
>
> *"Then," saith the Stranger, "Thou hast chosen the good part: follow me."*
>
> *Many there were who had entered the valley to speculate in worldly policy, religion, politics, finance, and to search for wealth and fame. These had heavy baggage of their own, and insisted upon taking all of it with them, which must greatly hinder their ascent.*
>
> *The journey commences. The encumbered travelers halt and disagree. They stoutly delay those who, having less baggage, ascend faster than themselves, and betimes burden them with their own. Despairing of gaining the summit, loaded as they are, they conclude to stop and lay down a few of the heavy weights, — but only to take them up again, more than ever determined not to part with their baggage.*
>
> *All this time the Stranger is pointing the way, showing them their folly, rebuking their pride, consoling their*

afflictions, and helping them on, saying, "He that loseth his life for my sake, shall find it."

Obstinately holding themselves back, and sore-footed, they fall behind and lose sight of their guide; when, stumbling and grumbling, and fighting each other, they plunge headlong over the jagged rocks.

Then he who has no baggage goes back and kindly binds up their wounds, wipes away the blood stains, and would help them on; but suddenly the Stranger shouts, "Let them alone; they must learn from the things they suffer. Make thine own way, and if thou strayest, listen for the mountain horn, and it will call thee back to the path that goeth upward."

He alone ascends the hill of Christian Science who follows the Way-shower, the spiritual presence and idea of God. Whatever obstructs the way — causing to stumble, fall or faint, those mortals who are striving to enter the path, divine Love will remove; and uplift the fallen and strengthen the weak. Therefore, give up thy earth-weights; and observe the apostle's admonition, "Forgetting those things which are behind, and reaching forth unto those which are before." Then, loving God supremely and thy neighbor as thyself, thou wilt safely bear thy cross up to the throne of everlasting glory.

Now, would we push the button? And yet is this not what the Scientific Statement of Being is demanding of us? To lay "our earthly all on the altar of Divine Science." And does it not burst the bubbles of earth — no life, truth, intelligence, nor substance in matter — and give us the sweet breath of heaven — the infinity of Mind as identity? So willingness to become as a child, no past to repine, no future to dread, no now as temporal, leaving the old for the new, renders thought receptive of the advanced idea. Sorry! It is too late. We have no choice. The Scientific Statement of Being has pushed the button. We are off. Everything is Go, A1 — OK. We have arrived. The ascension has taken place.

Christian Science has exchanged ME for I AM alive forever-more, and so I contemplate from my orbital flight, from the center and circumference of being, and see the delightfulness of being the morning, the eternal noon, and the everlasting day. Behold I AM. The fullness of His appearing."

So long as we accept matter as substance, we are look-ing into the glass darkly, and into the sepulchre, and will cry with Mary, "Where have they laid him?" But looking out from celestial heights, we cry, "Rabboni."

When it is seen that Science translates matter into its original language of Mind, the Scientific Statement of Be-ing shows us how to live the kingdom here and now. We must see that there is no personality, no objectivity calling itself me, and have no me but God, Spirit, as the All-in-all. Yes, we can give lip service to this, we can give intellectual assent, but are we willing to push the button and give the GO sign? Our textbook has a tremendous statement on page 324:2-4 and it is included in our Bible Lesson-Sermons over and over. Let us read it. "Gladness to leave the false landmarks and joy to see them disappear, — this disposi-tion helps to precipitate the ultimate harmony."

The hour has struck when proof and demonstration, instead of opinion and dogma, are summoned to the sup-port of Christianity, "making wise the simple."
Are we willing to precipitate the ultimate harmony? Mrs. Eddy tells us that Jesus' earthly mission was to translate substance into its original meaning, Mind. Mind is all; then all must be Mind, the All-in-all. We cannot say that Mind is all, then even for a moment believe we are dealing with a substance called matter. There is no matter. All is Spirit. This is the basis of Christian Science teaching. There is no mind to misstate. Mind as Principle is unerring in its state-ment of Truth, absolute integrity of statement.

"No man can serve two masters," Jesus warned, "for either he will hate the one and love the other, or else he will hold to the one, and despise the other. Ye cannot serve God and mammon."

"The infinite is one, and this one is Spirit; Spirit is God, and this God is infinite good. This simple statement of oneness is the only possible correct version of Christian Science. God being infinite, He is the only basis of Science; hence materiality is wholly apart from Christian Science, and is only a 'Suffer it to be so now' until we arrive at the spiritual fullness of God, Spirit, even the divine idea of Christian Science — Christ, born of God, the offspring of Spirit — wherein matter is neither part nor portion because matter is the absolute opposite of spiritual means, manifestation, and demonstration. The only incentive of a mistaken sense is malicious animal magnetism, — the name of all evil, — and this must be understood."

"Spirit is infinite; therefore *Spirit is all.* 'There is no matter' is not only the axiom of true Christian Science, but it is the only basis upon which this Science can be demonstrated." (*Miscellany*)

When Jesus fed the multitude with the five loaves, he did not say there were no loaves there. No, he took the loaves, "looked up to heaven and blessed and brake the loaves." Was this looking up to heaven not another way of saying he translated what he seemed to see into the being just at hand? He refused to accept the misstatement of lack. Looking out with Christ, Jesus saw the abundant being — these eternal verities just at hand. We can do the same; and the reason we do not do it in every line of endeavor, is because we still believe we are persons dealing with material objects called loaves and fishes. Jesus took everything back unto the Father. Jesus, living the Christ, knew that matter had no substance; he saw it was simply an imperfect view of the perfect and whole. Only the Christ can give us the right view. Students, let us see that we are not dealing with matter, young or old, blind or seeing, scarce or abundant. We are dealing with a misconception —animal magnetism, hypnotism. Everything must come to us as consciousness. Then we are not dealing with matter-substance. This is the whole of the Scientific Statement of Being.

"'The new tongue' is the spiritual meaning as opposed to the material. It is the language of Soul instead of the senses; it translates matter into its original language, which is Mind, and gives the spiritual instead of the material signification." (*Christian Healing*)

Remember the incident of the sick horse? Mrs. Eddy said, "I do not want anyone of you to treat a sick horse, but want all of you to know there is no mind to have such a concept." The sick horse had to come to consciousness as concept. It is here, and only here, we do the healing work. It must be healed in and as consciousness. Let us "give to Mind the glory, honor, dominion, and power everlastingly due its holy name."

Because Mind is All-in-all — all there is to our lives, our world, the movement, the government, the President — is this one Mind divinely, incorporeally, supremely, infinitely expressing itself as the All-in-all. There is and can be nothing else.

The law of the Scientific Statement of Being makes us free from the law of sin and death. It lifts us "ayont hate's thrall." The Prince of this world comes and finds nothing in us. The Prince of this world is the acceptance of the evil suggestion that identity was born; and if accepted, the law of sin and death begins to operate in behalf of this false identity. Only Christian Science can release us from this. Is not the Scientific Statement of Being telling us that man was never born? Let us see clearly here today that there is no birth, no beginning of days. There is only *day* and spiritual understanding constitutes this *day*. This is the eternal noon *day*. Are we admitting that identity was born, or that we gave birth to something? Death is the ultimate of this. We cannot die out of matter, because we never were born into it. Birth has nothing to do with Life or with Life's expression, man.

With chemistry and math, we have loosed atomic power; humanly it is inconceivable what can be done with this power. With the revelation of Christian Science, we have loosed identity from sinning, mortal personality to the glorious infinitude of eternal universal Mind's own self-expression. No limits in knowing, no restrictions to seeing, no regulations on how much beauty can be felt or experienced, no interference with the all-wiseness of eternal Being itself. Man is, as the image of God, Spirit, seen to be the fullness, the wholeness, the essence of God in being, knowing, seeing. Man is the infinite manifestation. Man is creation. Man is the grandeur, the universal beauty of holiness. Man is Mind's delight. The Father delighted in His beloved Son, saying, "Son, all that I have is thine"!

The Scientific Statement of Being has loosed us from personality, and shows us the individuality that reflects the individuality that is God's. How can we fully realize the basic potentialities inherent in the Scientific Statement of Being? How can we let loose this tremendous power available for the well-being of all? The power of good resident in the divine Mind has been freed through Christian Science treatment or prayer, so that this power can be utilized in present experience. It is called the Christ, and this Christ-power can move the mountain, still the storm, feed the multitude, raise the dead, transport one from here to there immediately, quicker than any thought process. This Christ-power offsets any human misconception. Let us here today feel this divine energy bringing us into newness of Life, not life infused into matter, but a released sense of Life in God and Life *as* God. The Scriptures declare Life to be the infinite I AM, not a dweller in matter. For man to know Life as it is — namely, God, the eternal good — gives him not merely a sense of existence, but an accompanying consciousness of spiritual power that subordinates matter and destroys sin, disease and death. This Jesus demonstrated, insomuch that Matthew wrote: "The people were astonished at his doctrine: for he taught them as one having authority, and not as the scribes." This spiritual power, healing sin and sickness, was not confined to the first century; it extends to all time, inhabits eternity, and demonstrates Life without beginning or end.

"Atomic action is Mind, not matter. It is neither the energy of matter, the result of organization, nor the outcome of life infused into matter: it is infinite Spirit, Truth, Life, defiant of error or matter." (*Miscellaneous Writings*)

The story of Christian Science continues with the infinite One that sustains its own self-expression — man, completeness. The daystar in the "Preface" of *Science and Health* gives us the clarion call, clear and definite; the human mind is not a factor in Christian Science. All is the operation of divine Principle, one divine Mind.

If we insist upon being persons knowing that God is Mind and this Mind is acting through and by human beings, we will always have a benighted understanding because there is no Science in this viewpoint. In order to experience the daystar lighting the way to eternal harmony, the student must yield up the ghost of personal sense and see that there is not a medium, avenue, channel nor agency through which Mind expresses itself. It seems too difficult for some students to see this fact. "Man is the expression of God's being." God being what? God's being perfect, eternal, infinite. Are we idea doing things under Mind's direction, or is idea the functioning on the part of indivisible all-wise Mind itself? Here is the point of great departure for all revelation. The daystar is the Christ-knowing that idea, man, is Mind's own conscious identity. This is reflection and brings forth the clarity of Jesus' statement: "He that hath seen me hath seen the Father."

"This infinite idea of infinity will be, is, as eternal as its divine Principle. The daystar of this appearance is the light of Christian Science — the Science which rends the veil of the flesh from top to bottom. The light of this revelation leaves nothing that is material; neither darkness, doubt, disease, nor death. The material corporeality disappears;

and individual spirituality, perfect and eternal, appears — never to disappear." (*Miscellaneous Writings*)

In the Scientific Statement of Being, man is forever dealing with and as the Father in operation as divine Principle. Man, phenomenon, is never dealing with man. Man is always alone with his own being, never alone with another being. It is this aloneness that armed Jesus with mightiness. It is this indivisibility of being, where cause and effect is *one*, which brings all the mightiness of God-being into operation as one's own experience, brings Soul in the fulness of satisfaction, Life in all its complete fulfillment, Love feeling its own immaculateness, directly and specifically. How can Immanual, God with us, as the only I or US, be the scientific fact unless the oneness of being is seen clearly? In the 'Preface,' our beloved Leader is leading us gently and firmly into the land of Christian Science. Step by step, this intrepid Discoverer shows us that man *is* the kingdom of God. Man *is* the land of divine Science, the consciousness of reality. It is the Father's good pleasure to give us, the only I or US, the kingdom.

Mrs. Eddy took the discovery of Christian Science into the laboratory of Spirit, and proved Christian Science to be of God, Spirit, and not of man. She proved that the revelation was not a person thinking, but the divine Principle present and operating as identity itself — man, Mind's idea, is the immediacy of Mind's knowing. No lapse of time between the knower and the knowing and the known, because all is infinite Mind immediately, directly, spontaneously knowing. This is the operation of divine Principle before which personal sense loses its reality as identity and disappears as darkness gives place to light. This understanding should make us appear as wise, brilliant, alert, intuitive, immediately knowing all, when the pale star with its benighted understanding fades out in the brilliancy of the Christ-Light or daystar. This comes only by way of humility — knowing no person to think, no personal involvement.

It is in this 'Preface' that our Leader shows us that there is no human to be involved, no finite sense of Ego. All is the operation of divine Principle, Love; all is the one infinite Mind operating as the Mind of its All-in-all.

Thus the 'Preface' gently takes the student into the true realm of prayer, and we then ask, "What is scientific prayer?"

Christ Jesus gives this answer: "For verily I say unto you, That whosoever shall say unto the mountain, Be thou removed, and be thou cast into the sea; and shall not doubt in his heart, but shall believe that those things which he saith shall come to pass; he shall have whatsoever he saith. Therefore I say unto you, What things soever ye desire when ye pray, believe that ye receive them, and ye shall have them. Your Father knoweth what things ye have need of, before ye ask Him."

The purpose of this Association today is to show how we can better say to this mountain: "Be thou removed." If there is no doubt in prayer to diffuse or adulterate the positive sense of prayer, the mountain of personal sense will remove because the Scientific Statement of Being, in its first scientific statement that there is no life in matter, removes the obscuring personality as reality, and the light of the ever-present Christ brings the proper focus. What better illustration could we have of the operation of this atomic power of Mind through prayer than in the experience of Paul and Silas in Acts? This positive power of prayer, this glorification of the God-Mind, this clear perception of reality, this conviction of being, dispelled the chains, opened the prison doors, and set the captive free. When thought is negative, doubtful and fearful, it acts as a nullifying agent or counter-acting influence and there is no answer; whereas joy, assurance, spontaneity, removes the mountain of personal sense. And the atomic power of Mind, this all-consuming power of Love, leaves nothing unlovely, leaves no trace of anything called hate or fear.

This power utilized has been called the descent of the Holy Ghost. The Bible records it as thunder. It is the activity of the universal solvent of Love dissolving the adamant of self-will, self-love, etc. Why should we stand aghast at nothingness? Why should we marvel or think it marvelous? Animal magnetism has been unmasked.

Love is the atomic energy that moves all and removes all unlike itself. Whereas the sun is needed for what is called human life, Love alone is divine Life. To experience the power of Love, we must loose ourself from all unlike Christ. "Love is impartial and universal in its adaptation and bestowals. It is the open fount which cries, 'Ho, every one that thirsteth, come ye to the waters.'"

"If we pray to God as a corporeal person, this will prevent us from relinquishing the human doubts and fears which attend such a belief, and so we cannot grasp the wonders wrought by infinite, incorporeal Love, to whom all things are possible." (*Science and Health*)

Without Love immediately available, where are we? The Scientific Statement of Being is the unassailable Truth immediately available. Unless we have this unassailable something that cannot be changed, varied, which is always dependable and will not yield in any direction no matter how great the seeming pressure — if there is not this unassailable Principle present and operating as its own *unassailable functioning presence called man*; if this Principle of the Scientific Statement of Being does not exist, if this truth is not eternally true — then there is no God, no man, no heaven, and we are not even here. But we are here because Truth is unassailable. We are here because the Scientific Statement of Being is absolutely dependable. We are here because Christian Science is this divine revelation and not personal. It is now that the Scientific Statement of Being is reality. It is that I that is divine saying I AM that I AM, because this one Ego is the I of all being. Even the infinitesimal is Mind saying I AM.

Prayer

The Scientific Statement of Being does not permit a personality called ME to mask the divine I AM. The Scientific Statement of Being permits only the Christ of God to be experienced as identity in perfect continuity. The Scientific Statement of Being is not a process of becoming; rather is it the being that was, is, and ever shall be, whom nothing can erase. Each is always alone with one's own being. Mary Baker Eddy made a marvelous discovery — she discovered the Science of being — that being which is both cause and effect, both Father and Son, in whom there is no impediment to eternal bliss. No separation, no division, no disruptive sense calling itself man here and cause out there. The discovery of the oneness and allness of being as Father-son, Cause-effect, Ego-God, Ego-man, is truly the Comforter that should come, because it comforts all with the Christ-understanding that now is man the eternal son of God, or the divine direct self-expression of the Mind that is God. What comfort to that which believed itself to be a personal ego trying to run everything from its own egotistical center! Now it finds itself not a personal ego or identity at all, for the Ego which is infinite has as its self-expression genuine man. And what comfort comes to the sinner to find his true selfhood is never involved with the insanity of sin! And the comforting Christ lifts the sick out of the belief of weakness into the glorious liberty of the Son of God! Truly, the Comforter shall come, and it has come in the name of the Science of Being called Christian Science.

Science is the impartation of knowledge being available for everyone willing to study and practice. Discerning that the teachings of Jesus had Science behind them, Mrs.

Eddy subjugated the personal sense of self and prayed for a clearer view, the Christ view; and this view is recorded in the Scientific Statement of Being. The Christian Science movement is founded on the impersonal nature of this Christ Science, or the Comforter.

In writing the textbook, Mrs. Eddy definitely must use English words to state scientific terms. What do we mean by the scientific term *prayer*? To many, it means one thing — going in and shutting the door and having audience with the Father. It is not asking; it is not petitioning; it is listening to what the Father is saying. It is the inward voice which said to Moses, "I AM that I AM." It is the Father saying I AM gently; and in this gentle stillness, we experience "Peace, be still." The willingness to go in and shut the door on the erring sense, the personal sense of existence, and permitting the Father to say I AM, announce His allness and oneness, completeness and satisfaction — this is true prayer.

In the textbook, our Leader says, "Prayer cannot change the Science of being." Why? Because true prayer is not changing anything, or asking for something; rather it is the deep feeling or acknowledgment of being, of reality, and the dismissal of that which seems to be. Mrs. Eddy continues, "God is intelligence. Can we inform the infinite Mind of anything He does not already comprehend? Do we expect to change perfection?"

Prayer does not change the seeming into the being. Prayer is deep consecration; it is complete subjugation, the absolute immersion of the personal sense of self into the infinite ocean of Love, where the drop with its sense of restriction, limitation, tension, etc., disappears, and the power and the glory and the dominion which is the ocean's becomes the power and the glory and the dominion of the expression or manifestation, man.

The Bible says we pray amiss when we pray for the personal sense of self. Jesus' "prayers were deep and conscientious protests of Truth, of man's likeness to God and of man's unity with Truth and Love."

Mrs. Eddy prayed constantly to lose all sight of the personal sense of self. Can we do less? Or do we insist upon praying for more matter, better objectivity? This is praying amiss, and you will fail at the outset. To use the human mind for praying is to pray amiss. The human mind is the problem, and we surely cannot use the problem to find the solution. No, we must go to that Mind which knows only present perfection and well-being. It is letting this Mind be your Mind which is also the Christ-Mind. It is permitting the I to go unto the Father and remain with the Father. This is true prayer. Prayer is shutting the door on the first sentence of the Scientific Statement of Being, and letting the second sentence be the All-in-all. This is the way Jesus prayed:

Father, give me the glory which was mine before the world was. Make them one even as we are one.

Where do we pray scientifically? We enter into the closet and shut the door, silently to commune with the Father. The torrent of words, the stereotyped borrowed speeches, the gushing theories, must yield to the heart and soul of prayer which is Love.

When we have shut the door, we are alone with our own being and the reality of things. We are then living the second sentence of the Scientific Statement of Being. Many times during the day, we should have resort to this secret place, and have audience with the Father-Mother, all-harmonious, and experience the adorableness of oneness. Man is incorporeal consciousness or the temple of the living God — and in this consciousness the activity of ideas becomes fruitful.

"In order to pray aright, we must enter into the closet and shut the door. We must close the lips and silence the material sense. In the quiet sanctuary of earnest longings, we must deny sin [the personal sense of self] and plead God's allness." (*Science and Health*)

Are we scientifically denying sin, the personal sense of

ego, and rejoicing in the allness and oneness of being, when we pray in the old way? We are not Christian Scientists until we leave all for Christ. Then let us pray as the Christ. It is here we are undisturbed by the ills of the flesh. It is in this sanctuary that we do not accept the sense of others. We are alone with our own being, the Science of Being. It is here we see our brother as having the face of God, Love. It is here we see our brother as the presence of God saying I AM. Here we rejoice in the allness and oneness of being. It is here where being becomes our own divine being. It is here where the Father says: "Be still — I AM ALL!" In prayer, when the answer does not appear quickly, study the chapter on 'Prayer' scientifically. See if you are pray-ing with the Christ method or praying amiss. True prayer is thinking no thoughts of your own. "Your thoughts are not my thoughts." "And which of you by taking thought can add one cubit unto his stature?" The Christ stills the "noisy waters" as we sail into the haven of Love's allness and oneness.

In any problem, immediately see the impossibility of it from the standpoint of the allness and oneness of the divine Principle, Love. If possible, never come into the problem, but see the truth so vividly that the aggressive mental suggestion as the problem is dissolved. At times, it is necessary to address the satanic suggestion even as Jesus did. Learning to still the "noisy waters" is not always easy. The aggressiveness of the suggestion and the tenacity of the belief that it is 'me' sometimes makes it most difficult to unsee the claim. But it is the refusal to accept the sug-gestion on its own terms, or to give it a man to fight with, that helps quickly to annul it.

Recently, the suggestion offered itself that I had cut my finger. Instantly the Christ-knowing was: If there is no acceptance, there is no punishment. Remember that "the belief is punished so long as the belief lasts"; in the German it reads "acceptance is punished so long as acceptance lasts." So the Christ-man, or conscious identity, could not accept something contrary to its own being, any more than light could accept darkness. And immediately the hand was put behind the back. It said 'bleeding,' but the knowing was: If there is no acceptance, there is no punishment, and the bleeding would be the punishment of the belief that something had cut itself. It took constancy and immediacy to stand fast, but in a few moments the "noisy waters" were quieted, and because nothing had accepted the belief, there was no believer. The healing was immediate.

When the suggestion offers itself that you have lost your keys, your joy, your job, your health, do you run around looking for it? Or do you see the impossibility of it from the standpoint of the allness of the infinitude of Mind, and man as the knowing of this allness and oneness? The certainty of the Christ stops the din suggesting itself, and we can hear the sweet song from heaven. The water has been pacified. As long as thought is knowing the Truth to change something, find something, stop something, then it is not Christian Science. Even wanting to be healed, which seems so legitimate, must be hushed. Suggestion offers its specious wares and says: Give me another treatment, pray for me. Now apply what you are hearing here today on me. Say to it: There is no 'me' but God. Christian Science has unmasked this finite personal sense of self called 'you' or 'me' and leaves only the Christ to be experienced as the song of the Scientific Statement of Being. Say: You, malicious animal magnetism, in the guise of physical personal body, cannot defile the Christliness of being, because the I of my being and all being lives, moves and has being *as* the *eternal now* of perfect being. All is God's expression of Himself.

You, mental assassin, cannot kill, murder, incapacitate, paralyze, destroy one God-given faculty or function or action, through any claim of a natural law. There is no such law. All law is divine law and alone present to act, or cause action — the law of perfection, the law of harmony, the law of perfect functioning. Nor can you operate through any claim of heredity. Man has not a single quality underived from Deity. Man's disposition is safe in Mind, showing forth the essence of Mind itself. Nor can you, animal magnetism, operate through the suggestion that this is an effect from some accident in the past. You are a present lie, for there has never been a lapse from nor return to perfection. Man is God's reflection of Himself. In this scientific prayer, the only possible I says: BE STILL. The fear is dissolved by the universal solvent of Love; perfect Love has cast out fear and the sweet song is heard: "This is My beloved Son in whom I am well pleased." This prayer is the law to this case and every case. And only the Father-Mother's adorableness is left to be experienced and felt here and now, directly and specifically. This is the ever-present kingdom enabling us to know Thy will of perfection. This prayer has fed the famished affections and leaves only the graciousness of being, where Love is reflected in its own loveliness, and the temptation has been annulled, and the song of Christ comes forth in all the kingdom and the power and the glory of being All-in-all!

Our textbook says: "The highest prayer is not one of faith merely; it is demonstration." Demonstration is Immanual, or God with us. Again our textbook says that "Self-forgetfulness, purity, and affection are constant prayers."

"Be still and *know* that I AM God." BE STILL! Quiet, calm, poised, in the knowing that the I is God. Don't try to use the revelation of Christian Science for some end, some proposition, but be still and *KNOW*. Stilling the personal sense of self, knowing becomes spontaneous. Reflection is always still. The I AM that is God, maintains His own image and likeness without being reminded of it through prayer. God, Principle, unerringly sustains its own self-expression, man. The I that is Love keeps its self-expression, man, in the state or condition of loveliness and lovableness. The I that is eternal Life identifies its own sustaining infinite in eternal perfection, well-being and unbroken freedom. Pure Soul satisfies its own self-expression of being — man. Man is the presence of God's being.

Why do we seem so reluctant to yield up this ghost of personal sense for the Mind that is unerring in its directness? Why should it be so difficult to yield up this personal sense of mind with its variableness, its erring nature, fearful transitory thoughts, its doubtful and negative sense, for the Mind which knows only perfect being. Is it because we have not seen the awfulness of the human mind, its enmity to God, its murdering thievery? Jesus surely looked into it and saw its illusory nature. He lifted the curtain from its birth to its death, and said it was a liar and the father of its own lies.

Then Mrs. Eddy could write later in *Retrospection and Introspection*: "Into mortal mind's material obliquity I gazed, and stood abashed. Blanched was the cheek of pride. My heart bent low before the omnipotence of Spirit, and a tint of humility, soft as the heart of a moonbeam, mantled the earth. Bethlehem and Bethany, Gethsemane and Calvary, spoke to my chastened sense as by the tearful lips of a babe. Frozen fountains were unsealed. Erudite systems of philosophy and religion melted, for Love unveiled the healing promise and potency of a present spiritual afflatus. It was the gospel of healing, on its divinely appointed human mission, bearing on its white wings, to my apprehension, 'the beauty of holiness' — even the possibilities of spiritual insight, knowledge, and being."

Let us be willing to bury this false sense of self today, here and now, and let us have the baptism: "Purification by Spirit, submergence in Spirit."(*Science and Health*) Then we can say the personal sense is dead; long live the Christ!

Being still in the Scientific Statement of Being would surely mean resting in, abiding in the Sabbath Day, in which no thinking, no reasoning is permitted. We should have frequent Sabbaths. Are we willing to accept without any mental reservations that our present Mind is the Christ-Mind? Do we go along in the old belief of knowing that God is Mind, and thinking man is the reflector of this Mind? Do you remember what was said on reflection last year? Let us read some of it again.

It is only the personal sense of self which insists on being a reflector. Yes, we hear it said that God is divine Mind and I am reflecting this Mind. Is this true? What is the I that is reflecting the divine Mind? Mind reflects itself, and this reflection is termed *man*. Have I been so long time with you and you have not seen the Father yet? There is no wall of partition where the Father begins and where man ceases. Or where man begins and the Father ceases. Let your center go from self-centeredness to God-centeredness; then we have both the center and circumference.

A great preacher once said in *Ways of Praying*, "With every breath I am breathing the breath of God." This seems so humble. But Mrs. Eddy writes of "deep drawn breath fresh from God." Man is this deep drawn breath. Man is not separate from I AM — I AM saying I AM is the beloved Son. Paul said: "Now we see through a glass darkly; but then face to face: now I know in part; but then shall I know even as also I am known." Christian Science says: I do not know in part, but I am the fullness of Mind in manifestation, the functioning presence of Mind.

Jesus warned us to go in and shut the door. What does this mean but shutting the door on the first sentence of the Scientific Statement of Being, and opening it wide to the great light that *all* is infinite Mind and its infinite manifestation.

"Acquaint now thyself with God" as the only Mind and be at peace. So the Scientific Statement of Being gives us prayer as acknowledgment. There is no personal man to pray. Only the I that is God being its own infinity of presence and power.

Unless the Scientific Statement of Being is seen, we

have faith Science instead of Christ Science. Faith Science is robbing our churches of its vitality. Faith Science seems to work to save in our early days of study, but then comes some problem and it is not solved through faith, then the real student digs deeper and finds spiritual understanding to be his own conscious identity; but unless the Scientific Statement of Being is recognized as one's own identity, we are building on the sand and the storms will shake our building, and great is the fall.

This statement of true being does not permit a finite mind or finite you to arrogantly array itself against the infinite. It was not until Mary Baker Eddy gave us this statement of being that we could understand the Biblical statement I AM that I AM. It is God, Mind, revealing Himself as the great and only I AM. The unillumined human mind has no comprehension of this statement. Only a deep and lasting feeling of humility permits the student to let the I go unto the Father and remain there. Only true humility permits us to feel the depth and might of this statement.

In *Miscellaneous Writings*, Mrs. Eddy tells us, "The five personal senses, that grasp neither the meaning nor the magnitude of self-abnegation, may lose sight thereof; but Science voices unselfish love, unfolds infinite good, leads on irresistible forces, and will finally show the fruits of Love. Human reason is inaccurate; and the scope of the senses is inadequate to grasp the word of Truth, and teach the eternal." And from the same book, "The scientific sense of being which establishes harmony, enters into no compromise with finiteness and feebleness."

The Scientific Statement of Being does not permit a compromise. The satanic suggestion that one is finite, or that consciousness is identified with finiteness, must be dispelled. This dispelling of personal sense and the coming of the Christ-man is quickened and clarified through prayer. Be still and know!

Marriage

Now, with the true sense of prayer and atonement, we are ready to experience the marriage feast. Bring on the wine. In the 'Glossary' we read: "Wine. Inspiration; understanding." We can drink all of this wine. Then let the bride appear. The purity of our being, the innocency that God, divine Principle, creates in man, His own spiritual idea. Let the marriage be made in heaven, male and female one, womanhood and manhood one, bride and bridegroom one; in this eternal oneness, there is no impediment to eternal bliss. Keep your marriage in heaven. Never permit it to leave heaven for earth, and have two beings trying to demonstrate oneness. If you permit your marriage to fall to earth, you will experience animal magnetism, and every belief of malpractice concerning that marriage will show itself in your experience. What God has joined together let no man put asunder. Principle and idea is one. This is the marriage from eternity. This marriage is before Abraham. This is the marriage feast — Love wedded to its own spiritual idea. Let no man put it asunder!

Marriage as it is humanly known, is a concession. It is a suffer it to be so now! After we become students of Christian Science, we must take the marriage from earth and put it back in heaven. It is most important to see Principle and its idea one, and ratified from all eternity. In this true sense of marriage, we are always alone with our own being, not trying to adjust or readjust, not acting or reacting. This Christ-understanding does not have us ignore what appears as husband or wife, but rather draws us nearer and nearer. True sense of husband, true sense of wife, all are blessed in this true understanding. Never let suggestion put a wall between husband and wife, by suggesting that one is spiritually beyond another, or that one knows the truth better than the other, or perhaps doesn't know the truth at all. If you put up this partition, the marriage will fall apart. You may blame it on the other one, but remember, are you not the one putting up the wall, the moment you have another? See that the wall is the belief that there is another. What appears as another is really not another at all. It is the way the Father is appearing; it is the way Life is exhibiting itself; it is the way Mind is manifesting its intelligence. Marriage is your recognition of spiritual completeness! This Christ-understanding may appear as one expressing both male and female qualities in such balance that there is no outward show called marriage, or it may appear in the language of today, but be sure that you never malpractice by believing there are two. What is called another is not the medium for happiness. Your textbook says, "Happiness is spiritual, born of Truth and Love." Husband or wife is not a medium through which heaven comes to earth. Remember, husband or wife is not a medium for hell either.

Personality is not a medium. The love, intelligence, kindness, integrity that we so admire in another, is never present because of another. It is present because that integrity, that love, that intelligence is a present fact of your being, and cannot be obscured by what is called another. Never look to another for anything. Always see that everything comes direct from God. Man is not person. Man is divine expression. Marriage should never be based on physical attraction. What is called physical attraction is not Love — it is lust. Man being divine, can only be attracted by spiritual qualities. Always be alone with your own being. Never be alone with another.

When marriage appears as two, you instantly have animal magnetism. Constantly take your marriage back into heaven and keep it there. In the textbook, your Leader says, "In Science man is the offspring of Spirit. The beautiful, good, and pure constitute his ancestry. His origin is not like that of mortals, in brute instinct, nor does he pass through material conditions, prior to reaching intelligence. Spirit is his primitive and ultimate source of

being; God is his Father, and Life is the law of his being."
Your Leader begins to sum it all up, for she says marriage
should signify a union of hearts. Furthermore, the time
cometh of which Jesus spoke, when he declared that in the
resurrection there should be no more marriage or given
in marriage. Man would be as the angels. Then shall
Soul rejoice in its own, in which passion has no part. The
white-robed purity will unite in one person, masculine
wisdom and feminine love, spiritual understanding and
perpetual peace. The union of the sexes suffers fearful
discord. To gain Christian Science and its harmony, life
should be more metaphysically regarded. Yes, when two
try to become one, there is fearful discord. Never accept
a union of two. Two can not become one. The starting
point of divine Science is: God, Spirit is all. Start from
One, identifying itself as all, and we end up with one.
Never start with two and try to be one. It is impossible
in Christian Science. Jesus started from the Father. See
that what appears to be another is really not another. It is
the one body, the one presence, the one Mind, identifying
itself as *all*. So let us see that husband is not a medium for
anything. Husband is but a symbol. Keep marriage in
the symbol, and see that the symbol is not a medium, but
that Love is present because Love is God, and cannot be
obscured by the symbol. You will always have the Love of
God present and being experienced. This Love will have
the husband or wife more nearly conform to the ideal; but
never be fooled; it is not becoming more thoughtful, more
loving, more honest; it is the disappearance of what we call
personal sense and the coming of the Christ which makes
what is called husband or wife appear more thoughtful,
kind and loving. So keep your marriage in heaven; what
the Father has put together, let no man put asunder. So
your marriage is ratified from eternity.

Keep your marriage in heaven. This is prayer being
experienced. This is your true atonement — drinking your
Christ cup. The Bible says: "He that has the bride [purity]

is the bridegroom [understanding] ... Have I been so long time with you, and yet hast thou not known me. . . he that hath seen me hath seen the Father." Scientific prayer, experiencing true atonement, brings with it the glorious marriage of Father and son, Principle and idea. Now we have experienced the marriage feast, Love wedded to its own spiritual idea. And your Leader says, "Arise from your false consciousness into the true sense of Love, and behold the Lamb's wife, — Love wedded to its own spiritual idea. Then cometh the marriage feast. The Lamb's wife presents the unity of male and female as no longer two wedded individuals, but as two individual natures in one; and this compounded spiritual individuality reflects God as Father-Mother, not as a corporeal being. In this divinely united spiritual consciousness, there is no impediment to eternal bliss, — to the perfectibility of God's creation." (*Science and Health*)

Practice

There are too many failures in our practice. Why? We are dealing with Science; then why is it not demonstrated more as infallible? Is it because we have become so engrossed in stating the letter that we have sacrificed the spirit for the "hecatombs of gushing theories, stereotyped borrowed speeches" and forgotten the Science, "aflame with divine Love"? Mrs. Eddy asks the question: "Why is there so much dissension among Christian Scientists? These 'ways that are vain' are the invention of animal magnetism, which would deceive, if possible, the very elect." (*Miscellaneous Writings*) Some are as involved in petty intrigues, gossip, politicians, and resentments as the Sanhedrin in the time of Jesus, who had no time for the Christ, only time to plot how to get rid of the Christ. We have had in our churches and movement so many politicians, actually planning on who the readers are to be, telephoning requests that members should vote in a certain way, gossiping about the problems of what appears as others, practitioners discussing cases with friends, all in direct violation of the *Church Manual*. Then how can we expect to demonstrate the Science of Being which has as its impulse Love? "Love is the liberator." Love is the feeling and knowing that only God is present to be experienced, so that we never see our brother less than Christlike. Do we go to church as person seeing other persons? Is this not the antichrist, the consciousness of corporeality which our Leader tells us is to be outgrown? Then is the failure due to the Science, or to the failure of the students to live and love the revelation? Christian Science is not to improve the human being with the Scientific Statement of Being. Christian Science is not to save the human being nor prolong its fabulous life. Christian Science is the Science of Mind, the infinite Mind being its own infinite manifestation. If in the Christ-knowing, this light of revelation, the human seems to be improved, becomes less sinful, and its life seems to be prolonged, remember, this is not the purpose of Christian Science. Christian Science is to prove to the world there is no human mind to have a human concept. All power, all presence, all action, all knowing belongs to the Mind which is limitless being. Then the healing is simply incidental; it is the dispelling of the ignorance of personal sense, and the coming of the man of Mind's knowing.

Students, don't fall to the level of "being a healer." Live the office of the Christ, keep the garment on, and the world will be blessed by your living and knowing. Jesus was compassionate. He never turned an honest heart away. He said, feed them; get up and walk; open your eyes; be thou clean. All this was incidental to his living of the Christ. But he was working out his own salvation, and if in this working out he could help, he was most happy; but he kept warning the disciples: Do not rejoice in this, but rejoice because your name, your nature, your essence is God's own essence. Man is God being. There is not God *and* man. There is just God being, and what God is being is man. Then are not the failures due to the failure on the part of the student to be more Christlike? Does not our Leader say, "Hold perpetually this thought, — that it is the spiritual idea, the Holy Ghost and Christ, which enables you to demonstrate, with scientific certainty, the rule of healing, based upon its divine Principle, Love, underlying, overlying and encompassing all true being"? (*Science and Health*)

Certainly she does. Then is it true? Of course it is true, divinely true. It is the Comforter itself. Then, because this is true, should we not lay off the old man as quickly as possible and put on the new man? Get rid of the ghostly belief of personal sense with its egotism, egotism that it did heal or that it did not heal. The one is the glorification of the false sense and the other is the non-glorification of personal sense. Its so-called humility and its so-called egotism are one, and this one is false.

Failures are due to the students not living enough the life that is Christ. Don't say the patient was not receptive, the patient was handled by jealousy or fear, the patient continued to sin. Have God, Love, so *all* that there is no possibility of a personal me to mask the eternal me that is divine. Oh, students, the culprit is this little mean finite me parading around, wanting to heal and to be recognized. It wants the highest seats. It wants to broaden its phylacteries. It is offended if it is not asked its opinion on church discussions. Never let a student of this Association fall to the level of politician or one who seeks position. Take no position unless you feel that God has put you in it, then it will be a glory to all.

Pray daily, pray ceaselessly, that this false sense of self-parading around in the first sentence of the Scientific Statement of Being, be seen for what it is, and see your own Christ, and let the first sentence fade into its nothingness.

Why should we stand aghast at nothingness? Our Leader says, "Jesus taught us to walk *over* not *into* or *with*, the currents of matter, or mortal mind."

Remember how, on the Isle of Patmos, John refused to bemoan his imprisonment? Rather, he used it to attain spiritual vision and let matter be squeezed into pieces of nothingness. This is what the word *Patmos* stands for in Greek. Through some terrifying experience, the human concept gives up the belief of being human, and yields up its pride, fear, egotism, personal sense, etc. It is not necessary to have a Patmos experience, but so many in Christian Science want to improve the human concept, pray to make it immortal, give it what it deserves, saying, "I am entitled to that." Our book says the human is sometimes beautiful, but always erroneous. Then can that which is always erroneous be brought into the line of truth or become truthful? In the Scientific Statement of Being, are we willing to permit the nothingness of matter to appear, be squeezed out of us as it were, and go the way of revelation, and ascend above the clamor and trash where the time-sense universe flutters, and in the brilliant light of Christ-revelation completely fades out?

Sometimes the gentle human must learn to be more like Principle. It yields up its human gentleness and permits the gentleness of Principle, Love, to appear. This gentleness can open the lily without tearing it, and yet it is so almighty that it holds the universe in its eternal grasp. Thus the human yields up its sense of gentleness and takes on the strength of spiritual nature. The healthy human has to yield up human health and find divine health, even as Mary Baker Eddy once said: "As Mary Baker Eddy, I am the weakest of mortals, but as the discoverer of Christian Science, I am the bone and sinew of the world." So it is with us; as person, we are nothing; but as Christ Science in being, we are the bone and sinew of the universe. It is the Christ-knowing, the Christ-man which heals.

Everyday we seem to face the Red Dragon, some form of life and intelligence in matter, and everyday we are required to see the nothingness of personal sense and its material objectivity called personality.

Fallibility of Human Concepts

What appears to us as person, place, or thing, world happenings, church affairs, parading before consciousness and claiming to be our experience, are nothing more than shadow boxing, deflections. Challenge every human concept whether it is called your own or another's. Never let a day pass without cleansing the disk of consciousness. Are we accepting that someone else died that lived to be a hundred, or are we challenging this fallible human concept? Never rationalize concerning human finite concepts. What this decision should be or that decision should be — this wears us out. We get so confused trying to find the solution. See that the divine Mind is present with all the wisdom and understanding in the universe, and directly express this wisdom, and know here and now that this expression is identity. This Christ-knowing does not permit something unwise to be done. See that the Scientific Statement of Being is constantly operating uninterruptedly in and as experience.

Did Moses stop to figure out concerning the Red Sea? How deep it was, how long it would take to cross it? Would this have parted the sea? No. Moses, Jesus, Mrs. Eddy never gave way to such reasoning. They were all starting out from the starting point that *all* is infinite Mind and its infinite manifestation, for God is All-in-all. They were acknowledging God's presence and all-power. They were all living this Christ vision which opened the sea and permitted the children of Israel to cross safely.

When we must face the sea, let us not try to find out why or how deep or how long, Oh Lord, but let us pray:

Father, open their eyes that all may see that they that are for *us* are greater than they that are against us. Surely the second sentence of the Scientific Statement of Being is greater, infinitely greater than anything the first sentence can put up. In *Miscellaneous Writings*, Mrs. Eddy replies to a question: "If one asks me, Is my concept of you right? I reply, The human concept is always imperfect; relinquish your human concept of me, or of anyone, and find the divine, and you have gained the right one — and never until then."

Never see anyone, or yourself, after Adam, but always after the order of Melchizedek, never after the first sentence, but always after the similitude of the second. Let us leave the old for the new. Render thought receptive to this advanced idea. Don't look around you to see if other Christian Scientists are living it. Your work is your own salvation, and if we drop a few flowers on the way and others pick them up, fine; but our work is to ascend as quickly as possible out of the personal sense of existence into the infinite realm of measureless Christ being.

Let us carry this on a little further. Some students are afraid of what others are thinking about them. False concepts of ourselves in the past, etc. If I have accepted identity as spiritual and "before Abraham was, I AM," it is of no concern what the human seems to think or not think, because it is not knowing what I AM. If one has accepted the butterfly and left the cocoon, what does it care about anything that happens to the cocoon, or what others are saying about it; and what harm can they do to that which knows itself to be the functioning presence of the Almighty One? Fly above the cocoon stage, keep both wings up, and fly unto the mountain. Never be concerned about the caterpillar. We have left the sepulchre and can cry out, "Rabboni." It is most important, if someone is gossiping about the caterpillar, condemning it, judging it, that we keep absolutely disconnected from it, because it is not our concept of ourselves; and so all the malpractice,

ignorant or malicious, is harmless when we refuse to identify ourselves with the caterpillar concept. The revelation
is: Man has never been a personal concept. Let us take
the wings of the morning and dwell in the universality of
our being.

This abortive evil ego saying I AM must be seen to have
no identity nor in any way be connected with what I AM.
If we have left the old for the new, and others refuse to take
this same position and want to till the soil, this misconception cannot touch our Christ-self.

Jesus knew this and felt free. Mrs. Eddy knew this
and felt completely serene when the attacks came. Let us
bathe this finite concept in the infinite ocean of Love, and
nothing is left to condemn nor be condemned. All is Love
seeing only the brightness of its own glory.

"Lift up your eyes on high, and behold who hath created these things, that bringeth out their host by number: he
calleth them all by names by the greatness of his might, for
that he is strong in power; not one faileth," Isaiah wrote.

In her *Message for 1902*, Mrs. Eddy wrote: "Christ
Jesus reckoned man in Science, having the kingdom of
heaven within him. He spake of man not as the offspring
of Adam, a departure from God, or His lost likeness, but
as God's child. Spiritual love makes man conscious that
God is his Father, and the consciousness of God as Love
gives man power with untold furtherance. Then God
becomes to him the All-presence — quenching sin; the
All-power — giving life, health, holiness; the All-science
— all law and gospel."

Again from Isaiah, "And I will bring the blind by a
way that they knew not; I will lead them in paths that they
have not known: I will make darkness light before them,
and crooked things straight. These things will I do unto
them, and not forsake them."

To see that God is Love gives us immediate freshness
and newness which has no mental flashback, no mortal

man to harass us. The consciousness of God as Love and man as direct expression, or emanation, of this Love, opens wide the gates of heaven which suggestions seem to have closed, and we find man not in heaven, but as the heaven of infinite Mind's presence, complete and satisfied.

Animal magnetism has been unmasked. Let there be no reluctance. Matter is mortal error. Error is nothing. It is the absence of truth. Can you pray over nothing? Can you pray for an absence of God-man? Then matter is mortal error. Matter is unreal and temporal. What does temporal mean? Is man temporal? Does man exist in a temporal, supposititious universe? To some, it would mean that which is present now but won't be later. In Christian Science, temporal means that which has no reality now because it is not eternal. Temporal has no now existence that will later become nonexistent. Time has no continuity. Time is broken up into past, present, future. But there is no continuity. No one lives in the same time universe. Our clocks may be the same, but our actions and movements are faster or slower. We simply do not exist in the same time universe. This is what seems to cause friction. Living in the same time sense, we have no impediment, because our rhythm is unbroken. To accept that one was born on a certain date starts the temporal time clock. Preexistence is existence before time began; it is our Christ ability to offset this time fuse.

In *Science and Health*, Mrs. Edddy tells us: "Eternity, not time, expresses the thought of Life, and time is no part of eternity. One ceases in proportion as the other is recognized."

Mesmerism is not cause to have temporal effects. Mesmerism is not cause nor effect. There is nothing temporal in the experience of man. Watch your terms. You will hear: Let us suffer it to be so now. Why? There is no temporal identity. Matter is unreal and temporal. Then if it is unreal, can it even have a temporal sense? No, Mrs. Eddy means that which has no existence *now*. This is most important.

Every student must rid himself of the belief in a personal mind. It is pernicious to divine Theology to accept belief in more than one Mind. Jesus "knew of but one Mind and laid no claim to any other. He knew that the Ego was Mind instead of body and that matter, sin, and evil were not Mind." (*Science and Health*)

We must do likewise and reject completely the suggestion of a personal, private mind. There is no indwelling mind to have a time clock. Communistic techniques, Roman Catholic harassment, are all based on a private mind to be influenced or to influence. Christian Science is not one mind influencing another. Christian Science is the one Ego, self-expressing I AM, declaring itself as All. A false, personal, destructive mind is impossible from the standpoint of the Scientific Statement of Being. We must not be made to forget this. Nor must we be made to neglect this basic fact. Jesus said: "Ye are of your father the devil, and the lusts of your father ye will do. He was a murderer from the beginning, and abode not in the truth, because there is no truth in him. When he speaketh a lie, he speaketh of his own: for he is a liar, and the father of it."

In order to speak as one having authority, the student must learn to speak to this carnal mentality: "Ye are a liar and cannot tell the truth of where I am, what I am, what I am doing, seeing, saying, feeling, because that divine idea, man, is the functioning presence of the one divine Mind that is Christ." Then man feels as Christ, sees only from the mount of vision, hears only as the audience of Spirit, knows only from the standpoint of Mind's knowing. Time has no place in this Day. This Day is constituted of *now*.

There is but one way in Christian Science, and this is the way of the Scientific Statement of Being. This keeps on the robe of Christ. This Christ robe is not put on through any human morality, being humanly good, loving, etc. No, this

Christ robe is put on because of sonship. It is our sonship which makes us Christ-like. Jesus said: "If ye know these things, happy are ye if ye do them."

Learn to defend happiness as you would integrity, truth, and so forth. It is our responsibility to destroy every depressive, repressive suggestion. These so-called negative qualities do not constitute the Christ identity. Defend your happiness as you would your door. Happiness includes all. Depressive moods exclude all. It includes nothing but its own egotistical personal sense. We find in *Science and Health* this statement: "Happiness is spiritual, born of Truth and Love. It is unselfish; therefore it cannot exist alone, but requires all mankind to share it."

Let all that constitutes the mortal selfhood be burned in the flame of spiritual happiness born of Truth and Love. Divine Love will erase from the disk of consciousness every earthborn taint.

Our freedom from these contentious suggestions claiming to be our own thinking or mentality must be handled with absolute certainty and conviction — there is no truth in anything the human mind says. It is supposititious opposite and time sense mind, which is no mind. It has no yesterday. It can anticipate no tomorrow. Its claim of *now* is so evasive it ceases to exist the moment one says it is aggressive mental suggestion. There is no reality in matter, and it cannot tell the truth concerning body, church, home, finances, etc. No matter what the suggestion, there is never a material condition that needs to be healed. Healing takes place from the standpoint of allness and oneness of divine Mind.

Acknowledging and accepting the present mind of man to be divine, we can prove beyond doubt there is no source for suggestion, no mental home from which it can come.

Rejecting any other consciousness or mind, one can speak with the authority of Mind, act with the power of Mind, love with the impartiality of Mind, expand with the intelligence of Mind, rest in the exhaustlessness of Mind. One can express health with the will of Mind, be sinless with the purity of Mind, be allied with the infinitude of Mind. Man does not act at the direction of Mind. Idea is the activity of Mind itself, direct and absolute.

To accept God as present Mind rules out all sin, disease, death, and every limitation. Accept the revelation of Christian Science, and we put off the old man, the false sense of mind with its deeds, contentions, dissatisfaction, forgetfulness, quarrelsomeness and argumentativeness. "Let this mind be in you, which was also in Christ Jesus."

So long as we are trying to see the unreality of matter or the problem, we have not yet put off the old man or taken off the shoes. Moses stopped to see why the bush wasn't burning, and saw the nothingness of matter by seeing the allness and oneness of divine Mind or I AM saying I AM. If we remain on the level of personal sense, we will always be contending with what we call good matter or bad matter. All is Spirit. Matter is misstatement of Mind. Whose misstatement? Under the microscope of Spirit, matter disappears. Now let us here today take off our shoes and see that the ground on which we stand is holy ground, thus getting rid of the personal sense of existence. Don't stop to see why the bush is not burned. When we first come into Christian Science, we should stop and see why. That is, some healing takes place, and it is correct to stop and find out how and why the healing was effected; but later in our study, we must rise above the suggestion of healing, and rejoice that our name is written in heaven. "When mortals learn to love aright; when they learn that man's highest happiness, that which has most of heaven in it, is in blessing others, and self-immolation, they will obey both the old and the new commandment, and receive the reward of obedience." (*Message for 1902*)

"Now I ask, Is there any more reality in the waking dream of mortal existence than in the sleeping dream? There cannot be, since whatever appears to be a mortal man is a mortal dream. Take away the mortal mind, and matter has no more sense as a man than it has as a tree. But the spiritual, real man is immortal." (*Science and Health*)

Reluctance to take off the shoes, see the nothingness of matter from the standpoint of Christ-allness and oneness of Spirit, only prolongs the dream, the problem. Many students are reluctant because they want to see Christian Science demonstrated in what they call matter.

Reflection has no objectivity. God reflects Himself, and this is man. There is no mind to have a concept of mortal body, birth, death, etc. Nothing can get between Principle and idea. Why not? Because of *one* being.

Mary stooped to look into the tomb. How often in working out what is called a problem, the student will stoop down to see what is called matter, if it is responding to the prayer or treatment. So long as we stoop down to the material evidence rather than take off our shoes because the place on which we stand is holy ground, we will weep and have sorrow and fear and be frustrated; but when we cry out "Rabboni!" identity is not personal sense, but is Principle's own self-reflection or activity. Identity is the multifarious identification of living Principle, Love — Love saying I AM that I AM. Then like the Master, we will have ascended above the personal sense of self and its problem, and can say, "Touch me not." We will have risen above personal sense and found safety in divine Science. What are called healings take place when this true sense comes of Rabboni or the recognition of the Christ of all being. This is the divine manifestation which comes to the flesh to destroy incarnate error, and what is incarnate error? Error claiming to be a person, place or thing. Let us cry out, in joyful knowing, Rabboni, Master, Christ, and see the Christliness of our own identity. This gives us retreat from the unreal trials of carnality, and we gather all and bring all into the presence of Love, and hear the Father say, "Son, all that I, the only Ego have, is thine."

"Thus saith the Lord the King of Israel, and his redeemer the Lord of hosts; I am the first, and I am the last; and beside me there is no God." That is from Isaiah. And from Mrs. Eddy: "All is infinite Mind, and its infinite manifestation, for God is All-in-all." Upon this base, Christian Science proceeds. "God's law is in three words, 'I am ALL' and this perfect law is ever present to rebuke any claim of another law," from *No and Yes*. "Mind is the multiplier and Mind's infinite idea, man and the universe, is the product," from *Science and Health*.

Then this infinity of Mind brings forth the infinity of man, the product of all Mind's knowing. The Scientific Statement of Being hides all in the Christ Mind, hid with Christ in God. The office of the Christ is to transform what appears as life in matter and show Life to be eternal and divine, Life directly expressing itself and this fullness of expression felt here and now. " Let us feel the divine energy of Spirit bringing us into newness of Life." " We are not Christian Scientists until we leave all for Christ." We must, without any reluctance, leave the world belief. Then we either find nothing, or we find the fullness of Mind in being. The one infinite Mind manifests itself in and as one infinite conception. Idea is the essence of Mind's own conceiving.

Let go the personal sense of ego as the first sentence in the Scientific Statement of Being demands, and find the Ego, to be divine, all substance, all intelligence, all understanding, all ability, all accomplishment.

"A knowledge of the Science of Being develops the latent abilities and possibilities of man. It extends the atmosphere of thought, giving mortals access to broader and higher realms. It raises the thinker into his native air of insight and perspicacity," the textbook tells us. This knowledge of the Science of being, this raising the thinker into his native air of insight and perspicacity, is Christ-being. It is not what the student seems to know of God that is important; rather is it what Mind knows itself to be; this is man and this is important. And all that God knows about His own reflection is: I AM flawless. I AM perfect. I AM beautiful. I AM glorious because I AM that I AM.

The Scientific Statement of Being gives the student the firm conviction of the allness and oneness of God, and the powerlessness and unreality of evil in all its forms. It lifts us out of the frustrating suggestion of a human mind into the ascension where matter and its limiting beliefs are unknown. This Scientific Statement of Being teaches that the material form calling itself personality, experiencing sin, disease and death, is unreal and untrue, and we find the spiritual man of Mind's infinite knowing.

The Scientific Statement of Being gives the student unwavering certainty of reality. "Ye shall have a song, as in the night when a holy solemnity is kept; and gladness of heart, as when one goeth with a pipe to come into the mountain of the Lord, to the mighty One of Israel." (Isaiah)

Understanding this true statement of reality, makes the heart sing and the face glow with inner light. We can thank God through this revelation that the whole of the mortal human picture is unreal from birth to death. It lifts the curtain, and man in all the glory and perfection of the Father, shows forth as one's own immediate identity. Let the joy of singing come forth, the singing based on the Scientific Statement of Being the reality of spiritual identity, and the unreality of personality and its limitation and afflictions.

The human so-called mind is pure evil. Never forget this important point! We hear it said that the human mind is a better phase of mind than the carnal, mortal, or flesh mind, but this is not so. Mrs. Eddy does not teach this. Any good apparent in or as the human being is not present because of the human, but because of some absence of personal sense which permits the Christ-Mind to show forth in all of the brilliancy of the Christ itself. Nothing is present as personality. Jesus said: "Why callest thou me good? One is good, and that is the Father." So any good made evident as person is not present because of personality, but is present because of the omnipresence of God, the source of all good.

We must accept the full revelation as given in the Scientific Statement of Being. Animal magnetism is unmasked as having no life, truth, intelligence nor substance, whereas all is seen to be infinite Mind and its infinite identification.

Christian Science does not ignore mortal error. Christian Science disposes of it as negative. We must not be tempted to ignore this part of the Scientific Statement of Being. Nor must we run away from it by fearing some form it seems to take. No, Goliath today is still calling out: Give me a man. Christian Science does not give animal magnetism a man. Christian Science teaches and proves that the only man is the expression of God's being. The very fact that God is, that there must be expression, and that expression is God's, is allness and indivisibility, makes God instantly available. Then should not this reflection, this man, be as instantly available? Why do we have to sit around and have a process for man to appear? Is it not because the first sentence has not become absolutely true? Have we completely let go the personal sense of ego, or do we demand everything to work around this ego? Is it still lord of all it surveys — this abortive evil ego demanding obedience and obeisance?

Christian Science is divine law, and divine law is immediately present and operating. Prayer does not bring law into operation. To have success in the practice of Christian Science, we must unmask animal magnetism in the guise of practitioner or patient. Both are evil because both deny the infinity of being.

Remember when Mary Baker Eddy was writing the textbook, she could not finish it because of her refusal to unmask animal magnetism? It was her willingness to say *nay, nay* and *yea, yea* that made the fullness of the revelation possible. Some students of Christian Science feel they have left the absolute point of view because they must handle error.

In *Unity of Good*, Mrs. Eddy states: "It is dangerous to rest upon the evidence of the senses, for this evidence is not absolute, and therefore not real, in our sense of the word. All that is beautiful and good in your individual consciousness is permanent. That which is not so is illusive and fading. My insistence upon a proper understanding of the unreality of matter and evil arises from their deleterious effects, physical, moral, and intellectual, upon the race."

"Infinite progression is concrete being, which finite mortals see and comprehend only as abstract glory. As mortal mind, or the material sense of life, is put off, the spiritual sense and Science of being is brought to light." That is from *Miscellaneous Writings*.

We must accept the wholeness of revelation, the completeness and finality of it. Many are willing to open the eyes to the allness of God, but not so willing to show the nothingness of matter and evil. We must see the human mind for what it is — a liar and the father of its own lies. There must be no reluctance to see that there is no truth in matter, no substance in matter, no life in it — not even temporarily.

Man does not come to the practitioner for healing. Man is the expression, reflection, of God's being. Surely the reflection of Mind would not attempt to heal the original One. That which comes for healing is nothing more than the hypnotic suggestion that there is something present besides the Holy One. This Holy One holds within itself both cause and effect. For the practitioner to think that something he seemed to think or say healed, is a state of self-deception. The only demonstration there was, is, or ever will be, is already made, and this is God's. Man is the demonstration. The all-knowing One maintains this demonstration at the point of perfect knowing, perfect seeing, perfect functioning and perfect being. Man cannot demonstrate God. Man *is* the demonstration. God said: "Let there be light and there was light." So the treatment is: Let there be man and there is man. The all of God-Mind, all of eternal Life and universal Love, is present to be experienced as identity, directly, specifically, here and now. What the world calls healing is simply a belief coming to the Christ-light and being dispelled without conscious effort.

"The truths of immortal Mind sustain man, and they annihilate the fables of mortal mind, whose flimsy and gaudy pretensions, like silly moths, singe their own wings and fall into dust." (*Science and Health*)

It is Christ which heals, and what is Christ? Divine manifestation which comes to the flesh to destroy incarnate error. Now what is incarnate error? Error claiming to have a believer, or personality. See that there is nothing present to respond, only the Christ-light being lived and outshining sin, sorcery and witchcraft. This Christ — this divine manifestation of God — is the Father saying: "I AM ALL. A knowledge of aught besides MYSELF is impossible." See that incarnate error is not even temporary identity. Before Abraham was I AM. Before the personal sense calling itself "me" was, I AM. I have always been daily the Father's delight. This is preexistence. This is Melchizedek. The Scientific Statement of Being gives us this Christ-view. It is the base from which all practice should proceed. This incarnate error claiming to be personality and having identity must be rebuked.

One of the students had to appear in a Police Court recently. While waiting for his particular case to come forward, a young Negro boy was on trial for obstructing traffic. He was accused of refusing to permit a white driver to pass; the white driver took out a warrant. The white man gave his testimony in a most convincing way. Finally, the driver of the other car appeared, with his sister and wife. They said they were not drunk, but were returning home from church, and were driving intelligently and lawfully. The lawyer tried every way to convince all present as to the guilt of the young man. Finally, the Judge said, "Now, somebody is lying! So I want a lie test to be taken here and the one found guilty will be sent on the road gang for six months at hard labor." The Negro boy immediately said he would welcome the test. The white man began to become confused and to talk out. The Judge dismissed the case and said, "This is the most outrageous thing that has ever appeared in this court, the most contemptible," and he gave the white youth a complete overhauling.

Now what brought about this complete change in this court room? It was the knowing, the Christ-knowing present as the student of Christian Science. The student had seen so clearly that the Judge was not a person; that the only Judge is the operation of divine Principle, Love; and that his same divine Principle, operating as the Scientific Statement of Being, is the only lawyer, and the only testimony had to proceed from this as a Principle and could not be obscured by any pretense calling itself by any name, color or creed. So the world of symbols had to conform to the ever-present law. Always be the law to every situation. Never neglect your duty to God. When something appears as consciousness, never neglect to see that divine Principle is present and operating as the Scientific Statement of Being and producing the only witness. "Ye are my witnesses, saith the Lord." (Isaiah)

Man is not material personality,
but spiritual individuality.

Association Address of 1956

by

Clarence Steves

David, the sweet singer of songs, in what is known as the 36th Psalm, sings unto the Eternal One, "Thy love is high as heaven, thy loyalty soars to the very skies, thy justice is like mighty mountains, thy judgments are like the deep sea. Thy providence is over man and beast; how precious is thy love, O God! To thee men come for shelter in the shadow of thy wings; they have their fill of choice food in thy house, the stream of thy delights to drink; for life's own fountain is within thy presence, and in thy smile we have the light of life." (Moffatt)

So in this eternal uninterrupted Day, we have the streams of thy delight to drink; and drinking deep from the fountain of thy presence, we find man to be the smile of thy great love. Even the Indians saw a lake to be the smile of the Great Spirit. Christian Science shows man to be the fullness of God's joy, even as our Leader, Mary Baker Eddy, says, "The sinless joy . . . constitutes the only veritable, indestructible man, whose being is spiritual." So this sinless joy constitutes all there is to our being.

We are abundantly satisfied because it is the understanding of the all-knowing Mind in self-expression. As our Leader writes in *Pulpit and Press*: "They shall be abundantly satisfied with the fatness of Thy house." The river of His pleasures is a tributary of divine Love, whose living waters have their source in God, and flow into everlasting Life. We drink of this river when all human desires are quenched, satisfied with what is pleasing to the divine Mind.

So, today, we are not the getting together of many to bask in the smile of God's great Love; but we know ourselves to *be* the smile of God. Divine, infinite Love permits no disintegration to be integrated; but Love, Principle, remains its own integrated Self. One is always one; it is never more; it is never less. Nothing less than infinity can express God. Infinity is that which is in a state of perfect integration. It does not have to come from there and come here, but it remains infinite. Thus, we are not made up of parts, but we are constituted of divine impartation. It is Truth uttering itself, and this utterance, without a single exception, is the wholeness, the completeness, the essence of this Day. So, therefore, this Day does not begin and end; this Day has continuity.

Here in this eternal Day, there is only a clearer vision of our own integrating All. There can never be more than all. Allness is the measure of the infinite, and nothing less can express God.

In *Science and Health with Key to the Scriptures*, Mary Baker Eddy writes, "The divine Ego, or individuality, is reflected in all spiritual individuality from the infinitesimal to the infinite." So is the divine Ego, or individuality, saying I AM from the infinitesimal to the infinite, and this leaves nothing else present to say I AM.

In the same book, we find, "Mind, God, is the source and condition of all existence." So this joy-filled Mind, this spontaneous delightful Mind called God, is the source and condition of this Association, without a single exception. And this is from everlasting to everlasting. So we are in fine condition; we are in good, healthy, whole condition, for we are conditioned entirely and completely by divine ever-present Mind; and there is nothing else present to make any conditions for man.

Mindless matter, substanceless matter, non-intelligent matter, lifeless matter, a delusion of sense, can make no conditions for man. Man, divine idea, is the functioning of the Mind that is God, the only Mind; man is the very essence, the condition, that is Principle itself. So never permit suggestion to say that man is even temporarily a human person and not in good condition. There is nothing human concerning man to be conditioned by organs. Man is not conditioned by flesh, nor by blood, nor by air, nor by weather.

Man, divine idea, is complete, absolutely conditioned by the law of Love, for man is Love's own identification. Man is Love, God, saying I AM. So this ever-present law of Love conditions its own idea, man, and maintains the condition flawless, immaculate, as itself.

On page 344 of *Science and Health*, Mrs. Eddy has written of God as the only absolute Life and Soul, and man as His idea — that is, His image. "It should be added that this is claimed to represent the normal, healthful, and sinless condition of man in divine Science, and that this claim is made because the Scriptures say that God has created man in His own image and after His likeness."

So man is in a sinless condition, for man is the purity of Mind, God, in manifestation. Man is the healthy condition that is God's own self-expression. So we know without a single exception that man is not something separate from Mind, but is the direct expression of Mind itself.

Why would Jesus have said, "Have I been so long time with you and haven't you seen the Father yet?" — unless he meant that man is the functioning, the reflection, of the Mind that is God? Never lose sight of the basic fact that man is not something separate from Mind, but man is the reflection of the knowing that is Mind. Man is not the reflector, the expresser, of God's great love; man is the directness of Love's own self-expressing. God, divine Mind, the great, the only I AM, is the source of all reality, all truth; and man, as divine idea, is the expression of this reality, this truth.

Because this is true, we are the oneness of Mind in manifestation; and in this oneness, all finds its identity. This

Mind, the source of reality, is our Mind. We, then, are all-inclusive; and there is nothing outside wanting to be here, or feeling that it has been shut out.

There is absolutely nothing going on outside of the great I AM — Mind, effortlessly, spontaneously acknowledging what Mind is — this is called man. There is no reaching out for anything, there is no reaching out for more truth today, there is no trying to get a better understanding. Man is the understanding of God. So there is no reaching out going on at all.

Let us not talk about what is going on here. It is not secret; it is sacred. We fill the office of the Christian Science practitioner; and in the *Manual*, we are advised to hold sacred all communications between practitioner and patient. Then why not be obedient to the *Manual*? Resort to your higher selfhood and abide under the shadow of the Almighty. And in this resort and this abiding, we will not discuss others as persons, and will not malpractice on what is called oneself by telling what is going on to what is called another person.

Don't indulge in personal sense for a moment — it is so deadly. Let us so live the Christ that its very presence will be the presence of omnipresence, and this will heal. The Bible says, pray to your Father in secret, and the Father will reward you openly. Confide only in God, and there will be no secrets voiced from the housetops.

To make a statement that a person said this or that, is to pervert the meaning. Our Leader says that the human inevitably perverts what it touches. Are we humans gathered here today to learn more of God? This would be a denial of the revelation of Christian Science. It would deny Mary Baker Eddy's teaching.

The entire Ego is God, and man has no ego but God. Your Leader speaks of it as Ego-God and the Ego-man. Let us be done with duality. We are not even temporarily human beings; there is no duality or plurality here. The great fact is that the divine Mind expresses itself, expresses its own uninterrupted, infinite, eternal Self in its everywhereness; and this divine, infinite activity, this divine manifestation, is called the Son of God. Therefore, my existence as divine idea is uninterrupted, eternal, complete, full. It knows nothing of a birth sense, and certainly will never know anything of a death sense.

Our work, then, is to completely outshine the anti-Christ. The human concept of oneself or another is the anti-Christ. Don't be afraid to call it by its right name — the anti-Christ. Mrs. Eddy says in *Miscellaneous Writings*, "I warn students against falling into the error of anti-Christ. The consciousness of corporeality, and whatever is connected therewith, must be outgrown." Man is the Christ activity, which means that man is the direct expression of Mind itself.

There is no medium between Mind and its idea, man, called language. Language is not something that goes from mouth to ear by vibration. That would be a denial of omnipresence. So to accept this report as language is to have a medium between God and man called language. Truth utters itself; it utters eternal verities priceless and just at hand. Our Leader says, "Immortal Mind is God, immortal good; in whom the Scripture saith 'we live, move, and have our being.' This Mind, then, is not subject to growth, change, or diminution, but is the divine intelligence, or Principle, of all real being; holding man forever in the rhythmic round of unfolding bliss, as a living witness to and perpetual idea of inexhaustible good." (*Miscellaneous Writings*)

Mrs. Eddy says, "I cannot be a Christian Scientist except I leave all for Christ." This whole paper is to show us how to leave all for Christ. (*Miscellany*)

In *Miscellaneous Writings*, we read of "the ever-present Christ, the spiritual idea which from the summit of bliss surveys the vale of the flesh, to burst the bubbles of earth with a breath of heaven." This paper is the breath of heaven, and it is bursting the bubbles of earth. All there is to the human concept is a bubble. If you take the rim off of it you have nothing, "and acquaint sensual mortals with the mystery of godliness, — unquenchable Love. Hast not thou heard this Christ knock at the door of thine own heart, and closed it against Truth, to 'eat and drink with the drunken'? Hast thou been driven by suffering to the foot of the mount, but earth-bound, burdened by pride, sin and self, hast thou turned back, stumbled, and wandered away? Or hast thou tarried in the habitation of the senses, pleased and stupefied, until wakened through the baptism of fire?" No student is waiting for the baptism of fire, for every class-taught student acknowledges completely his divinity. To leave all for the Christ means never to discuss yourself as if you were once a person and Christian Science has impersonalized you. That is not true. Christian Science has not impersonalized us; Christian Science is the revelation that man has never been a person.

A lecturer recently told of a group of hunters, hunting for live monkeys. They found that monkeys like wild rice. They obtained some coconuts, cut small holes in them and filled them with rice. In the morning, they found a group of forlorn looking monkeys, each with a tightly-closed hand full of rice inside the coconut, unable to get them out. They had only to let go of the handful of rice, and would have had instantaneous liberation, or what our movement calls healing.

Are we hanging on to the handful of rice in our own little coconut? Does material existence mean more to us than spiritual existence? How are we identifying ourselves? Our Leader says that you can climb Mt. Blanc, and do many wonderful things, but you can never escape identification with God, Spirit, the one I AM.

Are we going to let mortal mind make monkeys out of us? Are we demanding that Christian Science get our greedy little hands out of that coconut, but let the hand be filled with rice? Do you ask for treatment to get your hand loose, but you have no interest in the basic error at all, the satanic suggestion that you have a private mind inside a private coconut? Do we put our greedy hands inside the coconut and say to the practitioner, heal me, make me more comfortable — but let me keep my rice? Let us have no monkey-shines here.

The Master, Christ Jesus, once told his followers a story that has tremendous import here today. The story of Dives and Lazarus — a rich man, in hell, says if you will just dip your finger in the water, it will help me get rid of some of my hell. The answer, "There is a great gulf fixed" — to the personal sense of love this answer seems cruel, harsh and unloving. Yet, because God is Love and therefore Principle, the gulf must remain between that which thinks of itself as a person, good or evil, well or sick, rich or poor, and that which knows itself to be the son of God, already the heaven of God's presence. The gulf is fixed and there is no bridging it mentally, physically, morally or spiritually.

In *Science and Health*, we read, "Darkness and light, infancy and manhood, sickness and health, are opposites, — different beliefs, which never blend. Who will say that infancy can utter the ideas of manhood, that darkness can represent light . . . There is no bridge across the gulf which divides two such opposite conditions as spiritual, or incorporeal, and physical, or corporeal."

The textbook says, "Between Christian Science and all forms of superstition a great gulf is fixed, as impassable as that between Dives and Lazarus." Yes, the gulf is fixed between that which is divine and that which is human. You cannot take your finger of divinity, and touch the human, and make it comfortable in the hell of personal sense. What appears as the healing of a human concept is not its healing, but its dissipation. To be unwilling to let go the old for the new, is the hell of crucifixion; to be willing to let go the old for the new, is the heaven of ascension.

To live as greedy mortals, trying to get better flesh, more matter, is the crucifixion. Matter is a misstatement of a fact, not a condition. Willingness to leave the old for the new renders thought receptive of the advanced idea. What is the advanced idea your Leader talks of? Man is not a person; man is divine idea. What is a divine idea? It is the functioning presence of the great and only I AM. Truly, all is I AM saying I AM. There is no bridge needed between Father and Son, between cause and effect, between Principle and idea. Why? Because Being is One, indivisibly One, supremely One, divinely One, infinitely One, eternally One. And because of the indivisible oneness of all being, man is the expression of God's being. Now, what is God's being? The textbook says, freedom, infinity, harmony and boundless bliss. So man must be God being freedom, God being infinity, harmony and boundless bliss. We never interchange the terms God and man in Christian Science, God is cause, man is effect; but cause and effect is one being, and this being is freedom, harmony, infinity and boundless bliss.

So let go the handful of rice called person, let go the handful of atoms, let go the breathing dust, all called man. Let go all the prejudices, believed to be mixtures, North, South, false religious teachings, etc.

Are we afraid to let go of organs called heart, brain, blood, or do we demand that Christian Science make them work perfectly up to some human standard? The moment we are willing to let go the handful of rice — the belief that brain, heart, and blood have something to do with life and intelligence — the moment we let it go, then what are called organs begin to function normally and naturally. They do so, not because they have been healed, but because it is seen that there is no material heart, brain, or body. The functioning, the action, is present because it is God, I AM saying I AM, and this functioning, this action, has never left its natural home, and its natural home is Mind, God. So everything is found in Mind as Mind.

So let's keep our hands out of the coconut — that is, the evil suggestion that man is personality — and let us see that slavery is abolished. We cannot afford to indulge in personal sense for a moment. Never discuss it with yourself or others.

What is called personal sense, material sense, mortal mind, is unwilling to put off the Dives, but wants Dives to be healed. It says come on, put your finger into that holy water called treatment, make me more comfortable, but don't say I'm not a person. We must be willing to leave the old for the new. Christian Science does not patch up the old; it completely abandons the old, and so demonstrates its divinity.

Choose ye this day whom you will serve. No man can serve two masters. Believing oneself to be partly human, partly divine, is to serve two masters. It is a state of dualism. But man, divine idea, has no choice, for man is the directness of Mind itself in self-expression.

In Ephesians, Paul admonishes us, "That ye put off, concerning the former conversation, the old man, which is corrupt according to the deceitful lusts; and be renewed in the spirit of your mind; and that ye put on the new man, which after God is created in righteousness and true holiness."

Mrs. Eddy said: "You must get rid of the old man, the old woman; you cannot make them better and keep them. You are not getting rid of the old man if you try to make him better. If you should succeed in making him better, he would stay with you. If you patch up the old and say it is good enough, you do not put it off, but keep it. If you try to make the old satisfactory, you are preparing to keep it, not to put it off."

Christian Science gives us this new man, and we follow the advice of Jesus when he said, "No man putteth a piece of a new garment upon an old; if otherwise, then both the new maketh a rent, and the piece that was taken out of the new agreeth not with the old. And no man putteth new wine into old bottles; else the new wine will burst the bottles, and be spilled, and the bottles shall perish."

In practice, we don't take the new and put it into the old. If someone calls and says that they have a bad material heart, do we pray for them to have a good material heart, or is it Christian Science to know that the only heart is the great heart of Love; it is a universal heart, and it belongs to the only body there is, the shrine of Love, the temple of the living God. This one, this only heart, beats with the rhythm of omnipotence and omnipresent good.

Christian Science gives us the new heart. Treatment does not make the old into the new; so when the so-called bad material heart begins to function normally and naturally, it is not because it has been made over, but the idea heart is present and functioning right where the symbol seemed to be. There is only one idea heart; it is infinite, eternal, universal, impersonal. There is no need for more than one heart because there is only one idea called man. This idea man has never been repeated, so there is no need for a repetition of heart any more than a repetition of body.

Mind, God, is the source of all action, the source of all function, and there is nothing to retard that perfect, harmonious action. Man, including all right ideas, includes the right idea called heart, and this one idea functions by divine ever-present law. Thus we have not fallen into the evil suggestion of trying to make a bad material heart into a good one; we have not put a piece of new garment upon an old. We know ourselves to be the sparkling, lucid Christ-body, the heart of Love.

We have conquered the suggestion that disobedient cells must be turned into obedient cells, disobedient children must be turned into obedient children. We do not fall into the pitfall that man, or body, is material and personal;

the attempt to change something is nullified. Oneness, all-ness, wholeness, infinite being, is realized.

We are not dealing with patients with little private bodies and minds. The healing Christ will dissipate the patient, and all will be radiant and bright. We call it healing, but it is not healing. It is putting off the old for the new. This is not healing, but revealing.

Romanism, medical theories, sciences try to patch up the old and say it is good enough. Mental sciences patch up the old by stopping wrong thinking and giving it right thinking. This is the reason the gulf is fixed between Christian Science and all else. Christian Science alone refused to make the old into the new; but this Science of being starts out with God-cause and ends with God-effect, called man.

In *Retrospection and Introspection*, Mrs. Eddy writes, "The divine hand led me into a new world of light and Life, a fresh universe — old to God, but new to His 'little one.' It became evident that the divine Mind alone must answer, and be found as the Life, or Principle, of all being; and that one must acquaint himself with God, if he would be at peace. He must be ours practically, guiding our every thought and action; else we cannot understand the omnipresence of good sufficiently to demonstrate, even in part, the Science of the perfect Mind and divine healing."

In *Retrospection and Introspection*, Mrs. Eddy records, "I had learned that thought must be spiritualized, in order to apprehend Spirit. It must become honest, unselfish, and pure, in order to have the least understanding of God in divine Science. The first must become last. Our reliance upon material things must be transferred to a perception of and dependence on spiritual things. For Spirit to be supreme in demonstration, it must be supreme in our affections, and we must be clad with divine power. Purity, self-renunciation, faith, and understanding must reduce all things real to their own mental denomination, Mind, which divides, subdivides, increases, diminishes, constitutes, and sustains, according to the law of God."

So Christian Science gives us the new man created in the likeness of infinity, therefore infinite; created in the likeness of eternity, therefore timeless; and there is no finite time-sense man. The new man is never born, and the new man never gave birth to anything. The new man is both male and female, perfectly balanced. Never for a moment in infinity is there an unbalance of male and female. It is always Father-Mother, Adorable One, harmoniously self-expressing. The new man is Love demonstrating Love, constituted of sinless joy, forever showing forth the Principle, Love.

Whenever you use the term *man*, be certain that you don't see something separate from God. The term *man* means God in manifestation. The term *man* means Life living, Love loving, Mind knowing. So Christian Science has revealed man as the glory of God. Man, the very immaculateness of God Himself. Man, the satisfaction of Soul.

It is so important to recognize that in Christian Science we are dealing with *the* Science, and we have certain scientific terminology, and our terms must be kept straight. No student could say, "I am God," because the terms would be incorrect. He couldn't say, "I am God," because he would be saying, "I am cause;" but all there is to man, is the effect of God's knowing. All there is to man, is the very activity of Godliness. Jesus said, "Have I been so long time with you and haven't you seen the Father yet?" Are our senses so dull that we still see persons? Nothing is present as person.

What seemed so evident as Jesus, what seemed so evident as Mary Baker Eddy, as Elisha, Moses — this is present because of the willingness to put off the old for the new; present because it is the Christ. It is our willingness to see that nothing is present as person, but everything is present because it is God — I AM saying I AM. No person can do anything for or against. It doesn't have the ability. If you take the first sentence of the Scientific Statement of Being and say, "There is no life, truth, intelligence or substance in personality," what have you got left? You've got nothing; you have completely nothingized the human concept. But here your second sentence says, "All is infinite Mind and it's infinite manifestation," that God is All.

Make the declaration, "My senses cannot be perverted and see persons, places and things, for my senses are God's senses and see only as God sees." There is no perverted mind-power that can make students of Christian Science see that which is not going on. Mind-power is God-power, and it cannot be perverted. There is no perverted mind-power irrespective of what name you call it. It is all a claim of perverted mind-power, which says, "I can make you see that which is not going on." It is a lie and the father of its lies. All power belongs to God, omnipotence, and there has never been a perversion of the God-power called evil.

You see, Christian Science does not take into consideration what is called objectification. Christian Science is wholly withinness. Man has been revealed as consciousness. Consciousness has within itself all reality. Man's consciousness is universal; man's consciousness includes the universe. So make the declaration daily, I cannot *be made* to forget that there has never been a perversion of Mind-power. There is no perverted mind-power that can make any student of Christian Science believe that Christian Science is not meeting his needs, or saying perhaps medical science can help him. There is no perverted mind-power that can produce dullness, apathy, inertia, lack of interest. It is the most important thing to know today. And that is why it is so important to acknowledge that we are not little coconuts with little minds inside.

Man is not a personality. What is called personality is only a dim perception of our spiritual individuality. I am not responsible for what someone else thinks about what is called myself, but what I know myself to be is most important.

Where is this so-called thinking going on? We are not thinkers. Christian Science does not teach us to think. Christian Science teaches us Mind is God, and Mind is All, and Mind expresses itself. Oh, yes, it appears this is right thinking; but daily make the declaration, "The present Mind I have is God, and right where I seem to be thinking fearfully, negatively, the divine Mind is expressing itself, and this knowing is myself."

The present life we have is God, and the present Mind is God, and right where we seem to be thinking erroneously — or even what we sometimes call brilliantly — the Mind that is God is present, and expressing itself, and cannot be displaced by this concept calling itself *me*.

One morning when in California, I seemed unable to get up. I opened the textbook and found one line, "The material body, which you call *me* is mortal mind . . ." Just a line, not even a complete sentence. I asked the question out loud, "Who is the you calling it *me*?" Like a flash that word *you* finity, the first iniquitous manifestation of sin, calling itself you, was saying it was you calling it me. Like a flash of lightning, Satan fell. "Thou shalt have no ME but God." Again I read in the textbook, "The first demand of this Science is, `Thou shalt have no other gods before me. This *me* is Spirit." Then the only thing here that can say *me* is Spirit, and Spirit is all right. But think of the audacity of it, this 'you' calling it *me*!

Never permit anything to say me. *Me* is God, a term for God, the same as I AM is a term for God. You wouldn't permit someone to say you were dishonest; then why permit someone to say that thing the body calls itself us. Christian Science does not heal a false concept; it reveals the true concept and leaves no false concept.

In *Miscellany*, we read, "Today the watchful shepherd shouts his welcome over the new cradle of an old truth. This truth has traversed night, through gloom to glory, from cradle to crown. To the awakened consciousness, the

Bethlehem babe has left his swaddling clothes (material environments) for the form and comeliness of the divine ideal, which has passed from a corporeal to the spiritual sense of Christ and is winning the heart of humanity with ineffable tenderness."

In *No and Yes*, we find, "Let the Word have free course and be glorified. The people clamor to leave cradle and swaddling-clothes."

The whole purpose of Christian Science is to take us away from the belief of cradle, that there has ever been anything cradled about us, or that we have been in swaddling clothes. The dictionary says swaddling clothes are to bind, wrap tight, or to limit.

Are we today willing to leave all for the Christ? Are we willing to leave the personalized restriction, localization — these are the swaddling clothes.

Never accept the evil hypnotic suggestion that man has been divided into millions of parts. The textbook tells us that God is all-presence, God is all-power, and nothing apart from God is present or has power. Also the textbook says, "The divine Science of man is woven into one web of consistency without seam or rent." In *Retrospection and Introspection*, we read, "Whatever diverges from the one divine Mind, or God, — or divides Mind into minds, Spirit into spirits, Soul into souls, and Being into beings, — is a misstatement of the unerring divine Principle of Science, which interrupts the meaning of the omnipotence, omniscience, and omnipresence of Spirit . . ."

Never permit anything to tear or mar the Christ garment that is man. You tear, divide, mar, the Christ garment when you think in terms of another. Let us leave all for the Christ. Oh, sometimes it's difficult to let the old go for the new. It isn't always unwillingness; it is sometimes the habit of what is called thinking, rather than letting Mind express itself. Let us stop thinking as persons, and let us live the spiritual individuality which is Mind knowing.

Jesus fed the multitude by knowing that man had not been millions of times repeated. Jesus knew that the only man is the infinite, indivisible expression of God.

The textbook says, "Give up the belief that mind is, even temporarily, compressed within the skull, and you will quickly become more manly and more womanly. You will understand yourself and your Maker better than before." Here the suggestion is that Mind is compressed within the narrow limits of physical humanity. Has man ever been nothing and becomes something at birth and then returns to nothing? Isn't this the swaddling clothes we are to leave today?

Man is the self-expression of God, the Self that is God giving expression to its own aliveness, giving vitality to its own aliveness, that is called man. Then can this man be compressed even temporarily in the skull, and called person, and that person carrying around by name? Is your name human, or do you have the new name? Isn't our new name, our new nature and essence, the truth as revealed in Christian Science? My name is the essence of Christian Science. By this true acknowledgment, we become what appears to be even better Christian Scientists, and we show forth to the world that Christian Science is all that our Leader says it is.

Can malpractice ever touch Christian Science, the divine revelation? No. But malpractice does seem to touch that which thinks of itself, even temporarily, as person doing, person not doing, person understanding. To think of ourselves as personal Christian Scientists, is to put up an object for malpractice; but to understand ourselves as the operation of Christian Science is to have complete protection. Never think of yourself as *a* Christian Scientist — that would be one of a series, one of many — but acknowledge, my nature, my name, my essence, my being is Christian Science. I am Christian Science in operation.

Freedom from aggressive mental suggestion always

comes when we refuse to identify ourselves as personality and to think in terms of *a* — "a this" or "a that." There is no *a* in the kingdom of God, and that is where man lives, moves, and has his being. It is *the*.

Christian Science is the law of God, the law of universal harmony. Therefore, we are not divided into parts. The movement of Christian Science exists only in one place, and that is in the consciousness of that which knows itself to be Church. The movement does not exist out there. The movement moves because God moves it. The movement is because it is consciousness; it doesn't exist in stones and churches and places. The only place the Christian Science movement exists, is in the consciousness of what we call its members. Let us see that we are not one of many, but let us see that we are the Christian Science movement. Would you not make the declaration, "I am Church"? Is Church something outside, or is Church idea included in true consciousness, true being? Man includes his church.

We are not persons with some understanding of divine facts, because we would wake up and find we don't know anything. I *am* understanding. Can Mind, God, be compressed in a skull? Did you ever stop to consider the word *compression*? Your Leader refers to being compressed within narrow limits. The dictionary says to compress would be to force into a narrow compass. Have you ever watched a pressure cooker? It builds up steam; if not watched carefully, it explodes or pops off. Is not this what personality does? It seems to stand something just so long, and then has had enough and pops off. Do you not see why it is so necessary not to think of yourself even temporarily as compressed?

In the First Edition of *Science and Health*, Mrs. Eddy wrote, "Spirit originating in matter, and Intelligence inserted afterwards, Soul pushed into a body, matter intelligent, and the body named man where personal sense takes the lead of Soul, is a myth."

Look at the words — intelligence inserted afterwards, Soul pushed into a body, and the body named man.

Also in the first edition, we read, "Soul is outside of matter, and not a person but Principle: unlimited and infinite, beyond all boundaries; it is not pent up in person or man."

We hear of pent up emotions. Should we not say, egotistical personal sense wanting to be something, finds in Christian Science that which knows itself to be the Christ?

Personal sense is nothing but a handful of dust thrown into the face of spiritual immensity.

Is Mind under compression, encased in a skull? "Skull" as Golgotha, is the place of the crucifixion. No crucifixion can take place unless there is indulgence in personal sense. Jesus permitted the crucifixion in order to prove the eternality of Life. We no longer need to prove it. Jesus was the Wayshower. If we accept the suggestion that evil, or personality, is even temporarily our dwelling place, we are believing in time . . . and have lost the eternal now.

The personal senses always betray us into turning Principle into right and wrong, Truth into theories, Life into organs — all of this compression is called man. What a delusion! The acceptance of any such belief brings repression, depression, suppression. Do you feel suppressed — cannot express yourself as you want to? You have not given up the swaddling clothes. If you want to be babes feeding on milk, all right. You may say, "Christian Science isn't meeting my needs. Practitioners don't help me any more, I don't think they're any good. In the old days, I called up and was healed immediately. Oh yes, I know Christian Science is true — *but*." As in the second chapter of Genesis, 'but.' God made all good — but. Doubt and fear come in, the first indication of personal sense on its rampage.

Are we going to constantly ask for help to heal a personal body? You can't be happy in a lie. Jesus says the human sense of self is a liar from the beginning, and can't be helped.

You've read of the healing of Mr. Mann in *We Knew Mary Baker Eddy, Third Series*. He was shot in the heart and was healed. Mrs. Eddy told him, "You were thrown violently out of the house, and picked yourself up on the outside; go not back into it."

Students of Christian Science are thrown violently out of their house called body when they say there is no life, truth, intelligence, or substance in matter. A violent displacement. How revolutionary. When we acknowledge that this statement is true, we either cease to exist, or we exist in the Mind that is God. Idea is the functioning of the Mind that is God — this is our home, this is our heaven, this is our church, this is our All.

No practitioner can help that which insists it is a physical body parading around calling itself man. Indulging in personal sense is dangerous. Let us leave the milk for meat, strong meat, the absolute facts of divine Science as revealed and written in our textbook. We must admit them, and admit them without any compromise. Man is the power of omnipotence in action. Man is the eternality of Life itself. Man is not something separate from God, the great, the only I AM. Man is the I AM saying I AM, and nothing else has presence to say I AM.

The very absence of this pressurized, atomic misconception called me, you, permits I, God, to be the only I present. Remember, in the chapter on 'Spiritualism' in the textbook, we find that error is not a convenient sieve through which to strain truth; and to believe that one is a person straining to know the truth and put it into action, is worthless.

Let us be willing to take off the swaddling clothes here and forever, and when the winds of God blow, the grand truths being uttered, don't hug your tatters of personal sense. When the wind of Mind — omnipotence, omnipresence, omniscience — blows, it removes fear based on finity; it leaves no mortal trying to become immortal; it leaves no suppressed, depressed, compressed personalities waging feeble fight; it leaves only the man of God's creating. When the wind of God blows, it leaves nothing unlike itself. It is the Father saying, "Son, all that I have is thine." Of course, all that the Father has is the Son.

There is nothing withheld. Strong meat, absolute Truth, God is the one good, the one I AM, the alone I AM. All ability, intelligence, function, action, perfection, faculties. The fullness of all that the Father has, is the Son. Hence man, as reflection, has no ability of himself, and because man has no ability, he can have no disability.

Reflection has no ability, hence no disability. Reflection must be obedient. Man is simply the term for the fullness of Mind's glowing knowing. Think of the joy of knowing that all there is to man is the glowing knowing of Mind, not something trying to know something. You just can't help yourself. Man does not exist as man; man exists as the effect of Mind's knowing. All this vital, spontaneous, glowing knowing constitutes the only man. There is no compression, or deflection, only divine reflection going on. The belief that Mind, or Life, was even temporarily compressed in a skull has been dissipated. This, of course, gives us instant freedom and liberation from the belief that man can possibly think. Man cannot think; man as man is nothing. Man has no organs; therefore, man has no brain; and if man has no brain, he cannot even think in belief. All Mind is God.

Jesus freed those who came to him from the evil suggestion of belief in a personal mind — whether it was a good one or a bad one. The Bible calls it those whom Satan hath bound. The satanic suggestion that would bind, is that personality exists. Mrs. Eddy says, "The understanding that the Ego is Mind, and that there is but one Mind or intelligence, begins at once to destroy the errors of mortal sense and to supply the truth of immortal sense." This brings liberation. That which sits in the chair is not the creator of thought. The textbook says, "Thought is borrowed from a higher source than matter," and, "Man shines by borrowed light." Reflection cannot think. All thought proceeds from divine Mind.

Now it is true that Mrs. Eddy uses the words *think* and *thinking*, but Mrs. Eddy uses them scientifically. She had to use terms that the world could understand; but she did not mean an activity going on in the head. If it did, and this is one of the most important points in Christian Science practice; if thinking means something going on in the head, then what appears to be a physical body must have within itself a mind; and in practice, we would have to deal with that private mind. Never forget that the basic truth is that all Mind is God, and the basic error is mortal mind. Mrs. Eddy tells us "the basic error is mortal mind."

So man does not have a private mind which he alone possesses. There is but one mortal mind. That which is called a mortal person does not have a mind. But it is simply an objectification of mortal mind. Our Leader says over and over, and you will find it page after page — mortal mind and body is one. There would be no Christian Science healing if each patient had a personal mind. We would be forced to handle the patient's mind, and thus would fall into the category of hypnotism. Christian Science is the Science of Mind-healing. It heals the suggestion that there is a personal mind. Mrs. Eddy uses terms quite differently from the way the world does.

"Lucifer" is simply a term for what we call mortal mind. Christian Science has brought it to hell, to nothing.

In *Science and Health*, we read, "If mental practice is abused or is used in any way except to promote right thinking and doing, the power to heal mentally will diminish, until the practitioner's healing ability is wholly lost."

Always remember that right thinking will not produce the Christ that heals. The Christ will produce what looks like human right thinking. Right thinking will not produce the Christ. The Christ appearing as one's own experience does seem to have one do what the world calls the humanly right activity, but no Christian Scientist would leave it there.

The cancer of today is nothing different than the leprosy of Jesus' day. Jesus healed ten; he could have healed a hundred. Why? There has never been a repetition of disease any more than there has been a repetition of body. Disease claims to be ever-present as mortal mind, but it has no more substance than mortal mind. Heal the hypnotic suggestion that there ever has been a Mind besides God.

If we fall into the mesmerism that we are healing disease, we are on the same plane as a doctor; and we had better turn them over to the doctor; they will be much better off. We would be 'matter' physicians if we healed on the same basis as a doctor.

What is called human right thinking, must be put off, for it does not produce the Christ. But the coming of the Christ produces what is called right thinking. Let's not be fooled. It is not the right thinking of a person; it is the Christ-Mind expressing itself independent of the personal sense. How could we be obedient to the command in the Bible, "Be still and know that the I is God?" How could we solemnly promise to watch and pray for the Christ-Mind if we had to think with the human mind which is enmity to God? At no place does Mrs. Eddy say that the human mind can think right, but she says that the human mind imbued with the Christ seems to think right, not because the human mind is better, but it is losing its claim of entity or reality, and the divine Mind is appearing as all.

If we are obedient to our Leader's revelation, we rejoice that there is no right thinking man, no wrong thinking man, no man rewarded for right thinking, no man punished for wrong thinking. This is not the Christ way.

Jesus did not say to Mary Magdalene, "What have you been thinking?" He didn't say to the leper, "It's your right thinking." He said, "Go, thou art *made* whole." God makes man whole. God makes man perfect. This is forever. There has never been a lapse from; there has never been a return to.

Ideas do not think. Idea is the emanation of Mind; idea is the functioning of Mind. We read in *Retrospection and Introspection*, "My own corporeal personality afflicteth me not wittingly, for I desire never to think of it, and it cannot think of me."

Crucifixion, resurrection and ascension — there is nothing mysterious concerning these words. Acceptance of the suggestion that one is compressed within the narrow limits of humanity is daily crucifixion. As one begins to let the swaddling clothes go, and the personal restricted thinking knows that there is something divine about himself, this is the resurrection.

Accepting anything as the nature of man which is not the nature of the primal cause, is crucifixion. It claims an ego apart from God, the great I AM. It claims rivalry, envy, egotism, fear, dullness, apathy, a ruptured sense of self. And in its so-called right thinking, the good it would, it does not; the evil it would not, it does; it is a constant pendulum. It's insistence that it has something to do with our identity, even temporarily, is the crucifixion.

Suggestion keeps needling, Yes, back there before you knew of Christian Science you did that, said that, saw that. This is the most satanic suggestion that can come. There has never been a moment in eternity when man was not the conscious identity of being as found in Christian Science. We have never betrayed our Christ into the hands of personal sense.

"Before Abraham was, I AM." Every student of Christian Science can say with the authority given to the Son of God, before the human concept was, I AM. Don't be afraid to acknowledge completely your divinity. You will not be absorbed; you are not making yourself God. You will find marvelous liberation from your human self.

We are not waiting for the moving of the water to free us; but man is the moving of the water; man is the immaculate, innocent water flowing straight from the throne of God itself. We are not waiting for someone called a practitioner to plunge us into the water, to put personal sense of self into the water to be healed. Let us dip the concept of ourselves now seven times into the river Hiddekel, and we will come out as divine Science understood and acknowledged.

To dip yourself seven times means only to acknowledge completely that there is nothing human about what I am; but if you continue to accept suggestions, and believe that they are directed at your true self, then you will be trying to demonstrate Christian Science. Never try to demonstrate. You are demonstration. If you try to demonstrate, it is crucifixion. But make the declaration, I am not trying to demonstrate the truths of Christian Science; I am the truth of Christian Science in being. This will hasten the crucifixion into the ascension, and there will be no need for resurrection. But living as good human persons knowing a little about our divinity, we do bring on the resurrection. But the trouble with the resurrection is that you slip back so easily into the crucifixion. It is so difficult not to be personal; it is so difficult not to have prejudices, to take sides on issues. But this is the crucifixion, so why be surprised when suggestion says there's a problem? Did you defend yourself against the aggressive mental suggestion that somewhere along the line there was a personal suggestion of yourself? Were you a person saying this or that? That is the crucifixion.

Are there little human persons clad in false mentalities? Can we possibly be human, even temporarily? Are we a fragment, a segregated being, one of many human units that go to make up a whole? Are we finite, localized, receiving impressions from the outside? Are we part of a great jigsaw puzzle, one of millions of parts trying desperately through Christian Science to put the parts together? Or is God what our Leader declares Him to be, the Adorable One? There is no Alpha to creation; revelation always has been. There is no Omega. There is always now. We have conquered the sound barrier, are eliminating the heat barrier, and then we will wipe out the time barrier. As we travel at the speed of light, we will exist in the continuous now. Christian Science does not teach us to travel at the speed of light; Christian Science says I am the light of the world; so therefore I must be the continuity of now; and in this now, I find nothing past, nothing future; I live as the light of the world.

In the textbook, our Leader says, "Breaking away from the mutations of time and sense, you will neither lose the solid objects and ends of life nor your own identity. Fixing your gaze on the realities supernal, you will rise to the spiritual consciousness of being." "The age has not wholly outlived the sense of ghostly beliefs. It still holds them more or less. Time has not yet reached eternity, immortality, complete reality. All the real is eternal. Perfection underlies reality. Without perfection, nothing is wholly real. All things will continue to disappear, until perfection appears and reality is reached. We must give up the spectral at all points."

Is not man conscious identity? Whose conscious identity? It is Mind, God, conscious of His own identification. It is God's conscious identity. Then we cannot accept the hypnotic suggestion that man is a receptacle of some kind encased in a body; this is crucifixion.

Some students think that there is some wonderful kind of knowing that can be carried on by this segregated unity, this shadow, this personal sense calling itself man for the purpose of self-improvement, for the purpose of keeping this corporeality whole, comfortable, satisfied, properly active, alive. That which believes itself to be a human person thinking of itself in this manner, is far from being oblivious of human self; it is animal magnetism; and this is crucifixion.

Let us know that all that is going on, is the operation of divine Principle, Life, and this operation in its directness, is called the Son of God. Let us not permit any pretense to call itself "us." What is a pretense? "Holding with something false, vain, presenting something deceptive, a mistake." And that is the only thing that can be crucified. Man never experienced it. It was Jesus' fate, but not the experience of the Christ. His resurrection was our resurrection. Then why do we not live in and as the ascension? Has the heavenly vision, divine Science, lifted us into the light? Christian Science teaches us man is light.

When the seventy returned to Jesus, he said, "Notwithstanding in this, rejoice not, that the spirits are subject unto you; but rather rejoice, because your names are written in heaven" — that is, that man is the identification of the Father, and man has never left and never returned to harmony. Man is perfection; he is God's perfection.

As the Jesus was laid aside for the Christ, the ascension took place — and it takes true humility to let the Jesus submit to the Christ, because the egotistical personal sense of self always wants to assert itself.

Let us rejoice, and throw all the swaddling clothes into the winds of God, and cling to nothing that will hide our Christ. Yield the spectral at all points, have no reluctance, step through the Shekinah, remove the veil. Man, divine idea, the functioning presence of the Mind that is God, is here and now, without any obscuration. We cannot be crucified, we cannot be resurrected, because acknowledging man to be divine idea, the function of the Mind that is God, is to have ascended above personal sense. But as long as I think I am a person trying to demonstrate Christian Science, and to ascend, then I am in the realm of crucifixion.

Let us know ourselves after the similitude of the Christ, after the order of Melchizedek. In this order, the brightness of his glory, we see whatever is not true concerning primal cause, is not true concerning reflection. Reflection is always obedient.

There is nothing difficult or mysterious in the ascension; it is to so live the Christ that we have ascended above the trash of human experience; it no longer impresses itself as reality, but is seen to be a dream without a dreamer.

Let us not look back longingly, but live the Scientific Statement of Being. To live the Scientific Statement of Being, is to have the ascension. There has never been any life in the spectral; there has never been a birth, swaddling clothes, no life in its assertions. Certainly it is mortal error and mortal error that is nothing. Recognition of this is ascension, recognition that *all* is infinite Mind and its infinite manifestation, that God is All-in-all. There is nothing beyond the All, there is nothing that can ever come into being that can be more than all, all is all. This understanding leaves no finiteness to assert itself; it leaves no swaddling clothes we have to burn, no dust that we have to shake from our beautiful garments, for man is seen to be the glory of the Father, the purity that is Principle, the Love that is divine, the Life that is from everlasting. All this is I AM, saying I AM; and what I AM says, is the beloved Son.

This is to live the ascension, to live as Love's own direct expression; to live the ascension is to see that man is Love loving. This is reality. We have taken all into the Father's house, and we find only flawless, unerring Principle itself.

AFTERNOON

We saw this morning that the only crucifixion takes place in the refusal to live divine revelation. Never permit thought to become personal. Let it always be from the standpoint that it is Mind, God, voicing His own truthfulness. In the chapter on Spiritualism in the First Edition of *Science and Health*, Mrs. Eddy called the chapter "Imposition versus Demonstration." Today it is called "Christian Science versus Spiritualism." It is not for a few people who believe in the return of spirits. Our Leader put it there to show that there are no mediums between God and His expression. There are no channels; there are no agents; there are no avenues.

You see, God, Principle, is self-expressing, so let's be certain that we see that there is no medium called language. Mrs. Eddy says human language repeats only an infinitesimal part of that which is divine, or that which is true. When you read the textbook and the Bible, always ask the question, What was the knowing going on when these words were recorded? Not what do these words say? Words change their meaning according to the dictionaries, but the knowing is changeless. So ask, what was the knowing going on when these words were recorded? Let it be knowing, for idea, man, is Mind's knowing.

As for the resurrection — if you have accepted the suggestion that there is something personal concerning yourself, then you must work through the resurrection, because that way material beliefs yield to spiritual understanding. But there is no resurrection needed to that which will accept the revelation which we call Christian Science. Are we living the revelation, rather than being good talkers? So many students have so much of the letter; they can quote; they know all the words; and yet underneath, there is no Science being lived. Unless we are living the Science, we are fooling ourselves. Let us live our Christ, and in living our Christ, we not only bless ourselves, but we have heaven everywhere.

A woman told of a guest who was so inconsiderate, was always late for dinner, for breakfast, for appointments. Finally, one day she had the dinner ready and the guest was already twenty minutes late; she went to the bottom of the stairway and was just ready to give the rebuke, when this came to her, "If thou the bending reed wouldst break by thought or word unkind, pray that His Spirit you partake who loved and healed mankind." Then she thought, "Oh, I'm not a person to correct another person; but God, Principle, Love, is present and expressing Himself, and that self-expression is not only lovely, but it is exact, it is punctual." And at that the friend came down the stairway and said, "I suddenly saw just now what a dreadful guest I've been," and apologized. The friend said nothing.

You see, living the Christ rebuked the error; but if a person in self-righteousness rebuked the error, then you have misunderstandings. Live your Christ, and let it rebuke the error. It will rebuke it without the other one even knowing it is being done. But never take the attitude of a person that knows more than another, that you're going to instruct, or rebuke, or whatever it might be; it is crucifixion, because then you have all that self-justification and guilt to go through with — why did I say it? Probably you are unable to rest at night. But you never have to handle that if you live your Christ.

Notice in reading Jeremiah, when he wanted the people to do something, he would always say, "Thus saith the Lord." Watch it in the home or at church. Don't tell them, "Thus saith the Lord."

But "if thou the bending reed wouldst break," go in quickly, and shut the door, and know, "I am not a person living with persons; there is just one thing going on here; Mind expressing itself." An adjustment will take place. It will take place only through living the Christ, and not through the words you say. The words will add fuel to the fire. How often we have the clever rebuke on our tongue, a needling thing. Be alert; it is constant crucifixion.

Live the ascension. It's so simple. It simply means the acknowledgement that Mind, God, is present, expressing itself; it simply means that there's one Life present, identifying itself. That's all there is to the ascension. You don't have to die to get there. Paul said, "I die daily." So if we would live this Christ, we would never have discordant things that seem to happen in our lives. Live it, but don't talk it.

For instance, if you are discussing Christian Science with another, what is their approach? Are they persons learning more about God? Don't touch it, they have a right to that view — unless they are people who have come to you for help in the practice. Then, of course, you can speak out. But not with church workers, church members, testimony meetings, etc. because it causes too much havoc in the movement.

When working with a science, you work out from it, not up to it. Be the living Christ; never be the talking Christ; it won't heal to begin with; and it will only cause disturbances in your life. Always determine the viewpoint.

In living this ascension, think what happens. We met a Navy Captain one time in San Diego. In showing us around the ship, we went from deck to deck, and everywhere you could see such love. I remarked, "I've never seen such love." He said, "These men know this is their home. While I do not approve of any of them getting drunk, they know that if they do get drunk, they must come back, and I have someone on the ship to take care of them. This is their home, and when they did see that, they stopped coming back to the ship drunk. They wouldn't desecrate their home." The Captain lived his Christ, and the men respected it. One with God is a majority.

Then what is going on as Christian Science, is not a local event for the privileged chosen children of God; this is a universal truth; this is all-inclusive. The monkey story is a good illustration of this. It shows how they want to hold on to the handful of rice. The student wants to hold on to human opinions, his little sense of ego. Our demonstration is the willingness not to get our hand out of the coconut, but to let go the handful of rice.

Then we went on to see that swaddling clothes that bind us. We have to be willing to let the wind of God blow, and never hold on to our swaddling clothes when it does. See that all challenges are an opportunity to let the swaddling clothes go. Don't use the truth to improve the human. Christian Science is not only a healing religion, but the revelation that man does not need to be healed.

I'll talk now on the word *reflection*. Recently in watching a very beautiful lake, I was suddenly aware that the quietness and tranquility had made itself felt in the water. The entire scene surrounding the lake was perfectly reflected in the water. The reflection was obedient; it had nothing that was not in the original. Every blade of grass was perfectly reflected. Suddenly a small duck came swimming by and away went the reflection.

This had a great lesson. If we accept the suggestion that the reflection called man is something in and of himself, separate from the Mind that conceives it, then we are believing that we are something apart from Mind; and this belief or apartness is the deflection that can be disturbed at any moment. We must see that reflection is going on *in* the Mind of God, Mind reflecting its own contents, without any outside upon which it could possibly throw its reflection.

Do you really understand the term *reflection*? Your Leader says few understand what Christian Science means by the word *reflection*. Why? Too many students think of the mirror and what is called reflection. The mirror reflects whatever is held before it. Remember, this is a poor illustration because it uses objects of sense, but Christian Science is ideas of Soul. Reflection in the mirror is unconscious; but man, reflection, is consciousness. It was not the water that was reflecting its surrounding; it was the shoreline that was reflecting itself in the lake. So it is with man — man is not a reflector, man is reflection. Let us see that reflection takes place in tranquility, serenity, peacefulness, when we stop thinking. It is, be still and know that the I AM is God. And in this stillness, we stop human thinking, or as your Leader calls it, the human mechanism.

Mind reflects itself. Man is not a presence on which God can reflect Himself. All presence belongs to God. Then where is the man-presence upon which God is to reflect Himself? Man has no presence of himself. If man had presence, he would displace omnipresence, and this is impossible. But man is the functioning presence of the Mind that is God. This is reflection. This is the reason the Christ of Jesus could say, "Have I been so long time with you and haven't you seen the Father?"

Deflection is not phenomena, because all is infinite Mind and its infinite reflection. The textbook says, "Divine Science, the Word of God, saith to the darkness upon the face of error, 'God is All-in-all,' and the light of ever-present Love illumines the universe." God said, Let there be light and there was light. On the marginal note we read, "Mind's idea faultless." Why would Mind's idea be faultless? Because Mind's idea is the faultlessness of Principle itself.

If we accept the suggestion that there is a reflector present, that we are in some way reflectors reflecting love to something, reflecting intelligence to something, being kind to someone, being good to someone, that is a reflector. If you think you are a reflector, don't be surprised if a duck (and you may not call it a duck) comes by and disturbs that reflection. There is no peace as long as we have two things going on. Peace is permanent. When we refuse to come down to the cheap human rubbish and wallow in it and soil our garments, we have peace, and only then do we have peace.

If you accept the suggestion that man is something knowing or not knowing, you are putting in the lake your own duck, and why be surprised if it disturbs the reflection?

Reflection is not something seen; reflection is Mind's knowing. Mind's knowing is called man. This reflection, or directness, is given the name *Christ*. Let there be no haziness on our part over the term *Christ*. The Christ is the substance of Love fully experienced, the feeling of Love feeling its loveliness. The Christ is not separate from Mind; the Christ is the glowing emanation that is God in manifestation. The Christ is the being still, and the knowing is Mind.

Identity is the reflection of Spirit. It is Spirit identifying itself. That is reflection; that is — of myself I can do nothing. Mrs. Eddy once said, "As Mary Baker Eddy, I am the weakest of mortals, but as the Discoverer of Christian Science, I am the bone and sinew of the world."

Reflection does nothing, but it is the doing that is Mind. Mind is the source of the knowing; Mind is the source of the seeing; Mind is the source of the being. The result is called reflection. Man, therefore, is reflection.

Mrs. Eddy says that the Ego-man is the reflection of the Ego-God. What joy should ring out today because I can of myself do nothing, but my Father works and I work. Here is reflection. If it weren't for the false teaching in the world, we would not have to draw such a fine line of distinction between Principle and idea, or reflection. Reflection can do nothing. We lose the meaning of the word the minute we have man doing something or saying something. Mind does the doing; Mind does the living; the result is the reflection.

Reflection then isn't a reflector; it isn't something reflecting God. See clearly that reflection can't say I AM. It is when there is the absolute absence of personal sense, when the I goes to the Father, when the I remains as the Father, then the I that is God can say I AM. Reflection cannot say I AM.

Mrs. Eddy says, "The verity that God's image is not a creator, though he reflects the creation of Mind, God, constitutes the underlying reality of reflection." So this knowing disposes of objectification. This also disposes of an object for malpractice. Thus the whole of the Ego-God is present, and the whole of the Ego-God in manifestation is called man. That is reflection. And there can never be more of God present than there is right now. All the presence that is God, is present now, and there is nothing here to displace that presence. There was no more God present for Jesus or for Mrs. Eddy than there is here. The whole I, the whole Ego, the great I AM, is present here now, and cannot and will not be deflected by any pretense. There is no little i to deflect God. Then all that God is, is here — and by here we mean infinitely here, not a time sense here, but here, infinitely here. The Bible says, "My glory I will not give to another."

There is no exception to this — the great, the only I AM is the whole, the complete, the entire being, now. And so let no false theological teaching prevent the full acceptance of this now. Reflection is immediate; it is not something that has to be done.

Mrs. Eddy uses the word *deflection* twice in *Science and Health*. "The decaying flower, the blighted bud, the gnarled oak, the ferocious beast, — like the discords of disease, sin and death, — are unnatural. They are the falsities of sense, the changing deflections of mortal mind; they are not the eternal realities of Mind." "This deflection of being, rightly viewed, serves to suggest the proper reflection of God and the spiritual actuality of man, as given in the first chapter of Genesis."

We read in *Science and Health*, "God fashions all things, after His own likeness. Life is reflected in existence, Truth in truthfulness, God in goodness, which impart their own peace and permanence. Love, redolent with unselfishness, bathes all in beauty and light." And, "Christ as the Son of God, the royal reflection of the infinite; . . . 'being a brightness from His glory, and an image of His being.'"

In *Miscellaneous Writings*, we read, "Man is God's image and likeness; whatever is possible to God is possible to man *as God's reflection.* Through the transparency of Science we learn this, and receive it: learn that man can fulfill the Scriptures in every instance; that if he open his mouth it shall be filled — not by reason of the schools, or learning, but by the natural ability, that reflection already has bestowed on him."

Miscellany says, "Bird, brook, blossom, breeze, and balm — are richly fraught with divine reflection."

Is man an object of sense that sees bird, breeze, trees? Or is man the experience of the breeze, is man the experience of birds, of trees? You see, man is the word for the compound idea of all that expresses God. We experience bird, weather, everything. It is not outside. We do not look *at* something. Man includes his universe. Don't ever be an onlooker, but be the thing itself. Be your weather; don't be something in weather; *be* your weather. Don't be something in the world; *be* your world — that is reflection!

Mrs. Eddy says, "God is glorified in His reflection." (See page 189 in Powell's biography of Mrs. Eddy.) There was but one God, and consequently, there could be but one full reflection, which, of course, was the compound idea man. She dwelt at length on the point that there could be but one full or complete reflection of one God, and that this must be the basis for all scientific deduction. She indicated that only as her students grasped this fundamental fact, that one God could have but one full reflection, did they have the right basic sense of Christian Science, and that there was no other starting point.

So reflection cannot have a past tense; reflection is always now. That is one of the most marvelous things about reflection — it is always now. Reflection is always innocent because it cannot know guilt, because it has no consciousness of its own, but is the conscious reflection of God. It can have no egotistical sense of having accomplished something, can have no memory, for reflection is nothing of itself.

Mrs. Eddy says in the definition of man, "Man is that which has not a single quality underived from Deity; that which possesses no life, intelligence, nor creative power of his own, but reflects spiritually all that belongs to his Maker."

Reflection has no ability, hence it has no disability. "Let us rid ourselves of the belief that man is separated from God, and obey only the divine Principle, Life and Love."

We read in *Science and Health*, "To show that the substance of himself was Spirit and the body no more perfect because of death and no less material until the ascension (his further spiritual exaltation), Jesus waited until the mortal or fleshly sense had relinquished the belief of substance-matter, and spiritual sense had quenched all earthly yearnings. Thus he found the eternal Ego, and proved that he and the Father were inseparable as God and His reflection or spiritual man. Our Master gained the solution of being, demonstrating the existence of but one Mind without a second or equal."

We find our Ego to be the only Ego, God, and this Ego irradiating throughout infinity. What seems to be so evident as person, is present only because it is I AM saying I AM, and cannot be deflected by person. So never attach qualities to what is called personality, either good or bad, well or sick. That which was so evident as Jesus, so evident as our beloved Leader, was not present as flesh, blood, bones; it was present because it was the absence of the personal sense, and the true understanding that the Ego was God, self-reflecting.

Jesus said to Peter, "Flesh and blood hath not revealed it to thee but my Father has expressed Himself." Mrs. Eddy said, "Because man is the reflection of his Maker, he is not subject to birth, growth, maturity, decay." Reflection can have nothing unless it is in the original. Reflection is obedient.

The temptation comes to accept the world belief of being a reflector. You often hear it said, "You know I couldn't do that. That was the Father working through me." God, divine Mind, does not have any little "me's" to work through. Mind expresses itself immediately, directly, without mediumship.

Be willing to let the old go. Jesus knew that the error of the age is the belief that personality is substance, and that in some way it is a transparency through which Truth works. He challenged this, and so did Mary Baker Eddy. Both were scientific workers, and they knew it was the subjugation of the personal sense that permitted the Christ to operate unspent. If you fail in healing a patient, why? Because you haven't sufficiently lived the life of Christ. Not because the patient wasn't receptive, didn't cooperate, but because you didn't sufficiently live the life of Christ. Jesus healed ten lepers. He didn't try to make them receptive. He said, "Be thou clean," because he would permit nothing to come before him that denied the purity of his Father. He was not dealing with ten mentalities, ten bodies, but with the hypnotic suggestion of what denied the purity, presence and perfection of his God. He healed the lepers; he didn't try to make them receptive.

Oh, you must be alert in practice, for the temptation is to talk to the patient. You wouldn't talk to that book. You say personality has no life, truth, intelligence or substance. Would you talk to the chair? The thing in the chair has no more intelligence than the chair. We don't heal what sits in the chair. We know there is no Mind but God, and it expresses itself. For instance, health is an ever-present fact of being. If someone calls and says, "I've lost my health," would you say, "Look in the closet?" You can no more lose health than you can lose God Almighty. Someone says, "God has lost some of His almightiness." Would you treat that? If someone says, "I'm weak," watch that you don't try to make them strong. Acknowledge strength as a quality of God, and the very activity of strength as man. Don't use mental quackery.

If the argument comes, "I didn't heal all cases," never permit that to stay. We are not trying to make humans eternal. We are knowing there is no being to be human. Being is God, and being has never been divided.

Let us discuss briefly impression. You don't realize how much impression plays a part in your day — newspapers, television, radios, noise in the street, what you see. You would think that we were impression rather than expression. Remember that if an impression comes to thought from without, it says it comes to consciousness; and if accepted, it will objectify itself. As man is infinite, man can receive no impressions. Man is not impressionistic. Your Leader says man is the ultimatum of perfection; he is not a means, a medium, of imperfection.

In photography, only a negative receives or retains an impression, or a picture; but as we maintain the positive point of view of divine revelation, which we call Christian Science, we will respond only to that which is in the camera of divine Mind. Never forget — only a negative takes an impression. Reflection cannot. Expression cannot.

Take what is called the human body. It is a series of false impressions from birth to death. Purely mental impressions from childhood, pre-natal, post-natal, educational teaching — all false mental impressions taken in and reproduced as body. Mrs. Eddy calls it sense betrayal. False mental impressions will betray you.

There was the story of a man who believed his legs were getting shorter. His little boy was impressed by hearing it, and one leg began to get shorter than the other. When request for help came, the practitioner thought, "Render unto Caesar the things that are Caesar's, and unto God the things that are God's." Render unto Caesar the claim that it can imprint itself, impress itself, and render unto God the ability to express Himself. Expression always wipes out impression. The next morning the child's leg was perfectly normal, and he was riding a bicycle. It was false mental impression, not a physical condition. Had it been a physical condition, no Christian Science treatment could have healed it overnight.

That's why all disease or false hypnotic impression, which has been taken into thought, is never localized, never in body, never on body, no matter what your senses say. It has nothing to do with body, for body is the temple of the living God, and the moment that you separate disease from body, at that moment the healing comes. As long as you think it is a material, bodily condition, you cannot heal it in Christian Science, no matter how faithful and honest you are. Christian Science does not work that way.

Here's a paragraph that is very interesting: "If you try to change your thoughts, you are caught in the maze of what is called mental science. If you try to change a condition, you are caught in the web of medical mesmerism. If you try to make the old over and say it's good enough, you're caught in the regeneration of Romanism. If you try to change bad matter into good matter, you're caught in the pernicious belief called Judaism. You should see that the whole picture is wholly dishonest, fraudulent, a betrayal of your senses which lie and defraud to break the Ten Commandments, the Sermon on the Mount, and the revelation of Christian Science. Acknowledge here and now, I am not trying to change anything, thoughts, conditions, matter — anything. Christian Science is the revelation of that which is true.

We are not caught in the maze of mental science; we are not caught in the medical mesmerism. The moment you accept it as a condition, you will bring on all the mental malpractice of that condition. A mother called for help with her child's case of measles. The treatment was, it wasn't measles. I wouldn't dignify it with a name, for the name is God, because the only name there is is Adorable One; and I will keep the name of my God holy, and will not permit any perversion to call it measles. The child was instantly healed.

Don't fool yourself by believing you thought something right that made those measles go — it is hypnotism. Christian Science is the Science of Mind-healing, never permit anything to take the name of God in vain. Don't permit what we call educated belief to name anything. Adam named everything, but let us let God name Himself, and God said, My name is Adorable, Hallowed. Hallowed, we say daily in our prayer, "Hallowed be Thy name," and how can you hallow the name of God and believe there is something called measles? Don't be caught.

Our Leader says in *Unity of Good:* "Jesus taught us to walk *over*, not *into* or *with*, the currents of matter, or mortal mind." He didn't say, that withered hand looks very real, you'd better give it a good treatment. He cut off its vain boasting; he destroyed human pride in it; he took away its evidence. "Jesus required neither cycles of time nor thought in order to mature fitness for perfection and its possibilities. He said that the kingdom of heaven is here, and is included in Mind."

Never be fooled. We are not dealing with outward conditions. We are dealing wholly and completely with a supposititious mind-force, or perverted mind power. We are not trying to make someone receptive; we acknowledge man is a state of receptivity.

Our Leader says there is no life in matter, there is no intelligence in it; then could you make it understand the Truth? It is attempting the impossible.

In our unwillingness to lay off the old for the new, do we see that there is no subconsciousness from which a flood of memories can flow forth to drown the Christ idea? Handle that belief daily. It is a very prevalent belief called subconsciousness. Subconsciousness is, of course, the lie called the dragon, the red dragon, that says it pours forth a flood to wipe out the Christ-idea. There is much talk today about there being a subconsciousness from which can pour out yesterday to wipe out today, or tomorrow which can wipe out today.

Consciousness is God, and there is nothing 'sub' or unconscious about it; it is conscious, and it can only be conscious of now.

All the mental sciences are built on the belief of subconsciousness in which yesterdays are stored away; but let us call this by its right name — red dragon. Your Leader says in *Science and Health*: "After the stars sang together and all was primeval harmony, the material lie made war upon the spiritual idea; but this only impelled the idea to rise to the zenith of demonstration, destroying sin, sickness, and death, and to be caught up unto God — to be found in its divine Principle."

Now, how do we rise to the zenith of demonstration? The only way we can rise to the zenith of demonstration, is to acknowledge here and now that man, idea, is the functioning presence of the Mind that is God.

Our Leader says, it "impelled the idea to rise to the zenith of demonstration, . . . to be found in its divine Principle." Now to be found in its divine Principle, would mean it has to be the functioning of the Principle, because in 'Recapitulation,' Mrs. Eddy says, "Principle and its idea is one." So let us rise to the zenith of demonstration to be caught up to our God, which means to acknowledge without any mental reservation that man is divine idea.

The textbook says there is but one way, and Christ in divine Science shows us this way, and it is to know no other reality than God, good, and to rise superior to the senses.

Now, there are some Christian Scientists who refuse to deny evil. Mrs. Eddy gave us her book *No and Yes*. She also started the Scientific Statement of Being with no and yes — the first statement is "no" and the second statement is "yes." Now, it is true that when the realization is clear enough, there is no need for any "no;" there is only "yes." But be willing to use the no and yes argument until you rise constantly to your own Christ. When it is your own Christ being experienced, you need neither no nor yes. You are living it then, and the living should heal. But be willing to deny reality to evil; be willing to see it doesn't have any place from which to send forth a flood; be willing to deny that it has any intelligence to make a condition.

Someone said recently that she was getting ready to go to her Association, and error was starting to be terrible in her life. I said, "I think error is pretty smart if it knows you're going to your Association." Don't you see what superstition that was — pure superstition. She got back exactly what she believed — that every year, at the time for her Association, error tried to prevent her going.

Be willing to deny evil having power, or presence, or entity, or avenue, or channel. It is necessary. Our Leader did, and certainly Jesus did. Jesus said, "Let your conversation be yea, yea, nay, nay." Be willing to do it. You deny it to wipe it out; it has no existence. You don't deny it as something; you deny it as nothing.

Now, the consensus of opinion is that we are persons with brains, and we think. Aren't you willing to deny that? Of course, you are. But you don't deny it as something. See that there isn't anything personal to respond to it. Frequently in practice, the moment the phone goes down, you say, "I AM, a universal false belief claiming to have identity; but identity is God saying I AM, and there is nothing to respond to it." Be willing to work in practice both ways. Sometimes it isn't necessary, but be willing. I have heard students say, "I just refuse to come down to deny evil." I have said, "Did you eat your breakfast this morning? You'd better deny. For Life is God, and Life is self-sustaining. "Suffer it to be so now."

I read in an old *Journal* of mortal mind claiming to have a body. Mortal mind needs no more space in which to deposit its objects than it needs space in which to   dream them.

When you learn to handle electricity correctly — your Leader calls it vibration; medically it is called nerves — when you learn as Scientists to handle electrical vibrations, called unrest, lust, thirst for narcotics, weather, tornadoes, you learn it is all magnetism, animal magnetism. Be certain that you know how to handle animal magnetism.

Christ Jesus said, "I saw Satan as lightning fall from heaven. Behold, I give unto you power to tread on serpents and scorpions, and over all the power of the enemy; and nothing shall by any means hurt you."

What called forth this statement? "The seventy returned with joy, saying Lord, even the devils are subject unto us through thy name." Jesus said, "I beheld Satan as lightning fall from heaven." Now, could Satan, electricity, fall from heaven? All power belongs to God, Mind, divine Principle; and nothing can fall out of the Mind of God because everything is in the Mind that is God. So Jesus saw this negative mind called mortal, called Satan, called lightning, fall in the presence of that which knows itself to be the Christ, and it will fall instantly. So we, too, can say, "I beheld Satan as lightning fall from heaven. I give you power to tread on suggestions.

This Christ ability neutralizes, nullifies, repels that which we call the anti-Christ. What is there to the anti-Christ but negative electricity. We have called it red dragon, animal magnetism. What is there to animal magnetism? It is a part of electricity.

Objectively, sensual body, calling itself us, is not us at all, because there is but one I or Us. Therefore, that which has been calling itself us is not a person, a place, a thing. Jesus ended his talk with the seventy by saying, "Notwithstanding in this rejoice not, rejoice not that you now have the ability to see instantly the nothingness of evil, or that the spirits are subject unto you, but rather rejoice that your name is written in heaven." Our name is written in heaven simply means that which proceeds from God.

Jesus knew that he was not dealing with matter substance, but with hypnotic suggestion. Christian Science is the only power today to neutralize and nullify the seeming suggestions sent forth — doubt, uncertainty, lack of conviction, many forms of tension, fear, hopelessness; but all of this comprise the one and only red dragon, which is the same as electricity.

If cancer were a disease in a matter body, Christian Science could not heal it; but the fact that what is called disease is nothing more than negativity, that can be healed instantly. In practice, we have seen every form of evil healed. Healing occurs because of the bringing of the Christ, or the pure power of God, into action. Are we going to stand aghast at nothingness? The only way to handle these electrical currents called animal magnetism — disease, broken bones, lack of money, fear, hopelessness, whatever called — we must see that the Mind that is God is present right where it seems to be, and this is its annulment. Right where one seems to be thinking negatively, the Mind of God is present expressing itself, and that is the annihilation of the belief instantly. If you permit it to stay and call it your thought, your knowing, your experience, you put up an antenna upon which all the negativity of the world can play upon.

That is why when fear tries to come, instantly say, this is not my fear, this is aggressive mental suggestion; this has nothing to do with what I AM. Don't be afraid to denounce it. Let the positiveness of the Christ come forth, not a person being positive, not a person being radical, but let it be the Christ of God. It will wipe out all negativity. There has never been the first birth; there has never been the first death; there has never been a time in which a minute existed; there has never been a time in which there was a day, an hour, a year. There is no presence but Omnipresence; therefore, there is no personal presence. There is no personal presence to have a personal mind. Omnipresence is God. Yes, the suggestion argues for the reality of a personal mind, but never argue with it from the standpoint of something. See its nothingness, and this is the end of the argument.

In building the wall, Sanballat came up saying, "Come on down. Stop your work. I've got something to tell you. I think it will interest you. A choice morsel about what Mrs. Jones did in church, it's so choice — come on, Gashmu said it." Nehemiah said, "I have a great work to do. Why should I come down and talk." Then he said, "Why don't you go to church. They won't come in there after you." He said, "No, I have a great work to do. I will not come down off my wall." What is the wall? Not something we are building. It is simply the recognition of your own Christliness. Never come down!

Gossip is the inability of the gossiper to maintain its own Christ. Never defile the Christ that you bear by gossip; it is denying your own Christliness, the Christly image that one should be bearing.

Sometimes it seems easy to fall into the habit of gossip, and that is because we must be enjoying the crucifixion. No one would gossip knowingly. Make the declaration, I cannot be made to say or hear, something contrary to my natural inclination.

Let's talk for a moment on Article 8, Section 6, in the *Manual*. We must not be made to forget. If we accept the suggestion that thinking, so-called, is going on in the head, we have been made to forget. God is Mind, Mind is divine, and Mind is All. There is no personal, private thinking capacity. It is either the divine Mind, or the suppositional mind called mortal mind. You see, there is no such thing as private thinking. It is either God or the suppositional opposite. Never be egotistical enough to believe that you can think wrong. You cannot think wrong any more than you can think right. Mind is God, and the exterminator of error is the great truth that God, good, is the only Mind.

Our Leader says in *Miscellaneous Writings*, "What will you do about it? Will you be equally earnest for the truth? Will you doff your lavender-kid zeal, and become real and consecrated warriors? Will you give yourselves wholly and irrevocably to the great work of establishing the truth, the gospel, and the Science which are necessary to the salvation of the world from error, sin, disease, and death? Answer at once and practically, and answer aright!"

So let it be your *Manual*. The word *manual* means hand, keeping your hands. All of Article 8 is called discipline, and discipline comes from the word *disciple*. The other day, I read Article 8 carefully. I was so interested in each section because I could find something that had been healed in practice through obedience to these sections. Don't think a person is obedient to the *Manual*. See that all there is to oneself is the operation of the *Manual* — the *Manual* in operation as one's own experience.

You see, it is the whole experience to have the altitude, this tremendous revelation is the altitude of all knowing, but our attitude towards what appears to be another must be our same altitude. That is why Jesus could heal instantly, because he never had the altitude that the ego is God, and then the attitude, 'Well, I wish they knew it.' You see, it really denies your own altitude, doesn't it? Don't you see that the gap is there between the revelation and the doing? You see the student who talks this tremendous revelation, but still has the attitude I am a person doing something — or I wish he knew the truth. You see, the truth is true. It isn't true because a certain number have accepted it. It is true because it is all that is going on.

Look Deep Into Realism
Association Address of 1957

by
Clarence Steves

NOTE: *This address differs slightly in form from others in this book, as it includes selections for study, presented as prefatory to the address itself.*

Scriptural selections for study

John 1:1,14,16
"In the beginning was the Word, and the Word was with God, and the Word was God."

And the Word was made flesh, and dwelt among us, (and we beheld his glory, the glory as of the only begotten of the Father), full of grace and truth."

And of his fullness have all we received, and grace for grace."

John 4:29
"A man which told me all things that ever I did: is not this the Christ?"

John 3:34
"For he whom God hath sent speaketh the words of God: for God giveth not the Spirit by measure unto him."

Ex. 3:1,10,11 to ?
"And Moses answered and said, But, behold, they will not believe me or hearken unto my voice: For they will say, The Lord hath not appeared unto thee."

"And Moses said unto the Lord, O my Lord, I am not eloquent, neither heretofore, nor since thou hast spoken unto thy servant: but I am slow of speech, and of a slow tongue."

"And the Lord said unto him, Who hath made man's mouth?"

Ex. 3:14 to:

"And God said unto Moses, I AM THAT I AM:"

1 Cor. 14:9,10, 14, 15, 19

"So likewise ye, except ye utter by the tongue words easy to be understood, how shall it be known what is spoken? For ye shall speak into the air."

"There are, it may be, so many kinds of voices in the world, and none of them is without signification."

"For if I pray in an unknown tongue, my spirit prayeth, but my understanding is unfruitful."

"What is it then, I will pray with the spirit, and I will pray with the understanding also: I will sing with the spirit, and I will sing with the understanding also."

"Yet in the Church I had rather speak five words with my understanding that by my voice I might teach others also, than ten thousand words in an unknown tongue."

1 Cor. 2:1,4,5,12,13

"And I brethren, when I came to you, came not with excellency of speech or of wisdom, declaring unto you the testimony of God."

"And my speech and my preaching was not with enticing words of man's wisdom, but in demonstration of the Spirit and of power: that your faith should not stand in the wisdom of men, but in the power of God."

"Now we have received, not the spirit of the world, but the Spirit which is of God; that we might know the things that are freely given to us of God."

"Which things also we speak, not in the words which man's wisdom teacheth, but which the Holy Ghost teacheth; comparing spiritual things with spiritual."

Zeph. 3:8 to 9

"Therefore wait ye upon me, saith the Lord, until the day that I rise up to the prey: for my determination is to gather the nations, that I may assemble the kingdoms, to pour upon them my indignation, even all my fierce anger: for all the earth shall be devoured with the fire of my jealousy."

"For then will I turn to the people a pure language, that they may all call upon the name of the Lord, to serve him with one consent."

Acts 2:1-4

And the day of Pentecost was fully come, they were all with one accord in one place."

And suddenly there came a sound from heaven as of a rushing mighty wind, and it filled all the house where they were sitting."

"And there appeared unto them cloven tongues like as of fire, and it sat upon each of them."

"And they were all filled with the Holy Ghost, and began to speak with other tongues, as the Spirit gave them utterance."

Isa. 55:3 to: 8-11

"Incline your ear, and come unto me:

"For my thoughts are not your thoughts, neither are your ways my ways, saith the Lord."

For as the heavens are higher than the earth, so are my ways higher than your ways, and my thoughts than your thoughts."

"For as the rain cometh down, and the snow from heaven, and returneth not thither, but watereth the earth, and maketh it bring forth and bud, that it may give seed to the sower, and bread to the eater."

"So shall my word be that goeth forth out of my mouth: it shall not return unto me void, but it shall accomplish that which I please and it shall prosper in the thing whereto I sent it."

"Felt ye the power of the word?" (Hymn 298)

Mis. 363: 24-27

...hold fast to the Principle of Christian Science as the Word that *is* God, Spirit, and Truth. This Word corrects the philosopher, confutes the astronomer, exposes the subtle sophist, and drives diviners mad.

"Let the Word have free course and be glorified. The people clamor to leave cradle and swaddling-clothes." *No. 45: 24-25*

"I see Christ walk, and come to me and tenderly divinely talk."

"This day is Soul's day, a radiant, divine, day, no persons gathering together, no coming, no going. Only Soul. Soul appreciating what Soul is, is called man. Not persons with souls, but Soul knowing itself. One-thousand years of belief in a soul separated from body cannot change the forever fact. There can be no personal soul, no personal man, because there can be no personal God. God manifests the reflection of God."

The Bible
1. John 1: 1,14,16
2. Ex. 4: 1,10,11 to ?
3. 1 Cor. 14: 9,10,14,15,19
   John 4: 29- A man
   John 3; 34
4. 1 Cor. 2: 1,4,5,12,13
5. Zeph. 3: 8 to
6. Acts 2: 1-4
Isa. 55: 3 to :, 8-11
"Felt ye the power of the Word?"
"—hold fast" 363 *Mis.* 24-27.
No and Yes 45: 24-25

Let the Word have free course and be glorified. The people clamor to leave cradle and swaddling-clothes.

This Association is already free from cradle and swaddling clothes because it has permitted the divine wind of omnipotent Mind to blow, so the Word *has* free course and *is* glorified.

Look Deep Into Realism

In our textbook we are told, (129:22), "Look deep into realism instead of accepting only the outward sense of things." We must look deep into reality. We do not accept the outward sense of things, but we are, "alone with, (our), own being and with the reality of things." (*Mess. 01'*, 20: 8-9). Looking deep into the divine Principle of the universe we find that Principle interprets its own being to itself, *as* Itself, all principle being. We know that Church is what is resting upon and proceeding from divine Principle. Association is resting upon and proceeding from divine Principle. Let it rest there. (Apply this to our work).

Is there something present beside God? In Church or in Association, could there be something present beside God? Is there a man present — or is *man* the *presence* of omnipresence? Man does not have a presence, he *is* Presence. (gentle presence — man — divine nature) R.H.
Mess. 02', 7: 11-21

The Latin *omni,* which signifies *all,* used as an English prefix to the words *potence, presence, science,* signifies all-power, all-presence, all-science. Use these words to define God, and nothing is left to consciousness but Love, without beginning and without end, even the forever *I AM,* and All, than which there is naught else. Thus we have Scriptural authority for divine metaphysics—spiritual man and the universe coexistent with God. No other logical conclusion can be drawn from the premises, and no other scientific proposition can be Christianly entertained.

Mrs. Eddy uses three words to define God, omnipotence, omniscience, omnipresence, and adds, "nothing is left to consciousness but Love," the forever I Am, and All. God alone is present in this Association day to say, "I Am," no cradles, no swaddling clothes in this day. This day has eternal duration. The most powerful thing that can happen in this day is that God alone has presence.

Our Leader states it in the Scientific Statement of Being, (S.&H., 468), she says there is no Life, Truth, intelligence, nor substance, in the *outward sense* of *things*. There is no Truth in objectivity. All is infinite Mind, *without exception*. Is there any possibility of dividing infinity into infinites? There is no person to look deep into realism to declare what it is or is not. Mind alone is present to say, I Am, All in all; immortal Truth; not mortal error. I Am — the real and eternal; I Am God, and man is My image and likeness, *Now*! There is no person, knowing, to say I Am. Moses did not say I Am, Mind said, I Am.

It is the presence of the Christ, this is the I that says I Am. Not even a student of Christian Science can say I Am for it will be duality and arouses the seven thunders and produces the earthquake.

When the I goes to the Father and remains *as* the Father, *then* it can say I Am.

Jesus so lived his Christ that he could say I Am the resurrection and the life. I Am the bread of life. These statements could never be made by a person. No person can no (know) God.

The Mind that is God is the Mind that is man, without exception. Omnipresent Mind is man, is God.

If this is not true, there could be no Association, no Science.

God and man, cause and effect, Principle and idea, are one being. "Principle and idea is one." (S.&H. 465) Principle is not separate from idea, it doesn't do something to idea. What God, Principle is being is termed man. Man rests upon and proceeds from divine Principle. No man ascends up into heaven or comes down from heaven, man *is* heaven, the heaven of oneness. Individual man does not ascend to Reality nor come from Reality, he is Reality experienced.

Jesus said, "All who come before me, are thieves and robbers." If you believe *you* or *me*, as person, you are a thief and a robber taking from God and calling it man. Never deal with effect or you are a thief and a robber. If you leave anything in objectivity, it is where it can be stolen. This belief of objectivity will steal your youth and leave you age; steal your wealth and leave you poverty, your eternity and leave you time, steal infinity and leave you with a limited concept of all you behold.

"Lay up for yourselves treasures in heaven." Cause — God — always interprets Itself to cause man, therefore no breakage can occur, no lapse from harmony, just perfect continuity.

In infinity, there is nothing, "out there," called a patient. If we yield to the belief there is something, "out there," we are tempted to change it.

"A Christian Scientist is alone with his own being," and has peace within and, "the gates of hell," the belief that we once were persons but now are sons of God — "shall not prevail against," that peace.

We are alone with our own being, with God, never alone with, "others," never alone with friends, with church workers, with others in business, in our homes, but ever alone with God, Father, our Father, which art in Heaven, Mind. This determines our day. God is All, (All we call, "others").

A poem in New Yorker, 1947; About a duck, floating in the ocean, about 100ft. off shore. There is a big heaving in the Atlantic, but the duck has poise. He doesn't know how large the Atlantic is, but he reposes in the universe as though all there were to it was where it touched him. He rests in infinity. This duck has religion.

Remember a man who was reposing in a boat on a heaving sea? He had poise, and rested in infinity. He was living his Christ and would never permit Jesus to intrude on his quietness. He knew no person called disciple nor

Jesus, to intrude on his peace or poise, and cry, "save us," "heal me," etc. Looking deep he saw the reality of his own being, and answered, Peace, be still. It was not Jesus, but the Christ speaking.

Looking at Christian Science as a remedy, we become mesmerized when the cry comes to heal and save. We are Scientists as we rest in the infinite and know the only healing is the recognition of eternal perfection. "And o'er earth's troubled, angry sea I see," "my own Christ," from divine revelation, "walk, and come to me and tenderly," declare, "Be still, and know that the only Ego is God." (S.&H. 216: 11-14) The Truth that we are not little fragments in a heaving world, but the Son of God.

Whittier, — "Take from us now the strain and stress, and let our ordered lives confess, the beauty of thy peace."

There is no peace in Twoness. Principle and its idea is one. Peace is found only in oneness. I and my Father are one. Mrs. Eddy said to a student, "The harmony of my being cannot be invaded because I dwell in the Infinite."

It is not a small, "my," but , "My," God being. (*Ret.* 56: 5-11), "Whatever divides Being into beings, is a misstatement of Science. "Never fear the Satanic suggestion — it is only suggestion — It will suggest, but remember it is suggestion, not condition. The creative ability belongs to God and he never gave it to another.

Remember the parable of the tares and the wheat. Suggestion said, "see the tare," but the good man who had planted the good seed answered, "Only what *I* have planted, is present. "All there could be to what appeared as a tare is a mis-conception of wheat." Don't be tempted to destroy it, remove it, to change it (see it as it is)!

Suggestion cries, "Personality," for individuality. God does not express Himself as a person, place or thing.

Is it our work to find out what the tare was thinking? It is never a condition brought about by wrong thinking, only a suggestion. (S.&H. 395: "Mental Quackery")

Good alone is present. "God is light and in Him is no darkness at all." Don't bring your work down to mental science. Historical records — Judge Smith. Mrs. Eddy feared Science would be brought down to mental science. (*Ret.* 57: "Man shines by borrowed light.")

We are not mentalists. If we were we would be [   ]. "Mental work," as used today means activity. When Mrs. Eddy used the term, she meant it as spiritual activity.

The tare is not becoming more wheat like, but the wheat is revealing the truth about what appeared to be a tare.

In the, "Scientific translation of mortal mind," (S.&H. 115-116), it appears as, "depravity," "evil beliefs disappearing," and then, "understanding," but the textbook plainly states that, "the last shall be first," there is no choice. (Always go to the textbook and ask, "what was the knowing going on?" There are too many human opinions.) When the last is perceived to have been the first and only, it will wipe out what had appeared to be real and was not, and may seem to produce a better human. Don't be fooled it is never a better human appearing, but *more Christ* appearing. There is no such thing as a better human.

Sentinel Poem — *Security*

"Naught was there that a carnal mind could touch or see." — Art Glass

Our security lies in looking deep into realism. Using the three words, omnipotence, omnipresence and omniscience to define Deity, "naught was there that a carnal mind could touch or see."

The distinction between Christian Science and mental science is that Christian Science treatment does not consider (?) the mind of a patient. Has the tare a mind? What is called a patient is mortal mind objectified. "Mortal mind and body are one" (S.&H. 177:8) The human mortal body does not contain mind. All other systems of so called mental healing have a mind to become educated or made aware, changed or informed. In Science this is impossible.

The art of healing with the divine Mind alone, is the position of Christian Science. Christian Science never deals with effects. Christian Science *knows* that man is ever in God-condition, and does not yield to the temptation to criticize man, to see him as sick, sinning or dying. Go into your closet and shut the door and be alone with the verity of true perfection. See only the Christ or God. This heals any case.

If we fall to the level of mental science, and see a drunken man and then attempt to heal him, he might turn and slap you and say he spent good money to get that way. If suggestion says, "a drunken man," God says, "No! Man is satisfied."

Don't *use* Christian Science for making drunken men into sober men, but know all that is going on is your own Christ being. Heal the suggestion that there are people, well or sick. Mrs. Eddy said, "It is more important to know there is no personality, than to know there is no disease."

When you use the word, "man," *see* the ultimate of perfection, the eternal noon, the eternal verity of Life, the full, vital, vigorous, effortless, self-expression of infinite Mind. "All that I have is thine," not outside consciousness, but *as* consciousness, individual / universal. "The phantasmagoric, (illusion of things either dwindling or enlarging), is a product of human dreams." (*Un.* 26:24)

"Man has never crossed the barriers of time, (either in what is called birth nor death), but he coexists with God and the universe." (S.&H. 266)

In practice, never try to make a person into spiritual individuality. Let the Christ outshine the flittering personality. Don't go out and get into the parade whether the music is sweet and low or rock and roll. Shut your door and look deep into realism!

Be I Am — the whole man, entire man, the full expression of being, the, "conscious constant capacity," of God.

The Christ does not labor, — is not a process. It is the gift of God. The world of personal sense hates this identification. It wants to be separate and cries, "This absorbs me" — "The human mind and body are myths." Can a myth be absorbed? Can light absorb darkness, Love absorb hate? Fear? God is All, and naught else is present. God, Mind, Principle identifies Itself. The conscious identity of being is man. Principle declares; "Ye are my witnesses." Could Principle absorb its own witness? Self-love cries out, "absorb" — Let the Christ shine forth.

"The material body, which *you* call me, is mortal mind," (S.&H. 416) Speak to this *you* (this finite corporeal mortal), "*You*, mortal mind, *you* Red Dragon, *you* Lucifer, you cannot call yourself *me*. There is no *me* but God, Mind, Spirit. There is nothing present here to break the First Commandment. Don't permit Lucifer to act as I.

"When will the world cease to judge of causes from a personal sense of things, conjectural and mis-apprehensive!" (*Mis.* 290:21) Cease to see persons, persons to judge or not to judge. "Make self-righteousness be still, break earth's stupid rest." Nothing more stupid than to believe in persons judging right or wrong. Mrs. Eddy defines person as mask. There is no person to mask the glory of God!

(*Mis.* 328) "The ever present Christ, the spiritual idea, surveys the vale of the flesh from the summit of bliss, to burst the *bubbles* of *earth* with *a breath of heaven*." The bubbles of earth are personal sense, coming from the soap of mortal mind. Don't let mortal mind soft soap us and blow more bubbles. Let the breath of heaven dispel them.

"Hast thou not heard this Christ knock at the door of thine own heart and closed it against Truth," and accepted the belief of being a person, even a *temporary* person, the pride of being a person?

"Give up thy earth-weights and thou wilt bear thy cross," not a cross of agony, but the cross of joy and gladness, free from all the old soap which has no more substance in the waking dream than in the night dream.

We don't rejoice that *now* we are no longer persons, we never were anything but the Christ of God. The only Ego there is, is the Ego that is God.

We don't believe that we were once prodigals, eating the husks of materiality to fill up persons or bubbles. *Let God be God!* It is not a cry of *heal me*. Goliath said, "Give me a man, that we may fight together." But don't *absorb me!*

Let the sweet breath of heaven blow the bubbles away, with no struggle, no labor, this is your birthright. Man is the perfection that is God. He was never a prodigal. He does not return to the Father's house to be fed with the fatted calf, to be clothed with the best robe nor to have the ring of sonship placed on his finger and then to be kissed by the Father. Man *is* the kiss of Divinity, he has forever been embraced in the ring of sonship, clad in the robe of indivisibility, without rent or seam, forever One with the Father.

Burst the bubbles to see the reality. Survey from the summit of bliss and see that which seemed, "by flesh embound, was but thy shade." In the eternal noon there is no shadow. See man as reflection with no shadow because there is nothing to cast a shadow. *All* is here and now. No divisibility in reflection. *All* that I have is thine.

(S.&H. 334:10-18 to ,) "The invisible Christ will remain imperceptible so long as we believe the human concept and our divinity are two separate states and will continue until the ascension. We must admit ascension today! There is no one in a state of crucifixion, no person trying to know the Truth to change something or to get something. There is no one in resurrection, a person knowing some of his divinity but believing it to be, "over there," and that he has to read and study diligently to attain it. In Christian Science perfection is gained only by perfection." You have constant crucifixion if you think of human concept Jesus instead of living the Christ. Never be *a* anything, *a* Christian Scientist, *a* Reader, *a* practitioner, teacher, lecturer. All there is to any of these *is* Christian Science in operation.

Never believe I know about Christian Science and nobody else knows it, or I know more than someone else. If you do this, *you* malpractice. Don't blame it on R.C. They know Christian Science is true.

Know there is nothing animal present to be magnetized.

In class, a student was given a case to handle in which was fear of the term, "animal magnetism." He answered: According to physics, everyone is made up of chemicals. If you set up a magnetic field it is in itself perfectly harmless. But, if you move a block of iron above it, it rearranges the molecules so they could be attracted. A block of wood moved above it would have no effect on the molecules. If we believe we are persons, we are always rearranging our molecules to make them more attractive and what we accomplish is all there is to animal magnetism.

(S.&H. 507) "Infinite Mind creates and governs all, from the mental molecule to infinity."

Don't put up a target to be magnetized. "Adhesion, cohesion and attraction belong to God." There is no other attraction. Never anything *outside*. The champion malpractitioner is the student who believes there is something or someone *out there* to malpractice on him.

Mind is God, the only present Mind is God. (S.&H. 204) "In Science it can never be said that man has a mind of his own, distinct from God, the *all* Mind." Man is reflection. The only knowing going on is the knowing that is God.

Ascension is not work — it is but yielding up the ghost ("illusion, belief, supposition" S.&H. 587) Let the Holy Ghost be our experience.

I am not *a* Christian Scientist, but I am Christian Science in operation. Think of the magnitude of it, the glory of it! When we see there is no error, then there is no longer either the fear of it nor the love of it. Ascension takes place when we lift the curtain on the material concept and find, "man as never born and never dying, but as coexistent with his creator." (S.&H. 557)

The Christ dispels the finite error that we are persons thinking. "We are Christian Scientists only as we quit our reliance upon that which is false and grasp the true. We are not Christian Scientists until we leave all for Christ." "Human opinions are not spiritual." (S.&H. 192)

Our work is not to redeem the tare.

(S.&H. 502) Deflection of being — the tare is only deflection. Personality is the tare. This deflection — rightly viewed — reveals even time as truly being nothing but the glory of eternity.

There is no Truth and Love in matter. Let's be consistent. Sing it out *Personal sense is dead! Long live the Christ! Be still! Don't permit the shadow to say, "You must get to your books!" Don't be like the man at the pool of Bethesda, waiting for a shove! The waters are fresh now, fresh from the throne of God. They are not making us whole but disclosing more of our wholeness and radiance.

Mrs. Eddy spoke of shadows. As shadows of various types come in contact and no harm ensues — so is the impact called an accident, nothing has really happened.

(3rd edition) "Impress indelible"

In the Bible the serpent promises, "Ye shall be as gods," having a private mind to think with, a private soul with which to feel, a personal love, but the serpent cannot make good his boast. It is wholly dishonest. It would make *you* a separate private ego and tempt you to compare your ego with your neighbor's ego etc. All personality is afraid of loosing itself to Christian Science. But what is it? What is this material body *you* call me? The bubble of depravity — all lying suggestion.

(*Mis.* 363:4) "The "Ego" that claims selfhood in error, and passes from molecule and monkey up to man, is no ego, but is simply the supposition that the absence of good is mind and makes man, — when its greatest flatterer — identification, is piqued by him who, "compensateth vanity with nothingness, dust with dust."

Why flatter this false ego with *my* claim, *my* body, *my* distress, *my* family? Only the serpent says, "I will make *you* as gods." Look deep into realism and hear the Christ which says, "man is like God, not gods, infinite, eternal, whole and complete." This does not make us God, but reflection, the wholeness which is man.

Mortal mind constantly sends forth a flood of what is called bodies. A touch of the brush paints them black, white, yellow. Looking deep into realism we find nothing born to die. Man is the functioning presence of the eternity that is God, the perfection that is God.

Personal sense cannot intrude. Am I accepting the revelation of Christian Science or am I seeing myself as a one of many instead of the Adorable One. Am I finite person *using* Christian Science or am I accepting the fact that the Adorable One is all there is present identifying itself. This is Science. (Never think of Science as a religion.)

Even though it seems necessary to feed and clothe the human concept, never look in the mirror and call it *my* face. See the face of God. Don't let the human concept make laws for oneself — take it for a walk but don't let it take you.

Infinity is experienced.

(S.&H. 14) "Entirely separate from the belief and dream of material living, is the Life divine," etc. Material belief says, "Yes, but Mr. Smith died!" *Demand*, who are *you* material belief, to declare that? No *body* ever died! The only body there is, is the Christ body, forever here — "no cradle song, no natal hour and mother's tear to thee belong." This body is universal, infinite, get the greater conception of the grandiose of this body, the purity called man. In answer to, "What are body and Soul?," Mrs. Eddy uses the word *identity* for body. The living Principle, Love identifies itself in multifarious forms — this is *body*. The only body is the God-body, the temple of the living God. Let all the earth keep silence. There is no body to grow, nor a body to have a growth, just one universal body — the shrine of Love, conditioned by God, saying, "I Am." It is only hypnotic suggestion when the telephone rings and says, "*my* body etc."

Go into your closet! The voice you hear is not the voice of your friend, the voice of man — but electrical reproduction of voice. Electricity is, "The sharp surplus of materiality," counterfeiting the true essence of spirituality. Are you listening to it, or treating it? Or are you aware only of the, "calm, strong currents of true spirituality"?

There is no personal man to wear out — manhood *is* eternal noon. "Deity was satisfied with his work." (S.&H. 519)

The infinite One remains One. We are never dealing with persons. We are never dealing with what is wrong. All that is wrong is the one suppositious opposite of the One reality. It is not 100 cases, just *one* belief in a mind apart from God. We never treat the mind of the patient, as though there were separate minds. There is none to have it. Mind gives body to Itself. Mrs. Eddy says, "Mortal mind is the criminal." The body sitting in the chair has no more mind than the chair. Would you treat the chair? (see 20) It is true because it is God.

If the suggestion is handled as though it were body, then you must handle fear, doubt, diagnosis, mortal mind, etc. If we handle the thinking of the patient we are psychologists. If we handle the morals of the patient, we are Romanists.

The God-Principle is all-presence, all-power and will never become anything else.

Mrs. Eddy has given us the rule that's the exterminator of error, (S.&H. 469) The great truth that, "God, good is the *only* Mind." What calls itself another mentality or another body, has no existence. God says I AM ALL — and that is all that is going on. Anything else is but the ghostly ghost of nothingness.

The one Ego is God. There is no other presence, just the Adorable One maintaining Its own individual being, expressing Itself adorably. This Association is the adorableness of God, the infinite satisfaction of God.

Have you told yourself, I am the light of the world? I am the bread of life? The innocency of everything, the purity of all that is? I Am that! Now blaspheme by believing yourself a person, do you look deep into realism knowing there *is* no personal ego?

"The understanding that Ego is Mind," etc., "begins at once to destroy the error of mortal sense and to supply the truth of immortal sense."

The only I is God. The one Ego is the only presence, alone with its own being, saying, "I Am." I Am perfect, I am free, I am satisfied. This is living Association.

Divine Mind looks deep into realism and sees its perfect being. "God saw everything that he had made and behold, it was all God!"

Our dauntless Leader says, "The starting point of divine Science *is* — and there is no other." (S.&H. 275)

Divine Principle is that from which all rests upon and proceeds from. Association rests upon and proceeds from divine Principle. Reality is so simple when it is just God — I Am — person cannot say, I AM. Personal sense will suggest but never be fooled. Personal sense will attempt to show you organs and say it is Life, show you time and say it is reality, eternity. Identity is not even temporarily connected with what personal sense suggests. Never permit the fraud to say I. Remember, the winds blow and conception is unconfined and we have looked deep and beheld realism.

We are not students looking deep into realism. (S.&H. 261) "Fixing your gaze on realities supernal you will rise to the spiritual consciousness of being," to experience that I which says, "Before Abraham was, I Am." To know no other gods — self — before the *me* which has always been.

(S.&H. 109) "Christian Science reveals incontrovertibly that Mind is All in all, that the only realities are divine Mind and idea." Man is the boundless freedom that is God.

If suggestion cries — too absolute, ask — Is Science too true? Science is absolutely free from mixture, *now* — Remember, we are *not* absolutists, not persons being absolute. Can Truth be too true?

The greatness of Jesus and Mrs. Eddy was in their ability to get Jesus and Mrs. Eddy out of the way and let their own Christ being express its own presence and immortality. Let Truth utter Itself because it's true.

All Christian Science is absolute — There cannot be two schools of thought. To be Science it must be absolute and exact. Is 2x2 too absolute? If mathematics be watered down it is not science. Christian Science cannot be watered down to suit religionists.

Manual — Sunday School — "children taught absolute Science in textbook." "Human opinions are not Science." Many say absolute Science is an abstraction. The dictionary defines abstraction as — a withdrawal, separation, a theory.

The universe responds to what I Am, it cannot withdraw.

If, — as a person, we make absolute statements of Truth, it will disturb rather than heal. There is no person to deflect the purity of Truth. (*Mis.* 250) "Love, (Divine Science), is not something put upon a shelf, to be taken down on rare occasions with sugar-tongs and laid on a rose-leaf. Love, (Divine Science), cannot be a mere abstraction, or goodness without activity and power."

(*My.* 113) "A child will demonstrate Christian Science and have a clear perception of it. Then, is Christian Science a cold, dull abstraction, or is that unscientific which all around us is demonstrated on a fixed Principle and a given rule, etc."

We are not Christian Scientists labeled abstract nor absolute. Live it, love it, be it, but don't talk it.

We are not doling out arguments having that Love, so divine, so *felt* it will melt away the mist.

Judaism would hold Spirit in the grasp of matter. (S.&H. 28:7) "The persecutor of Truth and Love" — no mortal, incorrect view, no substance, no reality, — nothing.

When students talk it and don't live it, even correct...

(*Mis.* 166:28) "This spiritual idea, or Christ, entered into the minutiae of the life of the personal Jesus. It made him an honest man, a good carpenter, and a good man, before it could make him the glorified."

We cannot say, "oh, that was not *I* smoking, that was animal magnetism." We are responsible for what appears to our neighbor. Told of a student who ignored a stop sign and who said, "Oh, I am a law unto myself." Also, told of a Christian Science child who had a belief of measles. Parents said, "Oh, he feels fine, he's out playing with the children." What *right* has a Christian Scientist to ignore the law. It is not what *we* feel, but what is right for my neighbor.

We are custodians of the final revelation of Truth. The Christian Science movement exists in the consciousness of its members.

"Moral idiocy"

These qualities do not belong to the I that is God, but we are custodians of the revelation and to the world we must present.

Don't let human concept appear to ignore the human law. Don't ignore it till it is redeemed. Remember how you were taught to watch, "ways that are vain." "I cannot be tempted to the committal of acts foreign to my natural Christ-being."

Afternoon

We are bursting the bubbles of earth with the sweet breath of heaven. Weather is not something outside. This

Association, acknowledging its own being, is producing its own weather.

Read from the address of Prof. Andrews. "Ripples and waves in atoms which can be heard. They form a musical pattern, as a symphony. Music surges all around us and creates what we see. We are not organized matter. In reality, we are music, unified and coherent. What we call ourselves is the music of the spheres." We live, move and have our being in the realm of the music of Soul, the reality of Spirit. (1951)

Don't say, "isn't this wonderful for a physical Scientist to see?" He is not approaching Science but backing in. There is no science *but* Christian Science.

(*Mis.* 23) "Reason and revelation declare that God is both noumenon and phenomena, — the first and only cause. The universe, including man, is not the result of atomic action, material force or energy; it is not organized dust. God, Spirit, Mind, are terms synonymous for the one God, whose reflection is creation, and man is His image and likeness."

(*Mis.* 190:1) "Atomic action is Mind, not matter. It is neither the energy of matter, the result of organization, nor the outcome of life infused into matter, It is infinite Spirit, Truth, Life, defiant of error or matter."

The knowing of this Association should be so universal that it should produce an anti-miss. **(??)** Don't ignore invention, Mrs. Eddy says it must have its day — it is the symbol appearing to counteract atomic power. Pray daily that God, Spirit be the interpreter of the universe. **(?)** Church is consciousness, constituted of beauty and love. As long as we seem to, (build), it must conform to highest visible form.

(S.&H. 252:15) Material sense — "I am wholly dishonest, and no man knoweth it" etc., a touch, an accident, the law of God, etc.

Atomic power being Mind, cannot be perverted.

(S.&H. 48:6) Jesus "held uncomplaining guard over a world." Don't ignore a suggestion of draught, but don't be tempted to work for rain, for you might get a flood! Handle the hypnotic suggestion that there is anything beside God.

Judge Smith was on the weather committee in Mrs. Eddy's home. One day during a severe storm, Mrs. Eddy sent someone to remind him he was still on it. God-Principle governs the universe. It includes no clashing elements. Heat and cold are products of mortal mind.

Evangelization

We must not shy away from evangelization as something belonging to old theology, but must understand it as a scientific term. Jesus looked deep into realism and saw every experience as Truth Itself. The scribe has no, "lens of Science." Jesus permitted the Christ to live him, so he lived in the realization that he was one with authority. The absence of Jesus permitted the Christ to have authority. He did not stand on the shifting sands of personal sense nor hide his candle under a bushel — a basket of personal sense. Jesus demonstrated Science. His work was not the result of the way he was born. He recognized Principle rather than person. Mrs. Eddy did not mistake person for Principle. Peter said, "God is no respecter of persons." Principle in perfect continuity expresses Itself. Yield up the bubbles of earth and experience your own divinity and the ghost of limited belief will disappear as the Holy Ghost appears.

Whatever is true about Jesus or Mrs. Eddy is true in absolute Christian Science. Here lies our inspiration, our all. Christ is the immediacy of Mind — Life, felt and lived.

(S.&H. 254:19) "The human self must be evangelized," by looking deep into realism. As the material person called you fades — more dominion is manifested over the symbols. The symbols become servants instead of masters and appear more abundantly and in fairer form. If you try to *get* more, we lose it. Expect it and we get it in more beauty and abundance. Living as the compound idea we have all as reflection.

Everlasting Christ is not organic but the consciousness of Truth and Love. Money is the inexhaustible self-expression of Good. Medicine is not matter in solution. The Christian Scientist's medicine is perfect God and perfect man. The scientific term — evangelize — means to preach the gospel, but don't allow it to fall to the level of old theology. There is no "from," "to," — but just good news. Not from matter to Spirit, but the good news that ever *is*. Regenerate means to be born again. Repent means to think over. Learn these terms scientifically not as they are used in false theological teaching.

Looking deep into realism, we can detect the false paths of scholastic theology, and are not tempted to *change* the carnal mind. "The carnal mind is enmity to God." Never try to clean up what is enmity to God. Christian Science is revealing Oneness, Allness, not man with a life apart from God. Man is not capable of wrong thinking. Christian Science is not mental science. Mrs. Eddy says, "The basic error is mortal mind," God is the *only* Mind. Don't respond to the belief that there is a mind apart from God. All there is to what is called the cancer, the T.B. is incorrect, improper identification. Watch that you don't flatter the false claim with improper identification.

Don't try to mentally project harmony and completeness into a discordant home. We can't *use* Christian Science It is *not* a remedy. Christian Science is Truth, revelation! *Let* God, Spirit, Mind, Life identify Himself. This is *man*. Students can't identify. Never try to identify yourself with God. *Let* God identify Himself. That is the only I. (S.&H. 512:25) "— this so called mind puts forth its own qualities and claims God as their author — the claim usurps the deific prerogatives and is an attempted infringement on infinity."

So many sincere, honest students who still name the nothingness and then try to heal it. It is bound to fall that way. They have withdrawn from Christian Science because they have failed to project harmony into a discordant situation. This is due to incorrect instruction by Teacher or Practitioner. They are trying to make the human concept into the divine idea. It is perfectly natural for the human mind to hate, to be miserable, and mean because it is a liar from the beginning. It never had any good in it. These students that work thus are so honest, but so wrong.

(S.&H. 395:21) "It is mental quackery to make disease a reality — to hold it as something seen and felt — and then attempt its cure through Mind."

Don't ignore what is back of human qualities — the belief of heredity. Use no more the proverb — "sour grapes — children's teeth set on edge." Man receives only from God. Handle heredity daily — given — not given back?

Remember the gulf is fixed. All that appears as human mind is but a negative appearing or negation of divine Mind. "By reversal, errors serve as waymarks to God."

If the suggestion says you are unemployed reply, "Yes, man is forever employed reflecting God." If it says you are fearful — know your divine nature as the Christ of God, and the power of Omnipotence, knows no fear. If it claims dissatisfaction, realize your completeness.

The Practitioner has no right to delve into what anyone thinks. We have not the legal right to diagnose disease. Never permit a name to be given, its only identification is an, "evil, hypnotic, suggestion." It is *never* a condition.

[A] woman stepped on a nail in the garden — went through foot. She realized the nail was Spirit — and anything contrary was hypnotic suggestion. — *not matter.* [She was] healed. "This is Science."

AM I NOT MYSELF

Don't talk one way and act another. We must meet

and fulfill our responsibilities with no deviation, whether it be in church, committee or board, etc., see it is all your own Christ – being.

Jesus was obedient, he paid his taxes, etc. He manifested his Christ in the minutia of daily living. Some are always late to church — learn to manifest exactness, graciousness etc. This *living* prevents the so called, "big things" from happening.

We hear too much about the prophylactic and not enough of the preventative side of Christian Science.

Always give testimonies from the standpoint of reality. Nothing inharmonious could enter God, and man lives, moves, and has his being in God. Don't give a testimony as though you still had a little *being in* God being. Is there God plus me? Identity of God is man. Don't leave the bubble of earth. Being is God. "Whatever… divides… Being into beings, is a misstatement of the unerring Principle of Science." (*Ret.* 56)

"Rejoice, because your names are written in heaven." *Know* that seeing is the ever-present fact of being. Life is universal, eternal. Mind is God, one. If the belief says, "no job," know the uninterrupted continuity of good, if it says, "no home," realize the fact that home is universal, ever-present. Rejoice always in the fact!

(*Rud.* 3) — Mrs. Eddy says, "physical healing is but the bugle call to higher thought and action." Are we just hearing the bugle call or the whole band? Look *deep* into realism! (*Un.* 44:13) "In the days of Eden, humanity was misled by a false personality, a talking snake —." This pretender taught the opposite of Truth. This *abortive ego*, this fable of error, is laid bare in Christian Science," "Bruise the head of this serpent," as Truth and, "The woman," are doing in Christian Science, and it stings your heel, rears its crest proudly, and goes on saying, "Am I not myself? Am I not mind and matter, person and thing?" We should answer: "Yes! You are indeed yourself, and need most of all to be rid of this self, for it is very far from God's likeness."

Identity is the directness of Mind Itself. What does an abortive ego think with? It is not a person thinking nor puppets — called *me*.

If you have personality you are one with mortal mind and *its* multifarious forms. Identity is the functioning presence of the Mind that is God. What claims to be a personal function or a person functioning is the carnal mind.

Truth lived is worth more than all the words in the English language. There is but *one school* of Truth. "From the infinite One in Christian Science comes one Principle and its infinite idea, etc." (112)

Suggestion — animal magnetism — would like Christian Scientists to believe there are different kinds of teaching, but there is but *one* Science and Health and it is a revelation from God. Mind, Spirit, is the one teacher, divine Principle. There is no evil ego. The rod of Divinity? From holiness? Into light. (nobody)

Us is not plural. Principle and idea is *one*, not two. (See "Personal Statements" — *Un.* 44-47)

(*Un.* 18:4) "Dwelling in light, I can see only the brightness of My own glory."

(18:25) "A knowledge of aught beside Myself is impossible."

(17:7) "Hourly in Christian Science, man thus weds himself with God."

Remember, it is never two becoming one. Always, the Adorable One, identifying Itself. "Love wedded to its own spiritual idea."

Looking deep into realism, Paul asked, "Is Christ divided?" It is ever the same Christ. What appeared as Jesus or Paul is incidental to the real Christ, my Christ being, "without seam or rent."

Jesus said, "Greater works shall ye do." What did he mean by greater works? Jesus healed the sick. The greater works must be the proof that there is no death. This Association should wipe out the belief called death. Can Christ be divided? All that is present is the Christ-power, the Christ-Life, the Christ Science which is the vital understanding now going on as one's own identity.

So live your Christ so that you will cease to struggle.

(*My.* 26:27-5) "Look high enough" —

Book — Jewish — New Testament.

On John, "Christ always existed. (existent) Jesus was but an incident in the eternality of the Christ.

Let the human concept be incidental. Don't permit it to take on such proportions that it is always demanding attention. "Get the behind me, Jesus," was what the Master replied to the Satanic suggestion of the human concept for identification.

Establish your day so thoroughly that the human concept is incidental. No medium.

If the world picture is not harmonious, do something fresh and new. Have a holy curiosity. Don't just read a lesson because you feel you have to. Always keep it free. If you don't like a lesson on Animal Magnetism, read about its being denounced! Modern necromancy is the belief that bodies have life in them. Ancient necromancy was the belief in witchcraft, calling up a so-called dead.

Don't permit thought to go to human concept. When you read about Everlasting Punishment, see it is only ignorance punishing itself.

Science is revelation — always fresh, new, sing it! Live it! Love it! But don't try to explain it.

In practice, never start with man. Always start with God. Where effect is cause has to be first. Where the Son is, the Father must be first, where man is, God must be first.

(Related early visit to a practitioner.) She said, All Life is God, Mind is God, Action is God, all power — every faculty is God. We don't need to treat God! (Mr. Steves said he was in an Aura of light for weeks.)

God is primal — creation secondary. The moment you start with God, man is all right. When you start with cause, effect is all right. Start with noumenon and phenomena is all right. The Father has given His promise, "All that I have is thine."

We must watch our terminology. If someone says, "wheel" — one may think of a tiny watch wheel, another, of a locomotive wheel. Each is correct according to his vision at the moment. Be glad if yours is a larger vision and live your concept.

The terms must be kept straight and scientifically understood. The terms in all science must be exact. The chemist or mathematician cannot confuse nor supplant terms.

Individuality, identity, Cause-effect — must be distinctly understood.

Man is not God.

Don't discuss metaphysical points in practice. Turn to the books. Let Jesus or Mrs. Eddy do it for you.

Letter from Mr. Mann.

A claim may be subtly malicious as to be mistaken for a physical belief and the temptation came to handle it as such. There can and must be no compromise as to handling it as a physical condition. It is never anything but malicious, vicious, suggestion.

Jesus so consistently looked deep into realism that he could not accept the religious teaching of his day. Jesus, living the Christ, made broad his phylacteries. One alone is master. Never accept the suggestion that, "I'm a Reader, a Practitioner," etc., All that is present *is God, not person.* There is no target for a, "carnal mind to see or touch." Don't put up something besides God. That is all there is because of the permanency of Principle.

Never think of yourself as a person. Sin would strike at persons. Love, innocency, lack of guile etc., constitutes the only Mind. That Mind, expressing Itself can say, "I did a grand job."

Never permit thought to drop to the level of human

persons. Nicodemus knew Jesus looked deep into realism and never accepted the outward sense.

Jesus refused to accept the suggestion that man is a habitation for God. The Christ of Jesus answered, "What things?" He identified himself always with and as the Christ. The tormentor says you must purge consciousness.?

Man never lapses from nor returns to harmony. There is no person calling itself myself. I am a priest of God, after the order of Melchisedec - no material history, as impersonal as God. Before Abraham, Melchisedec, or Jesus — I AM — not because of any virgin birth but because of the demonstration of divine Principle. Preexistence does not mean before something. Was it the way we were born? No! Man is never born, never dying but coexistent with God, because man is the Son of God.

Atonement is a hard problem in theology but no problem in Christian Science. There are no fragments, no Jesus, Mrs. Eddy, but the one Ego that is God, that said I and my Father are one.

Temptation — The only Satan is the satanic suggestion that one is person instead of Principle. "Get thee behind me, *Jesus*." Better results in practice are merely incidental. Don't *use* it for yourself. No deviation, *I Am All*.

Never be afraid to address the anti-Christ as *you* — you iniquity — you suppositious — you Lucifer — you — sick child or frantic mother — *you* are *all* animal magnetism and I thank God there is only perfect God and perfect man.

Bicknell Young, a Christian Science lecturer, was called at 2 A.M. by a woman who was determined to impress him with the seriousness of her ailment. When he hung up he declared, "*You animal magnetism* cannot assume the disguise of a selfish woman and disturb my harmony nor interfere with my rest." She was healed and told him she had had 26 practitioners. She was not only denying the healing power of the Christ, but persuading them to deny their own Christ. Mr. Young said she got all their scalps but not mine. See it as *you*. Never dignify it by identifying it as person. Animal Magnetism is as impersonal as Truth. Its greatest flatterer is identification.

We are not dealing with persons, but animal magnetism. Our only activity is just to glorify God. Art 8 (of the *Church Manual*) not using it, but glorifying God. *You* — animal magnetism.

If we feel the need of protective work we are being handled by self righteousness. Health is an ever-present fact. Christian Science is not something with which a few protect themselves, it is not just for a few, but is the revelation of God. No mine and thine, no wall of partition.

Reader in Mother Church testimony —

When we have a limited finite sense of Science it antagonizes rather than heals.

Looking deep into realism, there is no personality — the product of two mortals. The suggestion that one is a product of two would naturally produce frustration, a belief of two heritages, a split personality.

In Christian Science man is the product of One — the Adorable One. Acknowledge that blood is the essence of Life, of Love — blood — begin by knowing — the essence of the purity of God.

Heart — heart of lettuce — man has the great heart of divinity. Be ye therefore perfect as your Father which is in heaven is perfect. All that is going on is the heart of divinity beating, the divinity of the universe. Heart is always *Now* — beating the rhythm of the universe.

Obstetrician told Mr. Steves he could detect the heartbeat of unborn child before child was formed, showing the function was present before the organ.

Case of negative blood in unborn child. Treatment was — there is only one Father, Mother, God. The only blood is the essence of divinity, perfect, eternal, nothing present but perfection. Child born and had perfect type blood. Did treatment change anything or recognize the only blood was flowing forth from the throne of God and was always right.

Daymare

Lecturer used term and Mr. Steves found it in Dictionary, "a dream sensation with the eyes open." A nightmare does not contend with matter. But in a daymare you permit thought to get in a track believing the claim to be physical and this produces the delusion and it becomes an obsession. Just thank God — I am not the one in the dream?

Judge Smith's wife was working for a patient. As she sat in the room she saw a snake slide across the floor. Suddenly she saw the pattern of the rug through the snake. Then she looked at the patient and she said she saw the pattern of the Christ visible through what appeared as a patient. She realized all the claim there was was animal magnetism attempting to deny the Christ of the practitioner.

Let the sweet breath of heaven blow away all the mockeries of earth. Now are we the Sons of God.

No sub-conscious mind to pour forth a flood of accusations. All consciousness belongs to God, nothing subconscious, abstract, no accuser nor accused.

Peace I give unto you, my peace give I unto you.

We are not persons to become wiser. Wisdom distilled is the wisdom of this Association.

Walden — Shame — illusion — Reality.

God culminates in this present moment and will never be more divine. This is the whole of Christian Science.

From glory unto glory —

The Higher Meaning of the Textbook
Association Address of 1959

by

Clarence Steves

Mary Baker Eddy, in speaking of the textbook, *Science and Health with Key to the Scriptures*, said, "It is the voice of Truth to this age, and contains the full statement of Christian Science, or the Science of healing through Mind." In *Miscellany*, she writes, "The opinions of men cannot be substituted for God's revelation." In times past, arrogance, ignorance and pride have dimmed the power and glory of the Scriptures, to which this Christian Science textbook is the Key.

In *Miscellany*, Mrs. Eddy writes, "It was not myself, but the divine power of Truth and Love, infinitely above me, which dictated 'Science and Health with Key to the Scriptures.' I have been learning the higher meaning of this book since writing it.... I should blush to write of 'Science and Health with Key to the Scriptures' as I have, were it of human origin, and were I, apart from God, its author. But, as I was only a scribe echoing the harmonies of heaven in divine metaphysics, I cannot be supermodest in my estimate of the Christian Science textbook."

The purpose of this Association today is to give us the higher meaning of the textbook. It is to permit the Mind that is God to reveal itself. In Revelation, we read, "Go and take the little book. . . Take it, and eat it up; and it shall make thy belly bitter, but it shall be in thy mouth sweet as honey." Mrs. Eddy says, "Mortals, obey the heavenly evangel. Take Divine Science. Read this book from beginning to end. Study it, ponder it. It will be indeed sweet at its first taste, when it heals you; but murmur not over Truth, if you find its digestion bitter. When you approach nearer and nearer to this divine Principle . . . — thus partaking of . . . the primal elements, of Truth and Love — do not be surprised nor discontented because you must share the hemlock cup and eat the bitter herbs; for the Israelites of old . . . thus prefigured this perilous passage out of bondage into the El Dorado of faith and hope."

This means that we eat the book by acknowledging to one's self that this divine man is one's own identity, here and now; and approaching nearer and nearer the divine Principle, means that as we see man to be the functioning presence of the Mind that is God; then we cease existing as persons, as mortals trying so hard to understand, trying to find out what the book is saying, trying to demonstrate what we read; but when we read it, we eat it, and make it our own identification — no longer humans trying to be divine; but our divinity embraces our humanity, and from now on the digestion is sweet! There is no personal mind to digest the revelation. There is only the revelation to be lived and loved as oneself. When the human mind is believed to be digesting divine ideas, we have a dangerous situation. This intellectuality seems to get itself accepted as the Christ. But beware of intellectuality! It is the antichrist. There is no life in it! High sounding words of man's wisdom are not divine Science. Willingness to let the old personal sense of self go, is the greatest sense of humility, because it is permitting the personal sense of ego to disappear in the Christly realization that the only ego is Mind, or God.

No little ego, running everything from a personal, egotistical sense, but to experience this true sense of ego as Jesus and Mrs. Eddy exemplified, we permit the ego to go unto the Father and remain as the Father. It is this joyous willingness to let this evil, abortive ego go, and permit the

Ego God to express Himself as the Ego man. This willingness opens the very gates of heaven that the personal sense of self has closed. Let us not read the textbook as egotistical persons knowing something of the truth, but rather let us permit the Mind that is Christ to reveal itself. This humility permits us to eat the little book with the joyous realization of self-identification. In reading the textbook, it must be carefully ascertained whether our Leader is speaking from the divine standpoint of revelation or from the limited human standpoint — that is, the Christian religious viewpoint. Educational statements gently lead the student on to the acceptance of the absolute, or divine; but this acceptance comes only as the student lives and loves the educational statements, until he can let go of the letter and experience the revelation.

In *Retrospection and Introspection*, Mrs. Eddy writes, "For many successive years I have endeavored to find new ways and means for the promotion and expansion of scientific Mind-healing, seeking to broaden its channels and, if possible, to build a hedge round about it that should shelter its perfections from the contaminating influences of those who have a small portion of its letter and less of its spirit. At the same time I have worked to provide a home for every true seeker and honest worker in this vineyard of Truth."

It is interesting that our Leader shows us that she has endeavored to shelter the beginner and find a true home for every seeker. She leads those that are with young so gently and quietly that the babe is born without effort or struggle. All are with young when they begin to glimpse that there is something divine about themselves — something to man besides what the senses are seeing and knowing. The pale star begins to disappear, and the daystar appears. What a marvelous journey there is in going from page to page, chapter to chapter, and seeing the new way, the new view, the new man. Be gentle with those who are with young. Help them bring forth the Christ man. Let us say and see, "His name is wonderful. Truly unto us a child is born and his name shall be called wonderful." The wonder is that Mrs. Eddy could bring forth the Christian Science textbook. The marvel is that she could find English words to clothe this wonder — this divine revelation. Truly it is the descent of the Holy Ghost. Now be gentle with yourself. Let the Christ idea come forth. Mother it, nurse it, love it, cherish it. Then the babe ceases to exist, and the Christ man comes forth in all the glory of God. All can clap their hands and say, "My name is wonderful." Then we see that "by flesh embound was but thy shade!" And the light grows brighter and brighter, the shade disappears and the Christ man, reality, the daystar appears, never to disappear. So I ask you with all the love of Principle — be gentle with those who are with young, who are seeing something of their divinity, struggling to attain true manhood, but still believing themselves to be persons struggling forward. Be gentle, be kind, because Mrs. Eddy says that she has given them a home in the Christian Science textbook.

From the educational standpoint, we seem to be students studying this Science and endeavoring to put into practice what is being known, what is being understood. And this is perfectly normal from a standpoint of being a person — we use what we know; but the time comes in our study when this attitude will no longer work. If we are not alert, we will ask the question, Why has Science failed me? Why do I not demonstrate as readily? Why do I have to work and study so hard? We must stop and ask ourseves if we are at the place where we can no longer use Christian Science, and we must begin to live divine Science. The living Christ is the demand upon this Association. Only this living will bless the movement and the world. In order that this Association may live the Christ today, let us pick up the textbook with a new meaning.

Preface

The opening sentence says, "To those leaning on the sustaining infinite, today is big with blessings. The wakeful shepherd beholds the first faint morning beams, ere cometh the full radiance of a risen day. So shone the pale star to the prophet-shepherds; yet it traversed the night, and came where, in cradled obscurity, lay the Bethlehem babe, the human herald of Christ, Truth, who would make plain to benighted understanding the way of salvation through Christ Jesus, till across a night of error should dawn the morning beams and shine the guiding star of being. The Wisemen were to behold and to follow this daystar of divine Science, lighting the way to eternal harmony."

In the early editions, Mrs. Eddy writes, "Tomorrow is big with blessing." But as the light grew brighter for our Leader, she could write *today*! Now! A present fact. Mrs. Eddy knew that no time need to elapse for Truth to be true, and so she changed the very first sentence in the textbook from "tomorrow" to "today." The infinite One is eternally sustaining its own infinite manifestation. This is the Science of being. It is not a process brought about by study or thinking. It is divine acknowledgment. The sustaining infinite is big with blessings. The new student beholds the first faint morning beams and beholds what wonders these faint morning beams seem to bring. Darkness, ignorance, superstition are all wiped out and healing comes. John Young of Edinburgh wrote, "Light shone in the darkness." These men always see the daybreak and always describe the first breaking of dawn as a hallowed morning. Truly, it is a hallowed morning when the first faint morning beam comes to tell us, man is not a poor sick mortal, a miserable sinner. Then the full day breaks forth, and the Christ shows us the daystar — the daystar of divine Science — lighting the way to eternal harmony. Now, as the light begins to break, the dawn shines forth; and we begin to experience the eternal noon; and we find man, not something separate from the divine Mind — we find man to be the effect of Mind's own knowing. Then the 'peace be still' comes. The night of error is banished as the light of the eternal now breaks forth, and it is found that man is as essential to God as God is to man. Effect is as essential to cause as cause is to effect. In the oneness of being, cause and effect are both the being that is God-being. When we see the term effect, or man, do we ask, What is man the effect of? The answer must be *cause*. The effect is always the effect of cause. Our Leader says, "Man is the expression of God's being," or effect is the expression of cause in being. Man as effect has all the attributes, all the qualities of the Father, cause, with the exception of creativeness. Man is creation; man is never creative. Reflection is not creative. Reflection is creation. Always keep your terms straight, and there is no better place to begin than in the 'Preface.'

The substance, Life, intelligence, Truth and Love which constitute Deity, cause, constitutes its effect, man. Let us have a wonderful sense of true being as we travel through the textbook. Let us have divine adventure. Let it be a new land, eternal light, free from the baggage of personal sense. Each sentence, each paragraph, each chapter, becomes the new land of Christian Science; and it is here in this land that all the fetters of personal sense fall, and the daystar rises with the light of eternity. We cannot read the textbook as we would read another book. Never attempt to. Just read it phrase to phrase, period to period, sentence to sentence. You must have a divine adventure. The first command in the Bible is, "Let there be light," and the first command in the 'Preface' is light, daystar. Then the light breaks into another facet. The human mind is not to be a factor in Christian Science. What joy should come forth from this Association today. There is no human mind. All is Mind, and in this Mind the entire being is found harmonious. The sooner we let go the old for the new, the sooner we begin to live this divine revelation. As long as we respond to the suggestion that the human mind is digesting or assimilating what is being said, the digestion will be bitter.

What freedom, what dominion comes when the daystar of being shows us man — the glowing knowing of Mind itself. To those leaning on the one and only Mind for inspiration, for life, for joy, today is big with blessings. To those leaning on personal sense, trying to find out something about God, trying to demonstrate what they have found out about God, today is lean, and there is no blessing. The belief that one has a private mind separate from his brother, separate from the divine Mind, is to experience hell. There is no existence separate from your brother. Hell is believing there is another. Heaven is the understanding of the oneness of all being. The pale star is seeing and knowing that God is Mind. But to experience the daystar, one must see that man is the directness of Mind in manifestation.

Your textbook, over and over, says, "Man has no mind but God." So God is the present Mind of man. What we call thinking, is not actually thinking going on in the skull. It is the Mind that is God revealing itself. Physique does not contain a mind; certainly no thinking goes on in a head. We do not use brains to think with, organs to live with, because Life and intelligence are purely spiritual. Again, your Leader wants it plainly understood in the 'Preface,' that healing results now as it did in Jesus' time from the operation of divine Principle. It is interesting that Mrs. Eddy, in the 'Preface,' shows the healing in Jesus' time was not something Jesus alone possessed; but that it was the operation of divine Principle. She says that this operation is called the Christ. It is the same Christ of Jesus that is present here as the Christ of this Association.

In mathematics, it is the operation of principle that dissolves the problem into its nothingness. In Christian Science, it is the acknowledgment that the God-Principle is present, and that the God-Principle is operating, and this Christ understanding does not permit a problem to assert itself. So simplicity in healing is simply darkness giving place to light. How simple your Leader explains healing in the 'Preface.' Students make it so difficult. It must be something I am thinking that is wrong. It must be something I am doing. Something I am seeing! This is *not* Christian Science, and your Leader, in the 'Preface,' shows you that the human mind is not a factor.

How can we understand the textbook, if we do not understand the 'Preface'? We must leave the argument of a personal mind and let the Mind that is God, the Mind that knows no problem, no false traits of character, no depraved appetite, no mental blocks, no impediment, govern. The Christ Mind is the only Mind of man. As we approach the textbook with newness and freshness, let us permit the textbook to state the fact, and not something we think it says. Do not let familiarity with the statement rob you of the freshness of now. Be willing to let the old go for the new. Let us pour in new wine. It is not what these words say, but what was the knowing going on when these words were written. This Christ-knowing is the knowing here and now. This true sense of ego makes all things new. Reading the textbook from the standpoint of divine revelation will make all things new. There is no possibility of reading this book from a standpoint of scholastic theology, and then repeating certain phrases and sentences without the slightest spiritual understanding. Over and over, our Leader endeavors to make students see not English words, not grammar; but she is pouring into the bottle called English words, divine revelation. The bottle will break and we will lose the inspiration, if we permit the human mind to interpret what is being read. Let it be the Christ Mind which we have solemnly promised to watch for. Now are we the sons of God — the Christ Mind — so let us behold the Christ in our universe.

We have seen that leaning on the sustaining infinite, today is big with blessings. The human mind is not a factor in healing; man's present Mind is God. We are now ready to experience the quietness and the freshness of the chapter called 'Prayer.'

Prayer

What is scientific prayer? True prayer is not an instrument for altering or moving the heart of God. Our book shows that when Jesus prayed, he withdrew from the material senses to refresh his heart with brighter, more spiritual views. Christian Science shows us that there is no self apart from God to pray. We are not mortals praying to a vast God outside, worshipping a God, falling down, saying certain words that we think will appease this man-formulated God. Paul rebuked this kind of prayer. "Whom therefore ye ignorantly worship, him declare I unto you." True prayer is the practice of God's presence — permitting the personal sense of self to fade into its native nothingness in the realization of the God-presence, the God-power. In this divine presence, no finiteness can possibly remain.

In true prayer, Jesus "held uncomplaining guard over a world." He never complained about what the neighbors did. He never complained about what anyone did. He maintained his oneness with his Father. This is true prayer.

Mrs. Eddy has revolutionized prayer. She asked, "What are the motives for prayer? Are we benefited by praying?" She says, "Prayer cannot change the Science of being, but it tends to bring us into harmony with it." So we do not pray to change a sick mortal into a well one, or a discontented person into a contented person. True prayer is not to change anything. Your Leader says that it tends to bring us into harmony with the Science of being. So true prayer is to bring us this harmony of our own being. Now let us ask the question, "What is the Science of being?" Our book states that there is no life, truth, intelligence nor substance in the belief of being a person. Then comes that all-embracing statement, that all without a single exception is infinite Mind, infinitely manifesting itself as all. There is no possibility within this infinity of being for there to be a finity calling itself you, and that this "you" must pray to a great ego outside to remind Him what we need or what we want, or we are in trouble. And if he does not do something quickly, we shall cease to exist as a "you." Well, let us face it! The sooner we get rid of the "you," the better off we will be. Remember, in class teaching, the "you" was "the first iniquitous manifestation of sin." Sin is simply the evil suggestion that there is a "you," there is something present besides God. How can you say that God is all-presence, all-power, and still have a personal sense — "you"?

Prayer is not to change the human "you." True prayer is to leave the human mind completely, not to try to change it; the human mind is the problem, so why stay within the problem? Acknowledge that the Mind that is God, is present and that this Mind knows no problems. Your Leader makes a tremendously sweeping statement, "The mere habit of pleading with the divine Mind, as one pleads with a human being, . . . humanly circumscribed, [is] an error which impedes spiritual growth." The impediment is that we have been praying incorrectly. Fruitful prayer will be denied as long as we pray in such a manner.

God is divine Principle. God is Love. Can we ask God to be more? God is intelligent. Can we tell this intelligent Mind anything? Do we expect that prayer will change the perfection, when the perfection that is God is the perfection of Mind in expression? Divine Mind concedes our perfection. Too many students stand before the blackboard and pray the divine Principle to operate, and yet the problem remains on the blackboard. The wise student in mathematics, finds out more concerning the principle, works with the principle and avoids the mistake. So it is in Christian Science. Prayer is recognition that Principle's idea, man, is the functioning presence of the unerring Principle itself. The fact that Principle is present and is operating, prevents the problem from arising. What if there should be an unsolved problem of long standing which refuses to budge under the most searching prayer, the most intelligent declarations? Could it not be that we are praying to solve the problem, rather than seeing the impossibility of the problem? I have seen the most stubborn cases called incurable which had been given treatment for years, yield when you can get the patient to pray from the standpoint that the revelation of God, as revealed in Christian Science, makes the problem impossible. I have seen the most earnest, conscientious students work day after day, and not solve their problem, because they insist they must solve it. What is wrong? They say, "Why am I not getting results as I used to?"

When we first approach Christian Science, dim perception seems to work; when we become students of this Science, we can no longer *use* it. Christian Science shows that the nature of God is the nature of man, and makes problems impossible. This is the only way scientific healing can be brought about in Christian Science. Mrs. Eddy tells us in the textbook, "The physical healing in Christian Science results now, as in Jesus' time from the operation of divine Principle, before which sin and disease lose their reality in human consciousness."

We have those who come to us and say, "Oh, but I do have a problem. It is my husband, he simply does not understand me. It's amazing; he is a member of the church, he works on committees, but he simply does not understand me. What is wrong?" Is it not that the student is permitting the aggressive mental suggestion that it is a person living with a person? But it is Mind that is God that is present; and the only will there is, is God's will; so let that will be done. Who are we to tell another what to do? How to read the lesson? They are not studying enough? Self-righteous mortals! Perhaps our prayer is unanswered because we are thinking we are divine idea. We know the truth. We are so certain we know it, yet everything in our home remains unchanged. Have you asked yourself the question, Who sees the problem? Mind's expression, man, is not that which sees the problem and struggles so hard to solve it. Is there a human mind to even be aware of the problem? To have such a mind would be to have a mind that is enmity to God! For a practitioner to take such a case and believe that somebody has a problem, but that he will help them solve it, is not prayer in Christian Science. If one sees others as disobedient persons, sick persons, but that we must pray to make these personalities good ones, then we are praying in vain, making vain repetitions even as the heathens do.

Prayer in Christian Science is not to change anything, not to alter, not to heal. True prayer in Christian Science is acknowledgment of your own oneness with God. You heal yourself in Christian Science. You never heal a patient. Your knowing is that there is no patient, for God is *all*. Being is One. Being is indivisible. Never let your prayer fall into vain repetition. God is the same yesterday, today and forever. Never forget the immediacy of Christian Science prayer. The immediacy, the nowness of Christian Science, does not heal man of sin. Christian Science shows the impossibility of sin attaching itself to the man of God's creation! How could darkness attach itself to light? Man is the light of the world in its eternal noon, undimmed by a declining sun, the purity of being, the immaculate Father-Mother God in manifestation. Mrs. Eddy writes, "In proportion as the spotless selfhood of God is understood, human nature will be renovated, and man will receive a higher selfhood, derived from God." Always keep your prayer on the level of divine Science. Never permit it to fall to the level of a human prayer to some God outside. There is no such God. Roman Catholics pray to the Mother of God. God never has a mother. God *is* Mother. Your prayer will be just as vain if you pray to a God outside!

God is now at once the center and circumference of your being. Mrs. Eddy asks this question, "Dost thou 'love the Lord thy God with all thy heart, and with all thy soul, and with all thy mind'?" Watch what she answers, "This command includes much, even the surrender of all merely material sensation, affection, and worship. This is the El Dorado of Christianity." What is the El Dorado? It means piled with gold and every good thing. It is to have no concept of yourself as a person acting or reacting to what another says or does. It is most important to see that we are not persons acting and reacting to what is called another. We have surrendered the belief of merely material affection. She says, surrender it! We have no identity as person. Mind identifies itself. Let us be willing to surrender anything that would deny the oneness and allness of God. Mrs. Eddy says, "Prayer cannot change the unalterable Truth." Why? Because Truth is true. Truth then is something we live! We never use truth, we live it, we love it! Our prayer must be as scientific as Science itself!

Demonstration

One of the students of this Association, took a case of a woman who had had much treatment, and many practitioners, a patient dying with cancer. The student recognized the fact immediately, that if the condition called cancer was true, nothing could be done about it. She said to the patient, "If this is true, you are stuck with it, and it would be foolish for us to waste our time praying." Then she said to the patient, "If it is not true, it would be just as foolish to pray over it. Now, because it is untrue, it simply isn't present. It has no presence, because if it were present, I would also have it. I do not have it! Because the only I is God." The patient appeared to respond almost immediately, and in a few days, went back to her normal activity — all because this student knew what scientific prayer is! She refused to pray over nothing. She prayed from the standpoint that this suggestion, being no part of the divine Mind, was no part of man. She did not attempt to find out what was wrong with the patient's thinking. She immediately went straight to God, and saw its nothingness from the standpoint of God's allness. Never permit your prayer to leave heaven for earth. Keep your prayer in heaven. Become so conscious of the oneness of all being — Father and son, Principle and idea — that the knowing is Mind's own knowing, Mind's experiencing its own perfect self, unerring knowing — the knowing of one Mind only.

Prayer is shutting the door on the possibility of the problem. Become so conscious of the oneness, the allness of divine Love that the problem, the patient, the practitioner, all disappear, and leave only the Love of God experiencing its own loveliness. Self-forgetfulness, purity, affection are constant prayers. Think of that — self-forgetfulness is constant prayer; this is praying without ceasing. Live your prayer, be your prayer, be the presence of prayer, so that your living is praying and your prayer is living. Pray without ceasing. Be your prayer. Let your very presence be prayer. All you come in touch with will feel that something holy has touched them. The seventeenth chapter of John is prayer, seeing the being of oneness. True prayer is seeing there are no persons to know or to be known. No persons to act or react. We are not persons with persons. There is only Love, Life, joy experiencing itself, so sweet, so gently. Not persons trying to get along with persons. Not persons trying to understand persons. Live your prayer. Just be the presence of God to everything. True prayer brings such a titanic force into being that these results may seem incredible. True prayer is going in and shutting the door on personal sense and its clamor of "Pray for me, Oh! help me!" Shut the door and permit the Christ to come forward. This is prayer. So we can say, "Our Father which art in heaven," because we know it is "Hallowed be Thy name."

Atonement

In this eternal, joyous prayer, we find the true atonement, or the oneness of being. Jesus' whole life was a constant atonement. Jesus so lived the Christ that he had continuous resort to his true selfhood. This resorting with the Father, with prayer, recuperated Jesus for the day's work. What a marvelous definition this is for prayer. That it is resorting with the Father! Living the Christ simply means the full acceptance of your divinity. It is never to think in terms of duality. It is alone with your own being, always resorting with the Father. To Jesus, oneness with the Father was the greatest of reality. No being was so present to Jesus as God. To him there was but one creator, one creation. It was always the way the Father was appearing at the moment. It was no effort to this pure Christ, shining, to see the nothingness of personal sense. It simply was not a reality to be coped with. Jesus' oneness with God was not occasional; it was in perfect continuity. It was not partial from a sense of duty. It governed him as the original law of his being, God's being. This is the one and only being. This is the reason he could always speak of Father and son as one. It never occurred to Jesus that he was usurping the divine prerogative to say, "He that hath seen me hath seen the Father." He never had a personal sense of himself. He knew that if anything good was occurring, it was his Father. So he said, "He that hath seen me hath seen the Father." He that has seen effect, has seen cause in operation.

Then Mrs. Eddy says, "Jesus acted boldly, against the accredited evidence of the senses, against Pharisaical creeds and practices, and he refuted all opponents with his healing power." They hated him because he exposed their creeds and dogmas. Catholicism would hate him today, for the very same reason — because he would expose their creeds.

Mrs. Eddy says, "The atonement is a hard problem in theology." When theology is trying to get fallen man back to his God, in that theology, atonement is a hard problem. "Jesus taught mortals the opposite of themselves, even the nature of God." Paul later wrote, "Let us lay aside every weight, and the sin which doth so easily beset us, and let us run with patience the race that is set before us." The moment we are willing to put aside the personal sense of self and permit the Christ to come forward, at that moment we are experiencing the atonement. Mrs. Eddy once declared to her students, "All is infallible now. I am infallible." These same students rebelled, and said to their Leader they were expressing quite the opposite. Our Leader held her ground, and said, "All is infallible now. I have told you the truth." But it riles the personal to be told the infallibility of Principle is man. What is man but Principle's infallibility in operation. But mortal mind insists it is a person that must learn of God. Christian Science says man proceeds from Principle, man rests upon Principle, is Principle's own operation. This is your atonement. This is your infallibility. Man is not in the process of becoming man. Man is emanation — emanation coming out from God. Jesus was so constantly conscious of his oneness with the Father, he refused to think of himself in a dualistic attitude. He acknowledged that the faultlessness and the perfection of that which he called God, was the faultlessness and perfection of that which he called the son. He honored his Father by admitting the immaculateness of all being. He constantly maintained this oneness in the face of all opposition. That is how he healed. He said, "Which of you convinceth me of sin?"

There is no record in the Bible where Jesus had reproached himself or regretted anything he had ever done or said. He never uttered a word to indicate that he had taken a wrong step, neglected a single opportunity. He constantly acknowledged his own God-Being. Animal magnetism is constantly asserting that you know something of your divinity today, but remember two years ago or ten years ago, you did not know it. Remember the harsh words? Remember the sins? Always see that animal magnetism is always talking about its own concept. It is not talking about yourself. The Bible says, "Though your sins be as scarlet [as person] they shall be as white as snow [as divinity]."

Animal magnetism says there is guilt or condemnation, but be your bright shining self here and now. There must be no sense of condemnation. When something seems to appear to deny your Christ-being, suggesting we were thoughtless, unkind, sinful, let us have resort immediately to our true selfhood and rejoice! " I never left heaven for earth." Animal magnetism, in the guise of thought, cannot hide the purity of my being. Purity does not necessarily mean the absence of sin. Purity means to have God absolutely all. Too frequently, students think of impurity as sin. That isn't true. It is to have something besides God. That is impurity. To have God all, is purity. It will make the human concept appear to the world as pure and wholesome. Jesus said, "He that sent me is with me; the Father hath not left me alone; for I do always those things that please Him. Which of you convinceth me of sin? . . . the prince of this world cometh, and hath nothing in me." Satanic suggestion of separation comes to the Christ-consciousness and finds nothing in the Christ-consciousness to respond to it. Because one can never respond to two. Which can convince the Christ of personal sense? Sometimes the suggestion says, because of past sins of omission or commission or some inability to meet or resist temptation, we are undeserving to experience our atonement now. Handle this satanic suggestion by knowing, "I have never left heaven for earth."

Heaven means the consciousness of oneness. Earth means plurality. Jesus not only acknowledged his God-Being, but acknowledged the God-Being of all. He said, "I and my Father are one." He acknowledged the oneness of Father and son. This is our constant atonement. Jesus never lost sight of oneness. He maintained a sense of incomparable dignity and sacredness in oneness. Just think of that purity. "I and my Father are one." The consciousness that uttered those words could never belong to that which thinks in terms of personal sense. It would be blasphemous for a student to utter such words from a personal sense of self; but this same sense of truth uttered from the standpoint of the Christ, reveals true being. So we have put off all personal sense and laid all on the altar of Divine Science, and we can say, "I and my Father are one." Never make that statement to what appears to be another. Live it. Know it. Never say to someone, you and your Father are one. That is not true. It is I and the Father are one. These grand ideas uttered in this tremendous atonement were too great to be uttered by a person knowing something of divinity. No! These truths were uttered by the Christ. Remember Christ is the activity of God Himself. Only the Father can know the indivisibility of being. Only the Father can say, I AM. Time is not a factor in the atonement. The atonement is in perfect continuity. Jesus acknowledged no ties of the flesh. Can we do less? He admonished us to call no man on earth father, mother, sister or brother. He recognized Spirit, God, the Father of all.

In this chapter, Mrs. Eddy shows the difference between the cup of Jesus and the cup of the Christ. Jesus was the Wayshower. Is it necessary for every Christian Scientist to drink his cup? He did it for us. When someone shows us a better way to do something, do we go back over that step? Edison gave us the light bulb; we do not go back and do it over. Marconi gave us the wireless; we utilize it. Bell gave us the telephone; we simply experience their enlightenment today. Then let us not drink the cup of Jesus; let us drink the cup of the Christ, which means to constantly acknowledge your oneness with the Father. Your textbook says his resurrection is our resurrection. Then why is not his ascension our ascension? It is in reality, if we would cease thinking of ourselves as miserable sinners.

Something separate from God — suggestion says it constantly. Evil hypnotic suggestion, all day long, is trying to argue that we are person; and yet man is safe in the kingdom of God; and, thank God, there is no picture of us. No statue. No mortal picture of us anywhere; not even termed senses. Never take a picture of yourself and say, this is what I looked like twenty years ago! That is not true! That is death in slow motion. Never permit it. You cannot take a picture of man! Have you ever tried to take a picture of love? Kindness? Gentleness? Thoughtfulness? Maintain your atonement constantly.

Don't be fooled by the suggestion called memory. Mrs. Eddy says that Jesus ascended above their apprehension. All right, let's do the same. How? By refusing to discuss ourselves as persons, good or bad, young or old. Never admit that we are persons with persons. This is to experience animal magnetism. Let us ascend above their apprehension, and live the prayer which is atonement. We can unite with this church only as we are new-born of Spirit. Then let us be new-born today. Stop malpracticing on ourselves! To be new-born is to be only as old as *now*. No time can delineate itself on this now. Never defile our own Christ by gossiping about our brother. "Man is the expression of God's being." Then why defile yourself by gossiping about another? Mrs. Eddy says, "I warn students against falling into the error of anti-Christ."

Anti-Christ is to see man less than the expression of God. Mrs. Eddy says, "The belief that man has existence or mind separate from God is a dying error." Let it die here today.

In writing this paper, I turned to the word *burial* in the 'Glossary,' and this is what I found: "Corporeality and physical sense put out of sight and hearing; annihilation. Submergence in Spirit; immortality brought to light." Let's have a good burial today. Let us be so submerged in Spirit that we won't leave anything for anyone to bury. Oh, students, it is so important. Mrs. Eddy says that human law had condemned him, but he was demonstrating divine Science. The divine overcame the human at every point. Living this revelation, we are overcoming humanity at every point. What is going on as Association is going on at the conference table. It is our government going on throughout the world. This is not isolated or localized; this is Truth. Then our Leader goes on to that marvelous statement in Atonement, "Glory be to God, and peace to the struggling hearts! Christ hath rolled away the stone from the door of human hope and faith." Remember, she does not say that treatment rolled away the stone, or this did or that did. It is your Christ that rolled it away. It is your own Christliness. This Association is rolling away this stone of personal sense, that tried to put itself between us and the Father. This is the atonement; and we are proving that the Christ is not subject to material conditions; and so it is with living the Christ, putting personal sense aside that we become masters, never servants. Then as if ending up the chapter, our Leader says, "Whosoever layeth his earthly all on the altar of divine Science, drinketh of Christ's cup now, and is endued with the spirit and power of Christian healing. In the words of St. John, 'He shall give you another Comforter, that he may abide with you *forever*.' This Comforter I understand to be Divine Science."

So this is the glorious message of Christian Science: Principle and idea one. Now, have no regret, no condemnation, no unhealed condition, no unhealed situation. Only man basking in the light of eternal light, for man is the light of the world. He is Mind's own identification, and so the crucifixion is over. The pale star has disappeared, the resurrection is finished, and now we are living after the order of Melchizedek, which means that we have laid our earthly all on the altar of Divine Science; we are drinking of Christ's cup now; and we are enbued with the spirit and power of Christian healing. All limitations, all inadequacy, all false traits of character and human restrictions have all been laid on the altar of Divine Science. The wind of God is blowing and blows them into their nothingness, nobody, not even a memory, and we carry the song away — the song of present divinity, infallibility, immaculateness. We are drinking of Christ's cup, and this leaves only the love of God to be experienced. Thus we have eaten the little book, and now we are experiencing the substance of reality, and we are perfectly at one with our Father.

We have seen in the chapter 'Preface,' the nothingness of personal sense, and the operation of divine Principle leaves no unsolved problem. We have seen that the chapter on 'Prayer' is the practice of God's presence, and now we have seen "I and my Father are one." This is to live after the order of Melchizedek.

Marriage

Now with the true sense of prayer and the atonement having been fully and completely made and being experienced, we are ready to experience the marriage feast. Bring on the wine. The Glossary defines wine as inspiration and understanding. We can drink all of this wine. Then let the bride appear — the purity of our being, the innocency that is God. Divine Principle creates man as its own spiritual idea. Let the marriage be made in heaven, male and female one, womanhood and manhood one, bride and bridegroom one; in this eternal oneness is no impediment to eternal bliss. Keep your marriage in heaven. Never permit it to leave heaven for earth, and have two beings trying to demonstrate oneness. If you permit your marriage to fall to earth, you will experience animal magnetism, and every belief of malpractice concerning that marriage will show itself in your experience. What God has joined together let no man put asunder. Principle and idea is one. This is the marriage from eternity. This marriage is before Abraham. This is the marriage feast — Love wedded to its own spiritual idea. Let no man put it asunder!

Marriage, as it is humanly known, is a concession. It is a suffer it to be so now! After we become students of Christian Science, we must take the marriage from earth and put it back in heaven. It is most important to see Principle and its idea one, and ratified from all eternity. In this true sense of marriage, we are always alone with our own being, not trying to adjust or readjust, not acting or reacting. This Christ-understanding does not have us ignore what appears as husband or wife, but rather draws us nearer and nearer. True sense of husband, true sense of wife, all is blessed in this true understanding. Never let suggestion put a wall between husband and wife, by suggesting that one is spiritually beyond another, or that one knows the truth better than the other, or perhaps doesn't know the truth at all. If you put up this partition, the marriage will fall apart. You may blame it on the other one; but remember, are you not the one putting up the wall, the moment you have another? See that the wall is the belief that there is another. What appears as another is really not another at all. It is the way the Father is appearing; it is the way Life is exhibiting itself; it is the way Mind is manifesting its intelligence. Marriage is your recognition of spiritual completeness! This Christ understanding may appear as one expressing both male and female qualities in such balance that there is no outward show called marriage; or it may appear in the language of today; but be sure that you never malpractice by believing there are two. What is called another is not the medium for happiness. Your textbook says, "Happiness is spiritual, born of Truth and Love." Husband or wife is not a medium through which heaven comes to earth. Remember, husband or wife is not a medium for hell either.

Personality is not a medium. The love, intelligence, kindness, integrity that we so admire in another, is never present because of another. It is present because that integrity, that love, that intelligence is a present fact of your being, and cannot be obscured by what is called another. Never look to another for anything. Always see that everything comes direct from God. Man is not person. Man is divine expression. Marriage should never be based on physical attraction. What is called physical attraction is not Love — it is lust. Man being divine, can only be attracted by spiritual qualities. Always be alone with your own being. Never be alone with another.

When marriage appears as two, you instantly have animal magnetism. Constantly take your marriage back into heaven and keep it there. Your Leader says, "In Science man is the offspring of Spirit. The beautiful, good, and pure constitute his ancestry. His origin is not like that of mortals, in brute instinct, nor does he pass through material conditions, prior to reaching intelligence. Spirit is his primitive and ultimate source of being; God is his Father, and Life is the law of his being." Your Leader begins to sum it all up, for she says marriage should signify a union of hearts. Furthermore the time cometh of which Jesus spoke, when he declared that in the resurrection there should be no more marrying or being given in marriage. Man would be as the angels. Then shall Soul rejoice in its own, in which passion has no part. The white-robed purity will unite in one person, masculine wisdom and feminine love, spiritual understanding and perpetual peace. The union of the sexes suffers fearful discord. To gain Christian Science and its harmony, life should be more metaphysically regarded. Yes, when two try to become one, there is fearful discord. Never accept a union of two. Two cannot become one. The starting point of Divine Science is: God, Spirit is All. Start from One, identifying itself as All, and we end up with One. Never start with two and try to be one. It is impossible in Christian Science. Jesus started from the Father. See that what appears to be another is really not another. It is the one body, the one presence, the one Mind identifying itself as *All*. So let us see that husband is not a medium for anything. Husband is but a symbol.

Keep marriage in the symbol, and see that symbol is not a medium, but that Love is present because Love is God, and cannot be obscured by the symbol. You will always have the Love of God present and being experienced. This Love will have the husband or wife more nearly conform to the ideal; but never be fooled; it is not becoming more thoughtful, more loving, more honest; it is the disappearance of what we call personal sense and the coming of the Christ, which makes what is called husband or wife appear more thoughtful, kind and loving. What the Father has put together, let no man put asunder. So your marriage is ratified from eternity. Keep your marriage in heaven. This is prayer being experienced. This is your true atonement — drinking your Christ cup. The Bible says, "He that has the bride [purity] is the bridegroom [understanding] . . . Have I been so long time with you, and yet hast thou not known me. . . he that hath seen me hath seen the Father." Scientific prayer, experiencing true atonement brings with it the glorious marriage of Father and son, Principle and idea. Now we have experienced the marriage feast, Love wedded to its own spiritual idea. In the textbook, your Leader says, "Arise from your false consciousness into the true sense of Love, and behold the Lamb's wife, — Love wedded to its own spiritual idea. Then cometh the marriage feast. . . . The Lamb's wife presents the unity of male and female as no longer two wedded individuals, but as two individual natures in one; and this compounded spiritual individuality reflects God as Father-Mother, not as a corporeal being. In this divinely united spiritual consciousness, there is no impediment to eternal bliss, — to the perfectibility of God's creation."

Animal Magnetism Unmasked

With this clear knowing of prayer, atonement, and marriage, we are now able to keep animal magnetism unmasked, and see that it is not a person, place or thing. Mrs. Eddy once said to Laura Sargent, "Animal magnetism is absolutely nothing, when unattended by belief." In *The Christian Science Journal* for 1912, an article by Mrs. Eddy states, "Did you but know the sublimity of your hope, the infinite capacity of your being and the grandeur of your outlook, you would let error kill itself. Error comes to you for life, and you give it all the life it has." So it is with animal magnetism; it only wants a believer. Refuse to believe it. Acknowledge there is nothing animal concerning man to be magnetized. There is no animal magnetism. Our Leader has, through the Christ revelation, unmasked evil as illusion, delusion, nothing. But remember, only from the standpoint of God's allness, omnipotence, omniscience, is evil seen to be nothing. It cannot be made nothing; it *is* nothing, from the standpoint of the revelation of Christian Science.

There are students of Christian Science who refuse to handle animal magnetism; they feel they have gotten beyond that stage of Science. They are too absolute to deny evil in its claim to activity called animal magnetism. Neither Jesus nor Mrs. Eddy felt that they had risen to the point where they had no longer any need to deny evil reality or place. It sometimes seemed that Jesus handled it as if it were person. It is true that Jesus did seem to handle it as if it were a person, but remember we only have the account of someone standing by. Did Jesus believe that man was possessed with devils, and told the devils to come out? Of course not. Jesus rebuked the belief in evil. Therefore his words were not to personalize it. They were to nothingize it. Surely Mrs. Eddy, with her dealings with the church, knew that evil is not person. We have the problems today, as they did in the time of Jesus; but Jesus said, "Which of you convinceth me of sin?" All students, as long as they drive cars, eat meals, bring forth children, must handle animal magnetism, and do it daily, not because we are afraid of it, but because the world belief claims to act as law.

Salvation is to leave the mortal basis of belief, unite with the one Mind, and bring out God's unerring direction. This can be done only by living the Christ. As long as there is a shred of belief in the substantiality of matter, or that there is pleasure in it, we had better handle animal magnetism. As long as we believe in heat or cold, as long as we believe in rich or poor, as long as we believe here or there, we had better handle animal magnetism; but handle it scientifically. This means that in the presence of the allness of God, the oneness of divine Mind realized, evil is seen to be without presence or reality. Great credit goes to Mrs. Eddy for showing us how to handle scientifically this claim. We handle this claim when we see its gaudy pretensions singe their own wings in the blaze of the Christ light. Students sometimes try to singe error's wings. Let the Christ-light so shine that this will dispel its gaudy pretensions. Never try to singe the wings of error, but see the light of Christ and let the error singe its own wings. This is important. Too many students handle error as something; but living the Christ handles it as nothing.

There are students who do not realize there is no disease. What is called disease is animal magnetism in its claim of activity, reality, existence. Cancer is malicious animal magnetism. It has no more reality than two times two is five. Only belief says that one error is worse than the other. We must handle the world belief concerning it. Never handle it as a condition. Cancer has been healed when seen as — not a condition of matter, not fleshly rebellion — but as evil hypnotic suggestion, claiming to mesmerize a patient to accept it on the basis that it is something. Suggestion says, "Yes, you see me, you hear me, you smell me," but all of this has got to go down in the presence of Christian Science treatment. Stay on your mount of revelation, and see that cancer is but another name for animal magnetism. See that animal magnetism is hypnotism or mesmerism. If you see it is mesmerism, you will never be afraid of it. Face it fearlessly, with absolute conviction as to its nothingness.

The moment you permit disease to name itself, at that moment the malpractice begins to operate in your experience. Never permit evil to name itself. Hallow the name of God, and the suggestion that evil could possibly name itself is wiped out. Man's name is written in heaven. Make the declaration that animal magnetism in the guise of thought cannot darken the Christ-consciousness that is yours. Animal magnetism in the guise of fear or doubt, cannot make any student of Christian Science deny present perfection, or argue that this approach is too absolute.

All of Christian Science is absolute. There is no other. Science is absolute. There is no relative Christian Science! Know that animal magnetism or hypnotism cannot delineate itself on body, and call itself by some educated name. It cannot be done, is the treatment. I am not afraid of animal magnetism or any of its claims, for the only I knows it not. The only I sees it not. I AM of purer eyes than to behold animal magnetism, to hear it, or smell it. Learn to address it. "You, animal magnetism, are not pain, not disease — you are animal magnetism, and you are a mere negation. My textbook says that you possess neither intelligence, power nor reality; and in sense, you are an unreal concept of a so-called mortal mind. I denounce you from the standpoint of the allness, the one-ness of divine Mind. Your nothingness is apparent." This understanding makes the Christ immediately available; for what I am from the divine standpoint, saves me from any animal magnetism. Our Leader sums it up in these words, "The truths of immortal mind sustain man, and they annihilate the fables of mortal mind, whose flimsy and gaudy pretensions, like silly moths, singe their own wings and fall into dust." (*Science and Health*)

We must disarm animal magnetism by seeing that it is not a person. When Goliath with its bullying sugges-tions comes, stand as David did and say, "I come to you in the name of Almighty God, and from the standpoint of the allness of God," and then the nothingness of Goliath is seen. In closing the chapter, Mrs. Eddy makes a most significant statement, "Mortal mind, not matter, is the criminal in every case." Can we not say, mortal mind is the patient in every case? Is it not mortal mind claiming to identify itself as mortal body? Your textbook says, "The material body, which you call *me*, is mortal mind." In practice, we never deal with bodies, with mortal bodies. Never be fooled. Mortal mind is the criminal. If you try to instruct it with Truth, it will argue back. If you try to say, "God is Mind," it will say, "Don't tell me I don't have a private mind." Don't talk to it. If you have a patient, don't discuss anything with it. Just quietly know — there is no possibility of a patient, there is no possibility of a practitioner, because the infinity of Mind does not permit either. Let divine Mind, God, say, "I AM ALL. Nothing else is." You remember in "Ways That Are Vain," in *Miscellany*, where it is shown how to handle animal magnetism and all its claims. In the same book, we find ways of wisdom. In this book, it shows how to have God, ALL.

Let us be sure, from the standpoint of God's allness and of evil's nothingness, that we see it cannot make us commit an act foreign to the natural inclination. In "The

Way of Wisdom," found in *Miscellany*, see God's allness. We cannot serve two masters. Let us see that all really means *all*. Your Leader put this chapter into the textbook so you would see that animal magnetism is mere negation, possessing neither reality nor identity. Be sure that you keep it that way. Never discuss it as if it is a person, as if it is a church problem, a home problem, as if it were a condition or a situation; but always see that it is mesmerism. If we knew that someone was mesmerized, would we try to enter into the mesmerism to help them? Let us be smart as a serpent and harmless as a dove, and treat all suggestions as unreality, and walk forth as some holy thing, the Father's delight. See that man has no private mind to mesmerize. Man's mind is the Mind that is God. Man is the glowing knowing of the Mind that is Christ. Let us handle animal magnetism as nothing, as no body.

Christian Science versus Spiritualism

In the early editions of *Science and Health*, Mrs. Eddy called this chapter, "Demonstration versus Imposition."

We are most unwise if we accept the world belief that we are avenues, or channels, or mediums through which the Christ comes to earth. Christian Science does not teach that mortals are mediums for immortals; or that flesh is a medium for spirit; that organs are mediums for life.

Jesus teaches us that we must be born again. "That which is born of the flesh is flesh; and that which is born of the Spirit is spirit." Flesh is not the medium for Mind, God. If we accept the suggestion that we have once been a medium for Truth, and we are now being persecuted for it, we had better wake up. The omnipresent Mind is self-expressing. It has no medium, but directly expresses itself, and this is the Christ. Life and intelligence are purely spiritual. There are no mediums for Life. Life is God.

All is God. The self-creative Mind needs no medium in this chapter. There are no mediums in Christian Science. Idea is not a medium. Idea is the activity of Mind itself. At one time, people said that Mrs. Eddy was a medium. She corrected this constantly. She knew what Jesus had known, "That of myself I can do nothing." She knew that spiritualism was absolutely erroneous. She tells us this throughout the chapter in unforgettable language. The gulf is fixed between what the world calls spiritualism and Science.

It is interesting that Mrs. Eddy started this chapter with a discussion of the word *identity*. She says, "The divine Mind maintains all identities, from a blade of grass to a star, as distinct and eternal. The identity of all reality continues forever." Why this scientific approach to the term *identity*? Is it not that Mrs. Eddy desires the student to see that the divine Mind identifies itself. No mediumship going on here — not even for error called a cough. It is a relief for the new student to find that he is not a medium for God. God, the only Ego, is present and self-identified. At no time does the responsibility fall on man that he must identify himself with God. Man does not identify himself with God. That would denote separation. Mind identifies itself. This is man. Be absolutely clear on this great point. Cause identifies itself. Effect cannot identify itself with cause. Does reflection identify itself with the original? Or is it the original that identifies itself with the reflection? This is the most scientific point. It is God present identifying Himself, and there are no mediums.

In this chapter, we find that marvelous statement, "When being is understood, Life will be recognized as neither material nor finite, but as infinite, as God, universal good." When this chapter is clearly realized, we are never tempted to believe that there is someone else knowing more truth, more reality, or someone more loving than we are. Nothing is present as person, nor is anything absent because of person. All is present because it is God, the Father saying, "I AM ALL." If a person could possibly be loving, kind, intelligent, this would be deflection. This would not be reflection. Christian Science is the Science of divine reflection. When we see a brilliant performance; experience a glorious morning, a fresh day; see the purity of a child, guilelessness of a friend; feel the cleanness of the air; see the beauty of a flower; never leave these qualities in person, place or thing. See that you are experiencing your own divinity. How could you experience something outside of consciousness? Consciousness is fundamental. Consciousness is universal. Let us be alert that there is no medium in our universe; not even a flower to give us beauty. The beauty is present, because it is God, not because flower can give it. If spiritualists understood the Science of being, this belief in mediumship would vanish. If Christian Scientists understood the Science of being, their belief in mediumship would vanish. Where would fear go? And hate? And anger? And stress, anxiety, self-will, envy, jealousy go? Are we not thinking of persons? Mediums? Of course we are. Let us be finished with such beliefs. There are no mediums in Christian Science. Let us be willing to leave all for the Christ, and have that marvelous experience of the whole Christ, where we all speak the same language.

We are constantly dealing in the world of symbols. Read this carefully because it is a most important part of our work today. Even words are symbols. Let us see that the symbol called *word* is not the medium for realization. It is not the medium for knowing. The symbol is simply an indication that the fact is present, and can be experienced without the symbol. We understand that money, silver and gold are called symbols for abundance; but we do not think that the money is the medium for the good, for the abundance. Symbols are not mediums. The symbol is the hint that the fact is present to be experienced. The Liberty Bell is a symbol, but is not a medium for liberty. If it were, we could send bells all over the world and have liberty. It is most important to see that the symbol is not a medium. Take the symbol called rose or flower; it is not the medium for color, beauty, perfume. If the color, beauty, perfume were in the rose, we would have pantheism, and our Leader denounced pantheism up one side and down the other. "There is no life, truth, intelligence, nor substance in matter." Beauty is a present fact because it is God. The rose can appear only because the fact is in God. We acknowledge home to be a very present fact. We say, "In Him we live, and move, and have our being." This is the fact. The understanding of the fact will have the symbol appear in the way that will bless mankind. It may be called a plane, train, trailer or house. The symbol appears only because the fact has been known first. The symbol is not the medium.

So it is with seeing, hearing, health, etc. These attributes are present because they are omnipresent. There is no absence of health because there is no absence of God. We do not see because of eyes. We see because seeing is ever-present. The symbol cannot see. It is not a medium for seeing. A realization of this fact will heal blindness. Let us be absolutely clear on this scientific point. There are no mediums through which God, Soul, Life expresses itself. Mrs. Eddy says, "Knowing that Soul and its attributes were forever manifested through man, the Master healed the sick, gave sight to the blind, hearing to the deaf, feet to the lame." Then we read this marvelous reference, "To understand that Mind is infinite, not bounded by corporeality, not dependent upon the ear and eye for sound or sight nor upon muscles and bones for locomotion, is a step towards the Mind-science by which we discern man's nature and existence. This true conception of being destroys the belief of spiritualism at its very inception, for without the concession of material personalities called spirits, spiritualism has no basis upon which to build." This is a wonderful definition of what Mind is and what Mind does. It shows us that nothing is present as person. All is present because it is God.

Mrs. Eddy says, "This Soul-sense comes to the human mind when the latter yields to the divine Mind." Then we come to this tremendous point. The great teacher knew both cause and effect. Mrs. Eddy says, "Truth communicates itself." If we could heal the belief of mediumship, we would be capable of accomplishing any worthwhile project. "Mind is not necessarily dependent upon educational processes. It possesses of itself all beauty and poetry, and the power of expressing them. Spirit, God, is heard, when the senses are silent. We are all capable of more than we do. The influence or action of Soul confers a freedom, which explains the phenomena of improvisation and the fervor of untutored lips." If we could study that reference everyday! Then she says, "Divest yourself of the thought that there can be substance in matter, and the movements and transitions now possible for mortal mind will be found to be equally possible for the body. Then being will be recognized as spiritual, and death will be obsolete." Let us divest ourselves of the belief that there can be a medium or symbol. Now our Leader gives us the great point of departure for all true spiritual growth. "Let us rid ourselves of the belief that man is separated from God, and obey only the divine Principle, Life and Love. Here is the great point of departure for all true spiritual growth." There is no mediumship, no avenue, no agents, no channel. Then Mrs. Eddy warns us, "Absorbed in material selfhood we discern and reflect but faintly the substance of Life or Mind."

Now, are we today absorbed in personal sense with its bondage? Are we ridding ourselves of the suggestion that we are separated from our Father? Are we permitting the personal mind, putting on its burlesque show, to be our mind? Or are we the wise men today heralding Christ's eternal dawn and describing its effulgence? We should represent the wise man, heralding Christ's eternal dawn. Then as if summing up the chapter, Mrs. Eddy says, "Beyond the frail premises of human beliefs, above the loosening grasp of creeds, the demonstration of Christian Mind-healing stands a revealed and practical Science. It is imperious as Christ's revelation of Truth, of Life, and of Love, which remains inviolate for every man to understand and to practice."

The chapter ends with the statement, "The calm, strong currents of true spirituality, the manifestations of which are health, purity, and self-immolation, must deepen human experience, until the beliefs of material existence are seen to be a bald imposition, and sin, disease, and death give everlasting place to the scientific demonstration of divine Spirit and to God's spiritual, perfect man." It has been seen that Soul identifies itself, and this is the glory called man. We have seen material existence to be a bald imposition. Belief in mediumship has gone down. We have seen that there is no matter for Spirit to work through. Let us see the whole illusory nature of human experience, and we will never be tempted to believe in mediums. Mind directly expresses itself.

This chapter gives us tremendous power because it has removed all mediumship, all symbols, and permits Mind to reveal itself as the only knower, the only power, the only all, and leads us gently past the shoals of spiritualism, the belief in mediumship, to Christian Science, to that which is spiritual, divine, unerring. Christian Science leads us gently past the stone of personal sense, and says, "The admission to one's self that man is God's own likeness sets man free to master the infinite idea." Our Leader shows us the golden thread, the oneness of all being, the nothingness of any other sense of existence. The student, grounded in the true sense of prayer, living the atonement, experiencing marriage — the Lamb's wife, Love, wedded to its own spiritual idea — and now, seeing the impossibility of a medium and a living divinity, we can say as Jesus said, "Of myself I can do nothing." My Father worketh this way and I work. This is the Science of divine reflection. This living, this knowing, is our defense against the wiles of suggestion to go elsewhere for literature. Never leave the purity of the teaching of Christian Science. All Christian Science is found in the Christian Science textbook. Do not permit the suggestion that someone can explain it better. Who can explain it better than the Revelator? The precious book contains all; and if our Leader could say, since writing the book, she has learned the higher meaning of it, how could we accept the possibility that the textbook is difficult to understand? Every moment it is fresh; every time we pick it up, it is new. Why? Because it is not a mediumship between God and man; it is Mind revealing itself, now and forever.

We have seen how we must let the pale star go into the daystar. We have seen prayer, — the practice of God's presence. We have seen the atonement is living the oneness. We have seen marriage — Principle and idea as oneness; we have seen that what humanly appears as marriage can be successful only as we take it back into heaven and see the oneness of being. Never malpractice by believing two. Then we have seen the chapter on animal magnetism unmasked from the standpoint of God's allness. We have seen its impossibility. We have seen in the chapter on spiritualism God's persistency to be all. Now we are going to take the next chapter.

Science — Theology — Medicine

What is the leaven which the woman took and hid in the three measures of meal? The revelation of Christian Science shows the revelation of true being. Mrs. Eddy speaks of this leaven as the final revelation of the absolute divine Principle of scientific mental healing. Then we find that this divine Principle is "the sovereign ever-presence, delivering the children of men from every ill that 'flesh is heir to.'" Christian Science teaching and practice proceeds from this science, theology and medicine.

Mrs. Eddy asks the question, "Whence came to me this heavenly conviction, — a conviction antagonistic to the testimony of the physical senses?" Is it the conviction of a person? Can a person be heavenly convinced that God is the only Mind? Of course not. This heavenly conviction, Science, comes only as we are willing to let go the human sense of mind, and let the Mind that is Christ be the present Mind of all. Heavenly conviction means that conviction which comes from heaven, or government by divine Principle. This heavenly conviction is the rock, the immovable rock, the Christ. A personal conviction is built on the sand of intellectuality, and can be shaken at any moment. Heavenly conviction is the rock upon which this Science is founded. For three years, Mrs. Eddy searched for the Principle of this Science with the Bible as her only textbook. Then the light broke into full-orbed day, the eternal noon. Mrs. Eddy discovered the Science of being.

The teaching of Jesus was not a ritualistic Jehovah's special gift. Jesus demonstrated this Mind of all men when he sent the seventy out to heal and preach, and they returned joyously recounting the works they had done. Remember that the Master said, "In this rejoice not, that the spirits are subject unto you; but rather rejoice, because your names are written in heaven." He wanted his followers to see that they were demonstrating Science. It was not faith in him, or faith in his teaching, but they were demonstrating the Science of his teaching. Then they would go into the world and give proof of the Principle underlying his teaching.

Mrs. Eddy was not satisfied to rest in good matter — healing matter. No, she must find the Science behind the healing. Einstein, Edison, Bell, were all spurred on by holy curiosity, going beyond what the senses were testifying, to see reality. Inventions must have their day, and that day must be followed by Science. Today is the day of Science, because it proceeds from and rests upon divine Principle. Mrs. Eddy saw that the human was the problem, and for that reason, could hold within itself no solution. She must go beyond the so-called human mind and find the solution. The answer came through prayer and revelation. The way opened up. She later wrote in *Retrospection and Introspection*, "Thus it was when the moment arrived of the heart's bridal to more spiritual existence. When the door opened, I was waiting and watching; and, lo, the bridegroom came! The character of the Christ was illuminated by the midnight torches of Spirit. My heart knew its Redeemer. He whom my affections had diligently sought was as the One 'altogether lovely,' as 'the chiefest,' the only 'among ten thousand.' Soulless famine had fled. Agnosticism, pantheism, and theosophy were void. Being was beautiful, its substance, cause, and currents were God and His idea. I had touched the hem of Christian Science."

When Mrs. Eddy discovered the Science of the Christ-teaching, she prayed that the religious world would accept her revelation which she named Christian Science. When the churches refused to accept Christian Science, she began to present Christian Science as Science, as the Science of being. She did not believe that she had brought this Science into being of herself — of herself, she could do nothing; it had always existed; it had not come into being by human reasoning. Science is — always has been — and always will be; and today, we are experiencing this same Science, this same letting go of the human mind, for this is the dam, the wall or partition — the evil one. Jesus answered them and said, "My doctrine is not mine but His that sent me. If any man will do His will, he shall know of the doctrine, whether it be of God, or whether I speak of myself." Some statements in your textbook are from the presence of God felt and realized. When you come to those statements, feel the presence of God as All-in-all.

The statements of education lead those that are with young until they are able to bring forth the Christ-man. The whole revelation is set forth in the following message, "The three great verities of Spirit, omnipotence, omnipresence, omniscience, Spirit possessing all power, filling all space, constituting all science, contradict forever the belief that matter can be actual. These eternal verities reveal primeval existence as the radiant reality of God's creation, in which all that He has made is pronounced by His wisdom good." Then your Leader adds, "Thus it was that I beheld, as never before, the awful unreality called evil." It is interesting that she says she saw from the standpoint of the allness of God, this awful unreality which is called evil. She does not say, I saw evil's unreality. She said she saw the unreality called evil.

The equipollence of God brought to light another glorious proposition —man's perfectibility, and the establishment of the kingdom of heaven on earth — here are the verities; here is the radiant reality; and this revelation has reduced evil and its objectification called matter to its unreality. Christian Science reveals matter as nothing. What great revelation! Nowhere in history has a woman been so dauntless as to challenge science, theology and medicine. Christian Science shook these three from their solid foundations and showed them all to be built on human opinion; they were not science at all, and must give place to the Science that is divine. Mrs. Eddy, through keen spiritual discernment, knew that some students would not be willing to live the Christ revelation and gave them evangelization. She did not deviate from the absoluteness of Christian Science. It is to show the student by way of argument the way of the Christian.

Here the wise ask the question, "Is there more than one school of Christian Science?" Then she answers it unequivocally, "There is but one method in its teaching." Then we find this statement, "From the infinite One in Christian Science comes one Principle and its infinite idea, and with this infinitude come spiritual rules, laws, and their demonstration, which, like the great Giver, are 'the same yesterday, and today, and forever' for thus are the divine Principle of healing and the Christ-idea characterized in the epistle to the Hebrews." From the infinite One come both cause and effect. Here man is shown to be the effect of Mind's knowing; man is seen to be the effect of Mind's own knowing. What revelation! Not God and man — two, but God's expression of Himself is man. Mrs. Eddy says, "Man is the expression of God's being." You hear the statement, "Don't go into your closet and shut the door." The one making the statement is being a good Christian and has not yet found the Science of being, — his own divine being. What joy it is to go in and shut the door. Never argue with a point of view; never try to convince a point of view that it is wrong. Let your light shine that men may see your good works; then the correctness of your position will prove itself. Talk little. I warn you and ask you with the love that is Principle — do not talk metaphysics in groups or with others. You stir up all manner of evil if you are in a group and they appear to be discussing Science.

Remind yourself that it is the Christ that heals. Nowhere in the textbook can you find the talking Christ! It is the feeling, being, living that makes us the bone and sinew of our movement. Quiet and peace will heal. There are students of Christian Science who fight for what they call a point of view. Let us not be followers of person, right or wrong. Let us live the Christ. This precious movement is so needed in the world today that we can't permit any views to come in the guise of semantics. The use of certain words mean so many things. The dictionary does not give us one meaning of a word. The dictionary shows us that history has decreed what a certain word should mean; yet they change constantly. Let us never be drawn into discussion. This is the Science of being. This is divine revelation. What persons think Mrs. Eddy said, or did not say, has no value. Go into your closet and shut the door and pray the Father in secret to reveal and show forth the light. If we were not thinking of ourselves as persons, we would not attempt to defend what is called the radical position. This is the revelation of Christian Science. This is the Science of being, the Science of Mind-healing. Your Leader shows it to be impossible for ought but Mind to testify truly and exhibit the true status of man.

Think of it; man is the exhibition of God; Mind exhibits the real status of man. All Science is divine. It is an emanation of divine Mind, and it is alone able to interpret aright. It is a divine utterance, the Comforter which leadeth into all Truth. With this Science, we look deep into realism, instead of accepting the outward sense of things. Christian Science is the leaven which the woman put into the measure of meal called Science, and has restored all things back to God.

Theology

Christian Science has given us God, the living God. Christian Science has defined God. This definition has been proven in every instance. Christian Science has shown us that the only priest is the spiritualized man. The only church proceeds from Principle, Love. This church has no denomination. Christian Science has shown us that there is no man separated from God. Man is the functioning presence of the Mind that is Love. Christian Science has shown us that there is no hell as a place, no heaven as a place. The only hell is the acceptance of the Satanic suggestion that we are persons separate from God. This is the only hell there is. The acceptance of the Christ Mind, our present Mind, is to experience heaven without any process. Christian Science has disentangled the interlaced ambiguities of being; has shown us that there is no private soul, that Soul is present and gives body to itself. What a release from the false teachings of old theology. Mrs. Eddy went straight back to the teachings of Jesus; then she could say, "Denial of the possibility of Christian healing robs Christianity of the very element which gave it divine force and its astonishing and unequaled success in the first century." This Christ-power is all that will keep the Christian Science movement above scholastic theology. We have no right to exist as another Christian church, unless we are healing in our services, in our lectures, in our Sunday Schools, and in our practice. There is no need for another Protestant church. There is no need for the Christ Church. It is about time that we woke up to the fact that healing is the expression of our knowing, our living, and the only reason for the Christian Science church existing. Mrs. Eddy says, "Jesus established his church and maintained his mission on a spiritual foundation of Christ-healing." Remember, Jesus asked his disciples who men said he was? He rejected their answer because it suggested spiritualism. He knew there was no medium, that divine Mind expresses itself directly and absolutely, and this directness of expression is given the term *man*. Seeing they misunderstood his mission, Jesus said, "Whom say ye that I am?"

Did no one understand his mission? Finally Peter said, "Thou art the Christ, the Son of the living God!" Jesus answered Peter, "Flesh and blood hath not revealed it unto thee, but my Father which is in heaven."

Jesus rebuked the belief of mediumship. He wanted Peter to understand that he, Peter, was not a medium for that great statement. He knew it was Mind, his Father, directly expressing Himself. Only Mind can reveal the Truth. Jesus' answer is fraught with meaning for all of us, "Thou art Peter; and upon this rock I will build my church." All the aggressive mental suggestion, hell, cannot prevail against the church built on this theological point. Mrs. Eddy called it "The living Rock." It was evident to Peter now that divine Life, Truth, Love, and not a human personality, was the healer of the sick, a rock, a firm foundation in the realm of harmony. "The supremacy of Spirit was the foundation on which Jesus built. His sublime summary points to the religion of Love. It was this theology of Jesus which healed."

Theology must be of the heart, not the head. This means not talking nor thinking Christian Science, but living it, loving it. Mrs. Eddy takes away Romanism and its claim to this tremendous burst of light. "For this principle there is no dynasty, no ecclesiastical monopoly. Its only crowned head is immortal sovereignty. Its only priest is the spiritualized man. The Bible declares that all believers are made 'kings and priests unto God.' The outsiders did not then, and do not now, understand this ruling of the Christ; therefore they cannot demonstrate God's healing power. Neither can this manifestation of the Christ be comprehended, until its divine Principle is scientifically understood. We must seek the undivided garment, the whole Christ." Then the leaven has been put into the measure of meal called theology, and the whole of theology is being leavened. How great is our God! Long live Christ! The church built on the rock, Christ. Again, the leaven is at work and scholastic theological teachings are being shown the light of the Christ Principle, and now in the twentieth century the whole must be leavened.

Medicine

Mrs. Eddy has lifted the word *medicine* out of the general belief of pills, poultices, doctors, hospitals, and restored the word back to Mind. Let us read this tremendous revelation, "Which was first, Mind or medicine? If Mind was first and self-existent, then Mind, not matter, must have been the first medicine. God being All-in-all, He made medicine; but that medicine was Mind. It could not have been matter, which departs from the nature and character of Mind, God. Truth is God's remedy for error of every kind, and Truth destroys only what is untrue." Think of the immediacy of your medicine. It does not have to be concocted by some druggist; it does not have to be taken from a bottle; it does not have to be prescribed by some man. It is always instantaneously available, because Mind's medicine is its own idea, and keeps that idea ever functioning normally, perfectly, feeding it with the bread of Life and keeps all running smoothly with the oil of consecration. This oil of oneness permits no friction, because the Adorable One identifies itself as All. It has no parts to get out of order. There is no part to God.

Have you identified yourself with this man? This man that is the glory of God? This man that is the power of reality? This man that is the functioning presence of God, Life? Or are you a person speaking about the truth of Christian Science? When you read a book to children, the children quickly identify themselves with the characters in that book. They are like the characters; they talk like the characters. Some readers of the textbook identify themselves with the revelation from the very first and are willing to let the old go for the new. They see that the infinite does not have a finite being called "me" — helpless or afraid. They see the allness of good, the immediacy of now. It is their one and only experience, and they find themselves healed.

Others read over and over again but never identify themselves with the revelation! This is because they do not eat the book — they read it. They plod on as good humans, good church workers, but they never eat the little book. Do you not see that you are reading your biography? That your conscious identify is found in Science? This is what I Am, and the human objectification called human experience is no part of my identification. This book tells me what I Am. What I have always been! Why, it says, before Abraham was, I Am. It says I am born after the order of Melchizedek. I have always been my Father's delight! This is the only I or Us. Never identify yourself with man's man. Identify yourself with God's man. There is no process in it. Some are healed quickly because of this divine identification. Others read and read, and what good does the reading do, unless you eat the little book? This is your medicine. This is the medicine of Mind. In this chapter,

Mrs. Eddy says that we should never permit mortal mind to give a name to itself. At that moment, you bring all the malpractice against the name into being. The name you give a thing will effect your whole attitude against that problem.

Many Christian Scientists become very good diagnosticians. They call on the phone and say, "I have a cold, flu, arthritis, etc.," You ask, "Have you had a doctor recently?" They say, "Of course not. I am a Christian Scientist. Don't you think I know arthritis when I see it?" Of course, here is mortal mind in full swing. The student has been made to forget and to neglect his duty to God. He has permitted the prince of this world to come and find something in him. Never name to yourself any name other than the name of God.

We know of a case that was instantly healed with the practitioner turned from the situation and said, "Well, dear God, I don't know what it is; I don't know what it is supposed to be; what it is supposed to do. This I know, if you made it, it is right, and if you did not make it, it has no existence." Now this looks simple, but the practitioner was refusing to let a lie name itself, and then sit down and do a lot of metaphysical work over that name. It is mental quackery to make a disease as something seen and felt and heard, and then attempt to heal it. That is on the same level as a doctor. Your Leader says it is mental quackery to make it something seen or felt or named.

Here's an illustration: If someone called on the phone this morning and said, "My falibeu is not working this morning," would you know what falibeu is? It all sounds rather foolish, but is there any difference when the student calls, and calls it cancer? Can you laugh? You can if you know it is a name for a lie! It has no substance, no more reality than falibeu. It is not my problem; it is not my anything. It is not a name for God; only God can name anything; it is a fraud; it is a liar; it is a deluder. Let us not be fooled. Let us say, "God never made it. Animal magnetism, in the guise of thought, you are nameless; you are not a condition. You are not a presence. You are evil hypnotic suggestion." Then is when the Christ comes in and does the healing work.

Take every term back to God and see, not what mortal mind says about the term, but make that term declare God. If the cancer were seen not to be a dirty, hidden, rebellious cell, and the cell were seen to be governed and controlled by Love; if a cell is seen to be Love's own loving, could the cell rebel against the Mind that conceived it? Against the Life that gives it its own living? Of course not. Even if there seemed to be such a cell, it would yield to the Christ and come under God's law of Love, and do what a cell should be doing, and show forth the purity of its being. Is there something that divine Mind does not create? Is a cell too simple to come under divine law? Is not all from the infinitesimal to the infinite, God, saying, "I AM ALL?" Listen to your Leader; what your Leader has to say in *Miscellaneous Writings*: "The only logical conclusion is that all is Mind and its manifestation, from the rolling of worlds to a potato-patch." If a potato-patch can be under divine law, could not the human body come under it also? God must be recognized as supreme in the physical so-called, as well as in the spiritual. What does this mean? The law can govern the world of symbols as well as the universe of ideas.

It is an important point to remember. The law of God can govern the world of symbols as well as the world of ideas. Your Leader says that God must be recognized "as supreme in the physical realm, so-called, as well as in the spiritual." Then take every work, every symbol, every statement, and make it declare God. Then how can you have more than all? Your Leader speaks of relaxing rigid muscles, restoring carious bones to soundness. But she says, "The effect of this Science is to stir the human mind to a change of base, on which it may yield to the harmony of the divine Mind." What is the change of base that is needed? Is it not to see that man is not a person with a mind? Is not a body formed out of mortal mind beliefs; not physical? It is not a body functioning. Man is the revelation of God Himself. Mind is body. This body or identity is man; so with the change of base having been made, we have put the leaven into the whole; and now science is purely divine theology, is the perfect oneness of all; and Mind's medicine is, "Be ye perfect, for I am perfect!" This is the leaven.

Physiology

Why does Mrs. Eddy open this chapter with a familiar chapter from the Bible? "Therefore I say unto you, Take no thought for your life, what ye shall eat, or what ye shall drink; nor yet for your body, what ye shall put on. Is not the life more than meat, and the body than raiment?" Is it not because that we are so familiar with the false sense of life, with all the false educated beliefs concerning it, all the false theological teachings about Soul and body, all the fears attached to the limited sense of self? Mrs. Eddy knew that she must challenge every belief at the very outset of the chapter. She did it with a well known verse of the Bible. The Master could say, "Take no thought for your life," because Jesus permitted the Christ to be so real, so tangible, that he had no temptation to believe in a personal body with a finite, temporal sense of life. Has he not said, "I am come that ye might have life, and have it more abundantly"? Not simply a hundred years; but life eternal — life that has nothing to do with birth, forever untouched by death. If eating is supposed to give forth body, then stop and see what kind of body we must have from our knowing? Knowing constructs the only body there is. Body is not a human fabrication. Body is not material. There is no material body to be sick or to grow old. There is a belief that body is material, that it needs to be healed. If you believe that matter is substance, and holds within itself the ability to give life or take it, then you are in a hopeless situation. It becomes a tyrant, a dictator; it says it is thirsty, give me a drink; hungry, give me some food. It says give me glasses so I can see better; give me a car to haul me around; give me money so I can do what I want. Have you such a tyrant hanging around, calling itself *you*?

Wake up! It is simply animal magnetism doing the talking, pulling the strings for its puppet. If you identify yourself with that concept, that puppet, you will dance to every one of mortal mind's tunes. We seem to know so much more of this physical man, than we know of God's man. The world is constantly holding it before our gaze. Medically speaking, this man is made of hormones and glands that have great power. They seem to know much more than the Mind that created them. Let us take no thought for this kind of man. Let us grasp reality, and live the man that God has created. Let us see that our poise is our savior from the belief of personal sense. The argument that man is emotional, made up of glands that give forth secretions — this is but a mask, for the carnal mind to attempt to perpetuate itself. Jesus and Mrs. Eddy maintained their poise when the hatred struck against their teaching. Steadfast, immovable, Jesus said, "My words shall not pass away." Mrs. Eddy knew that if the world burned to ashes, Science would stand forever. In family relations, church work, employment, let us identify ourselves as the son of the living God, with not a single quality underived from Deity. Man is the effect of God, Cause, Being.

Can you think that Principle could be emotional? There is nothing natural, normal about emotionalism. It is sympathetic mesmerism, aggressive mental suggestion. It says we are persons acting and reacting. It is the red dragon, delusion. Emotionalism is suggestion trying to get one to act impulsively, without the quality of vision that comes from the Christ-understanding — that man is the functioning presence of the Mind that is God. Man's present Mind is Principle, and there is no emotion about it. Emotionalism would say that one's feeling is due to circumstance. This is not true. Man does not have an indwelling soul to emote with. Soul is God, Soul is Love, Soul is Principle, steady, immovable. Soul is of purer eyes than to behold persons. There is no over-action, no reaction. It is all a matter of identification. Divine feeling, divine quietness, peace, poise, spiritual strength, gentleness, tenderness — these are Soul qualities, and man has no indwelling soul to feel with. Man is the feeling of God. Man feels as God feels. Therefore man is not a person with a soul to feel; man is the feeling of quietness. "Felt ye the power of the word?" Man is pleasing to the Father. Spiritual feeling is always spiritual sense. The true recognition that Soul's attributes constitutes man, wipes out emotionalism at its very basis. Beset with misguided emotions, we shall be stranded on the quicksands of worldly commotion and practically come short of the wisdom requisite in teaching and demonstrating a victory over self and sin. Poise is our savior from the emotionalism called personal sense. Poise is a mighty rock. It will save us from personal pettiness. We will never be persons acting and reacting.

Footsteps of Truth

What appears to be footsteps, is actually the dispelling of the mist of personal sense and the coming of the eternal Christ-man, forever showing forth the glory, the perfection of the Father. Again it is the eternal noon, the day star. Let us step through the Shekinah through which Jesus stepped and live from the standpoint of revelation. Your leader says in starting this chapter, Truth is revealed, it needs only to be practiced.

When we think of progress in Christian Science, of footsteps, we do not mean coming from one state of consciousness to another, or going from one state of limitation to one of abundance. In Christian Science, we live the revelation, and this living dispels whatever is unlike the Father.

Over and over again, the Leader of Christian Science says: All is Mind, there is no matter. And then she opens this chapter, "No man can serve two masters" — that is, a dualistic attitude is unacceptable. How can we serve God and mammon? Can we use the revelation of Christian Science to make the old man over? Would this not be serving two masters?

Mrs. Eddy, throughout her writings, shows the student, from page to page, and shows with great clarity, we cannot build safely on false foundations. Truth makes a new creature in whom old things pass away and "all things are become new." This is so basic. Christian Science does not improve the old, does not make it over, but all things must become new. Our starting point is always from the Father. From this vantage point, look out at the universe with the eyes of spiritual discernment.

Would we not be building on false foundations if we built on members, persons, money? Would not we be building on false foundations if we try to improve the human concept? Our Leader answers this — we cannot fill vessels already full. They must first be emptied.

"Let us disrobe error. Then, when the winds of God blow, we shall not hug our tatters close about us." Is not this what we try to do? We try to pour something into the human mind to make it holy, to make it good, when the Science of Being demands that we abandon it completely, and see the nothingness of personal sense and all its objectivity.

"Let us disrobe error," see that it is not a person, a place or a thing, and "then when the winds of God blow"

— that is, the winds of omnipotence, omniscience, omnipresence of the divine Mind blow — it leaves nothing finite, leaves nothing personal, leaves nothing limited. Christian Science does not permit us to hug the tatters of personal sense; it makes us leave the old for the new, and put on the robe of righteousness.

If there is delayed healing, if there is a problem that will not yield, ask yourself, am I hugging the tatters of personal sense about me, or am I willing here and now to lay my all on the altar of Christian Science and carry the song of divinity away, the song that only Mind is present to express itself? This is the way to pour in Truth through floodtides of Love.

Then your Leader says, "Grafting holiness upon unholiness" is foolish. We cannot make the old over. But students will try; they will pray and read, to try to make the human concept better, yet your Leader says that "grafting holiness upon unholiness" is foolish. So if the problem is unyielding, ask yourself, am I hugging the tatters close about me?

"The scientific unity which exists between God and man must be wrought out in life-practice and God's will must be universally done." The whole purpose of Christian Science is to show forth this unity of Principle and idea. Man is the term for all that expresses God. God, cause, identifies itself and this is man.

In this chapter, 'Footsteps of Truth,' the Leader gently leads us out of the belief of persons knowing something of God to the glorious revelation that man is the direct knowing of Mind in reflection, that man is not separate from the Father, but man is the expression of the Father. So gently, so wisely, does Mrs. Eddy lead us away from the false to the true that sometimes we are not aware of the transformation going on. We let the tatters of personal sense fall, and all the glory of the Father shows forth the radiance of the all-knowing Mind.

Read this chapter slowly, read it carefully, see how the tatters fall, and then let the winds of God blow, and let the tatters go into their nothingness, and only the robe of your divinity will be left. Our divinity will be the good Samaritan and the wounds of personal sense will be washed away, and the man of God's creating will appear in all the glory of God. This is called coincidence, but it is reality outshining unreality. It is depravity yielding to divinity. It is ignorance giving way to intelligence, the pale star to the day star, and eternal noon is experienced.

On page 226 the Revelator booms forth in language unforgettable; "Divine Science rends asunder these fetters, and man's birthright of sole allegiance to his Maker asserts itself." What are the fetters that need to be rent asunder? Personal fathers, mothers, husbands, wives, friends, personal bodies, etc. All of these need to be seen for what they are, symbols of reality, but not mediums, simply symbols, and your Leader says that your sole allegiance to your Maker asserts itself.

Our divinity, our birthright, our reality asserts itself, and will not permit us to be satisfied with a lie. Our divine Christliness, will not permit us to be satisfied with less than spiritual love, with less than spiritual perfection, spiritual substance. Sometimes, students try to be satisfied with love that is human; but your divinity will not permit you to be satisfied; you must see that love is spiritual. We can no longer rest in the thralldom of the senses, for Christian Science makes us uncomfortable in a lie; it makes us uncomfortable in the lie as long as we hold to the tatters. But when we let go and let our birthright assert itself, then Christ, our divinity, comes forth and says, blessed art thou, thou art the Son of God. We call this Immanuel; we call it demonstration. Man really is at the standpoint of demonstration. Mind, God, the Father, is always demonstrating Himself, and man is that demonstration, the image, the likeness of God. So Christian Science raises the standard of liberty and says, Follow me.

What is the me? God, Spirit, All. Jesus marked out the way. Then there is no excuse — the way is clear.

Your Leader makes this statement: "It is the illusion of material sense that has bound you." Make this declaration, silently and knowingly: You, animal magnetism, in the guise of material sense, you cannot bind the Son of God, you cannot entangle my free limbs, you cannot deface the tablet of my being, because as the Son of God I live, move and have my being in the Mind that is God. This is freedom. No material sense can touch me, no material sense can make any condition for me.

And now comes the grand statement that brought such healing when I first found Christian Science. "Nothing inharmonious can enter being, for Life is God." And that early morning, I asked the question, Where is this being in which nothing inharmonious could enter. Then so gently the Father said, "The only being there is is the being that is here." I suddenly saw that I was not a little being dying, fading out fast; but I was at that moment the very expression of the Being that I had been calling God. And then my God became so near, became my very Life, and became my very Mind. I saw that I was not a person dying, but that I was the eternal Son of God, alive forever more. And so nothing inharmonious can enter being, for Life is God. Then you say to yourself, this being has never been divided and all there is to this Association, is the being in which nothing inharmonious can enter.

Your Leader goes on to say in our textbook, that mortal mind produces every discordant action of the body. Mortal mind is the cancer, arthritis, insanity, old age; and in the presence of the revelation that all Mind is God, your Leader says, mortal mind is a name for nothing, as zero is a name for nothing in mathematics. It is a term for nothing, and mortal mind is a term for nothing. Never make it something.

Always the allness, the oneness, the universality of the Mind that is God forbids a secondary mind. As the human concept fades out of sight, it might appear to be more beautiful, more lovely; it might even appear to be more wise, kind, loving; but in the footsteps of truth, remember it isn't a human concept that has become wiser, more beautiful, more charming, more gracious; but see that the qualities of beauty, graciousness, charm, poise and balance, gentleness, these are all present qualities of Soul, and they are forever present. Make the declaration that these qualities cannot be deflected by what is called person, but the reflection is going on and this is man.

Whenever these qualities are seen in action, immediately say, how beautiful man is. Whenever you see something graceful; something gracious, something kind, charming, loving, say, isn't man beautiful! Remember, you are talking about the man that *is yourself*. We are not really alive unless we see all that is going on, a soft white cloud against the blue sky, the hum of the bee busy in the flower, the sound of the wind passing though the pine trees. Cut an onion, and look at it and see the beauty, the texture. Cut an orange and look at the symmetry. Go and turn on the water and see a modern miracle, the water flowing from the tap. Never turn on a tap where water comes from unless you have a sense of gratitude for the omnipresence, for that water flowing forth from the throne of God. Air-conditioning, heating, lighting, these are miracles.

The same way with Soul-senses, smelling, hearing, knowing. Be so grateful that these are spiritual, always testifying to the Father's presence. See that beauty is ever-present, and that you are simply experiencing yourself when you see the magnificent mountains, the grandeur of the valley. When you see the flowers, you are experiencing your own being, not something out there; it is yourself; see how grand you are; see how beautiful you are; be alert never to objectify anything; it is all subjective; it is all consciousness, within — a beautiful woman, a handsome man. And most of all, be alert that physique is not man, therefore it is not beautiful. We must see that the beauty that is present as the woman, the grandeur present as the man, is there because it is omnipresence, and it is never present because of personality, and never absent because of personality. Never get entangled in the world of personal sense. What appears to be kind, loving or beautiful in your friend, is not your friend; it is the Father appearing in the only way we can understand at the moment.

We come to the statement, "Love never loses sight of loveliness." Of course, Love is always lovely and Love never sees anything but love, and your Leader says its halo rests upon its object. Every now and then, someone will try to knock your halo off. Put it right back on, and see that it was their misconception and not yourself. Keep your halo on. Your Leader says a halo rests upon its object, and be sure and keep it on no matter what appears, and permit nothing to knock it off.

Your Leader says, "One marvels that a friend can ever seem less than beautiful . . . Immortal Mind feeds the body with supernal freshness and fairness, supplying it with beautiful images of thought and destroying the woes of sense which each day brings to a nearer tomb." What joy to know that it is immortal Mind that is feeding us with these beautiful images of thought.

"Let us accept Science, relinquish all theories based on sense-testimony, give up imperfect models and illusive ideals; and so let us have one God, one Mind, and that one perfect, producing his own models of excellence. Let the 'male and female' of God's creating appear. Let us feel the divine energy of Spirit, bringing us into newness of life and recognizing no mortal nor material power as able to destroy. Let us rejoice that we are subject to the divine 'powers that be.' Such is the true Science of being. Any other theory of Life, or God, is delusive and mythological."

She says let us accept Science and relinquish all theories based on sense testimony. It is interesting how Mrs. Eddy wisely begins to close this chapter. "Material sense lifts its voice with the arrogance of reality and says: I am wholly dishonest, and no man knoweth it. I can cheat, lie, commit adultery, rob, murder, and I elude detection by smooth-tongued villainy." How does it elude detection? It says, it was Mr. Jones, or Mr. Smith or that man down the street. But it was the carnal mind claiming to have identity, and our work is to see that it isn't fooling anybody. It is the work today of this Association to see its nothingness, whether Russia, Roman Catholic, it is nothing. From the standpoint of revelation, its nothingness has appeared. It isn't something to be made nothing.

"Imperfect mortals grasp the ultimate of spiritual perfection slowly; but to begin aright and to continue the strife of demonstrating the great problem of being, is do-ing much." But no student of this Association will identify himself with an imperfect mortal, so therefore we are not grasping the ultimate of spiritual perfection slowly. We are acknowledging, I am the ultimate of spiritual perfection itself.

"This task God demands us to accept lovingly to-day and to abandon so fast as practical the material, and to work out the spiritual which determines the outward and actual." Great words of a great Leader. Do it as fast as practical, she says. Live it, know it, love it, eat the book. This will prevent the footsteps, because then it will be Truth uttering itself, coming right out from Principle.

Creation

It is so simple. There is only one Creator and one creation.

Science of Being

What a tremendous heading! The whole textbook has been the Science of Being, so all the Association paper has been the Science of Being. The works of Jesus are now understood, and your Leader says, "In this revolutionary period, like the shepherd-boy with his sling, woman goes forth to battle with Goliath." The Goliath, with all of its bullying suggestions, went down when our Leader put the leaven into Science, Theology and Medicine. The testimony of the material senses has been questioned and proven to be illusive, and now your courageous Leader is daring to say to the world, "You have made the same mistake that Ptolemy made." You have believed your senses and have had the world stand still, and now believe the senses and have soul in body, life in body.

"Divine Science is absolute, and permits no half-way position in learning its Principle and rule — establishing it by demonstration . . . matter, examined in the light of divine metaphysics, disappears." Divine metaphysics, as revealed to spiritual understanding, shows clearly that all is Mind and that Mind is God. . . Hence all is in reality the manifestation of Mind." Mrs. Eddy has told us that the human concept is sometimes beautiful, always erroneous, and that a Christian Scientist never deals with matter, changing bad matter into good matter, dealing with young matter or old matter. The 'Science of Being' shows us that all is infinite Mind.

Summing up the whole Science of Being, we find this: "Undisturbed amid the jarring testimony of the material senses, Science, still enthroned, is unfolding to mortals the immutable, harmonious, divine Principle — is unfolding Life and the universe, ever present and eternal."

Every statement in this chapter is one to ponder. Permit no intellectual high-sounding words. Eat the little book quietly; and in this quietness of digestion, in this deep calm of meditation, the soft message comes, Be still and know that the Ego is God.

The chapter ends with the scientific platform, with 32 sections. She says if you understand the 32 sections, you have the Rock of Christ and no Goliath can ever touch you.

At the end she says: "Let us hear the conclusion of the whole matter: love God and keep His commandments: for this is the whole of man in His image and likeness. Divine Love is infinite. Therefore all that really exists is in and of God, and manifests His love." So the Science of Being rests on Love.

Some Objections Answered

The same objections are met by the student today. There is nothing new in the human mind; it is purely negative; it has no presence, no reality. Your Leader asks you in this chapter: "Dear reader, which mind-picture or externalized thought shall be real to you, — the material or the spiritual? Both you cannot have. You are bringing out your own ideal. This ideal is either temporal or eternal. Either Spirit or matter is your model. If you try to have two models, then you practically have none."

So we are not persons having models of other persons, but it is the Christ model, the Christ after the order of Melchisidek. The Scripture reads: "For in Him we live, and move, and have our being." "You command the situation if you understand that mortal existence is a state of self-deception and not the truth of being. Mortal mind is constantly producing on mortal body the results of false opinions; and it will continue to do so, until mortal error is deprived of its imaginary powers by Truth, which sweeps away the gossamer web of mortal illusion." Christian Science sweeps away the gossamer web of personal sense.

Christian Science Practice

This chapter on 'Practice' is most important. Why does Mrs. Eddy start this chapter with the story of the Magdalene? Because she wanted us to see how Jesus handled those who were with young. The very fact that Mary could weep with tears of repentance, was proof to Jesus that Mary was knowing that there was something divine about herself. She would never have approached Jesus had she not known there was something divine about herself. And how did Jesus handle those with young? He told the parable about those who forgave most.

Now, why did Mrs. Eddy start this chapter with the story of Mary? She wanted us to see that we must learn to be this same good Samaritan to ourselves, go down where the human concept seems to be, forgive it its seeming mistakes, its sins, but always keep identity in the inn of God's presence. It is amazing how many students will forgive others their seeming mistakes, but it seems so difficult for them to forgive themselves. Why is this? Because the personal sense of self, the egotistical sense of self, is so real to them. They are able to love their neighbor as themselves, and see their neighbor as really the functioning of the Mind that is God, and see their neighbor as Love's own loving; but they still maintain the egotistical personal sense of themselves. In other words, instead of having a center and circumference, they have only a center. Circumference means all-inclusive.

Learn to forgive yourself. Never talk about yesterday. Never nag yourself. Of course, never nag another, but never nag yourself. Students sometimes are not alert as to how they nag themselves. Bring your own Christ and bless the human concept. If it knew how to be better, Mrs. Eddy said, it would be better. Our work is to show it how to be better.

In the practice of Christian Science, we must always turn to the Christ. There is nothing in the human mind that can be helpful. In practice, it is sometime necessary to make an appeal, even as Jesus did when he said, "My God, why hast thou forsaken me?" The appeal was made to the divine Principle, Love, and to his own divine self, Love's pure idea. What man is, from the divine standpoint, will save him from human limitations. We must be very alert that we are not accepting the frightened, fearful mortal as ourselves. We must appeal not only to our God, Principle, but we must appeal to our true self to dispel this illusion of the senses. That is what Jesus did. He asked why had the God-Principle forsaken him. Has your true self forsaken you? But the moment you acknowledge your true self is present, it will instantaneously heal the personal sense of self.

Our Leader, through deep consecration, wrote: "If the Scientist reaches his patient through divine Love, the healing work will be accomplished at one visit, and the disease will vanish into its native nothingness like dew before the morning sunshine." Could anything be more simple? There is no intellectual proficiency needed, no argument to the patient. Your book says, "If the Scientist reaches his patient through divine Love," and divine Love knows no problem because it is Principle, it always maintains its immaculate divinity.

Then your Leader says in *Miscellaneous Writings,* "LOVE, What a word!" It is interesting that she said that "if the patient is reached through divine Love . . . the disease will vanish into its native nothingness like dew before the morning sunshine."

Did you ever stop to think of disease as being like dew, and how instantaneously, how immediately, when the sun touches the dew, it is dispelled into its nothingness? All disease will dissolve into nothingness the moment we let the Love that is God be present as the only Mind there is, the Mind that is immaculate, the Mind that is All — Love itself. Love fulfills the law. Think how quietly and gently the sun dispels the dew. No effort. And the disease will vanish into its native nothingness like dew before the morning sunshine.

It is our divinity outshining humanity. This should be as effortless as darkness giving place to light. Oh that we might pray for and live this Love that is Principle, the Love that never loses sight of its own loveliness, the Love that is never hurt by personal sense, never disturbed by what persons say, never interested in what persons do or do not do, but the love that our Leader had for the world when at the very height of her career she withdrew. Think of the yearning she must have had just once to have gone into the church, the extension of the Mother Church. Think how she must have said, "If I could only go in there once and have a service." But she never did, not once. Why? She knew that would personalize her, do what they did to Jesus. So she stayed away in her own little sanctuary and loved the world more, loved the movement more. Think of it! This New England woman was willing to put down personal sense at the very height of her career, and could withdraw, and not see the church. At that time, she gave us the *Monitor* and the final textbook. The Love that is Principle, surely.

Can we do less? Think of the blessings we have all received through the study of Christian Science. Think of what has happened to us since we found it. I am sometimes just speechless when I see what has happened to my own experience. It is beyond words. I couldn't give a testimony on it. Everyone here has had that same experience because they would not even be a Christian Scientist if it were not true.

Never permit personal sense to get in your way even for a second. This love does not mean a person loving another person. What is called a person may not be worth loving. We love, not a person, but we love.

Mrs. Eddy says in our textbook that infinite Love alone confers the healing power. Animal magnetism would try to interfere with divine Love. Watch telling another what to do, watch in your household the little foxes that would spoil your vines. Be so alert. Never tell the other one what to do. Let it be their own present unfoldment. How much better it is. Like the little three year-old boy playing with the blocks one day. He was trying to get them up into a steeple, they would fall because he did not start out right. His mother sitting in the room started to reach out three or four times and try to show him how to put the blocks, but each time she stopped. He finally said, "You know what I like about you, Mommy? You don't play with my blocks." We are often tempted to play with the other fellow's blocks. Watch it! It will spoil your vine, I promise you.

It's so easy when you see something that needs to be done, to tell them. If you were really knowing that the Mind that is God is the only Mind present and cannot be obscured by what appears to be another, the Mind that is God will have the orderly, intelligent thing done, and it might be contrary to what you were about to tell them. It's so easy. It was so easy for Jeremiah to jump up on a soap box and say, "Thus saith the Lord," and the Lord didn't say a word of it.

"A Christian Scientist occupies the place at this period of which Jesus spoke to his disciples, when he said: 'Ye are the salt of the earth.' 'Ye are the light of the world. A city that is set on an hill cannot be hid.' Let us watch, work, and pray that this salt lose not its saltness, and that this light be not hid, but radiate and glow into noontide glory."

And the light is hid the moment that we think we are persons doing something. Let us watch and pray that our salt lose not its saltness.

Now, what does it mean to be the salt of the earth? Salt is used for flavoring. In order to be the salt of the earth, we must flavor everything we touch with divine Love, our practice, our homes, our daily contacts — let us flavor them with this precious salt, the flavor of Love. Jesus knew the value of salt in daily living. Here was the great metaphysician using salt in metaphysics, because he knew in cooking everything would be tasteless without salt. You are the salt of your day. Salt every incident of this day with the true flavoring of Love.

Salt is also used to preserve, so let us salt or preserve this day in reality. Let us drench everything in salt, the flavoring of Love. We cease being the light of church, the salt of membership, the moment we feel we must do this or that. Why are we so egotistical to think we must run the committee or the board? Why not be quiet and know, and let the Mind that is God express itself. This Association is the salt of the world, and it has not lost its saltness. It is the light of the world, and has not lost its glowing. So let us watch and pray that we have not lost the salt that flavors good humor and good will. Joy and gladness should characterize our meetings.

> *[Part of the address seems to be missing at this point. Mr. Steves next goes into a summary of the entire address, including chapters in the textbook not covered in the above text.]*

We have seen now that every chapter, irrespective of its name or heading, is the practice of Christian Science, the practice of the one Mind, called prayer, the practice of the oneness of Principle and idea, the practice of the indivisibility of being. How could healing take place if a practitioner here was knowing the Truth for someone over there? The practitioner becomes the patient, the moment the call is accepted. At that moment, the Christ office defends itself against the evil suggestions, at that moment, we will not be made to forget or neglect our duty to God. All the practitioner really does is defend himself. He does not try to change a patient's thinking, does not try to do anything to the patient, and the best practitioner is the one that can slam the door so fast that he will not permit the patient to stick his foot in it — by that I mean on the telephone. When the telephone rings, have your armor on before you pick it up. Don't sit down and say, "Brother, what a mess!" So in Christian Science practice we are constantly defending ourselves.

We have had the 'Preface' and we have seen the sustaining Infinite is big today with its blessings. We have seen that the human mind is not the factor, and then that marvelous thing came forth that the healing is the operation of divine Principle before which sin and disease lose their reality. In other words, from the standpoint of the God-Principle, we have seen the impossibility of the problem asserting itself. Be as alert on this as you can; it is called preventiveness. The therapeutic, we have proven; but the preventive should be our medicine today.

In the chapter 'Prayer,' we have seen that Jesus prayed, he withdrew from the material senses to refresh his heart with brighter views. Isn't that a marvelous definition of prayer — he withdrew from the material senses to refresh his heart with brighter views. Then we have seen that true prayer is the oneness of Father and son, and Mrs. Eddy says that prayer is not to change perfection. She says prayer is not to tell God something nor do we stand before the blackboard and pray. We know from the standpoint of the all-knowing Mind the impossibility of there being a problem.

Then we come to the chapter on 'Atonement and Eucharist.' We did not talk on Eucharist because it is simply a Greek word which means thanksgiving. So you see, when you have made your atonement, you will always have Eucharist, because you will have thanksgiving. Atonement is simply the living of the oneness.

When we came to 'Marriage,' we saw Love wedded to its own spiritual idea. We brought on the wine, the inspiration. We saw the bride and the bridegroom from the

'Glossary,' and we saw that even what appears as human marriage must be kept in heaven, the oneness of the presence of Love. We have seen that both male and female are one; we are neither male nor female because of organs; we are male and female because of quality. Permit your womanhood to come forth and your manhood to come forth — see male and female one, Principle and idea one.

In 'Christian Science versus Spiritualism,' it has been so clear that Mrs. Eddy started it on "Identity" to show us it is always Mind, God, identifying Himself. Then we have seen that there is no medium, no avenue, no channel, but it is always the Father saying, "Look, Son, I am." And we saw that the symbol is not a medium; the symbol is simply an indication of the presence. We saw that the rose, the flower, is a symbol; it is not a medium for the beauty; it is not a medium for the purity, not a medium for the immaculateness; but we have seen it for what it is. Your Leader says it is a hint, a symbol; it is not a medium, for if it were a medium you would have pantheism. Christian Science denounces pantheism.

We saw that there are no mediums for happiness, personality is not a medium for happiness, and personality cannot interfere with your happiness, cannot give it or take it. Your happiness is born of Truth and Love.

'Animal Magnetism Unmasked' shown for what it is, negation, nothing — only from the standpoint of the revelation of God's allness.

Then we took 'Science, Theology and Medicine' and saw how our Leader has put the leaven into the three measures of meal, and we saw that Science is divine because it proceeds from Principle; and we have seen how our Leader shows us that it is the sovereign ever-presence, God with us, and we are demonstrating Science, not faith in God, but Science.

In theology, the only priest is the spiritualized man. We have seen that the only church proceeds from Principle since the only thing possible concerning Church is grounded on Principle. Jesus asked, "Whom do men say I am?" They said, "The Christ," and Jesus said, "Upon this Rock this Church shall be built," — the Christ of everything, the Christ of all.

We saw medicine is Mind. There is no such thing as an objectified medicine. We took the term back to God and left it with God, and from now on we know that our medicine is perfect God, perfect man. This is your medicine.

In the chapter on 'Physiology' we saw clearly that Jesus said, take no thought for this kind of life, what ye shall eat, what ye shall drink. The whole chapter showed that there is no physiological man and that life has always been independent of matter, for Life is God.

'Footsteps of Truth.' It is so marvelous how Mrs. Eddy phrased it, showing us we cannot serve two masters, cannot build safely on false foundations. Truth has made a new creature of us today. Do not try to fill the old vessel, empty it, disrobe it. The winds of God blew — omnipresence, omnipotence, omniscience — and we do not hug the tatters about us; we let them go, and now we are clothed in the robe of divinity.

Next we turned to 'Creation' and we saw there is only one creator and one creation.

We turned to the 'Science of Being,' and saw that the whole textbook is the explanation of the Science of Being, for God and man are one in being according to our Leader.

Then 'Some Objections Answered' was shown to be of no importance because our Leader has explained them all.

We then came to 'Christian Science Practice,' and we asked why Mrs. Eddy started the chapter with Mary Magdalene. It was because she wanted us to learn to be kind and patient with ourselves.

The Pale Star disappeared, the day star came, and we have learned to be tender with those who are with young, those who think that the educational statements are the important things, that they must stay with them, they are with young. We must work with them until they can bring forth the ideal, the Christ man. Our work is never to kill that Christ child, but to help to nourish it. They will go forward. Stay with them. Write the articles that can be acceptable, and the Christ Mind will come forth as the Science of Christian Science.

All through this chapter on 'Practice,' your Leader shows you that it is Love that does the healing. Not words, not intellectual brilliance, not grammar, not a lot of writing, studying, but eating the book, being the salt of the world and flavoring everything with the Love of God. Our Leader says, over and over, it is Love that does the healing. Of course, in teaching Christian Science, we do that in words. And in Class, we know that the teaching is clear as crystal flowing from the throne of God.

In 'Recapitulation' we had questions and answers until finally there was no question and no answer, because there was only the all-knowing Mind giving evidence as the all-knowing Mind, and so we then came to the Key to the Scriptures. Mrs. Eddy has given us the Key and says it is the Key of David, which simply means the Christ, Melchisidek, and has opened everything for us. Always remember, with that same Key that opened it, you can also shut it, or lock it with the same Key of knowing that no aggressive mental suggestion can ever touch your home, your church, nothing can touch your practice. Take the same Key that opened it and shut the door on aggressive mental suggestion. It is a two-edged sword; it works both ways. It is your defense. No arrow can be shot into your home, no arrow that would wound the dove can ever touch us because of the Key. She says from Genesis to Revelation it is shown that God is All-in-all.

And then she gives us that chapter on 'Genesis,' and we know what that magnificent chapter is.

Then comes the chapter on Revelation. An interesting thing about it is that Mrs. Eddy not only opened the seven seals of Truth for us, but also opened the seven seals of error for us, and then said, why should we stand aghast at nothingness. Remember, its nothingness is apparent only from the allness of God.

Now we come to that marvelous chapter called 'Glossary.' We are no longer permitted to deal with semantics; we are no longer permitted to deal with words. When I was a child, I thought as a child, but when I became a man, the Christ man, I put away childish things. We no longer deal with people, things, patients, practitioners — only from the standpoint of allness, I Am All.

The chapter of 100 pages called Fruitage, and those hundred pages show us the fruitage of the knowing, and in looking that over I found every known belief that could ever be put forward had been nothingized. Do we have to go over and over, if we have 12, 40, 80 cases a day? Do we have to heal them separately? It has already been done once. Because we don't accept the fact that it has been healed once, and if it has been healed once, it is nothing already.

We should be able to heal eighty as well as one, and we don't do it because we think a patient is a person. We don't see that the patient is a world belief claiming to personalize itself; it is not a person with a belief; it is a belief claiming to personalize itself. As we see that, we can heal the ten lepers as easily as Jesus did, because it is the same Christ here that healed those ten. Never limit your practice by what you have heard anyone say, never limit it by what anyone has done before. Have such a grand sense of the practice that you can answer the phone a hundred times a day and know they are not persons with minds that need to be instructed. It is the one lie multifariously denying that God is all, no matter what its claim. It is the one lie, one supposititous opposite. We are not dealing with bodies in Christian Science; that is the work of the doctors. We are no matter physicians; we are metaphysicians; and metaphysician means that which knows that all is infinite Mind and its infinite manifestation for God is All-in-all.

The Association has been given the Key of David, has acknowledged the Christ. And with this Key, we have opened the textbook from 'Preface' to 'Fruitage,' and with this same Key, we should lock the door against any suggestions that would try to rob us of our fruitage. Remember, the same Key that opened the door will always lock it again, this is the two-edged sword.

Now we are not going out into the world to practice what we know. We have eaten the little book; we are not going out into the world; the world is knowing what I am and my world is all right. So let us rejoice, not that the devils are subject unto us, but let us rejoice that our names are written in heaven, which means that we have eaten the little book, the digestion is over, and now we are the body of the book. And the Christ, so gentle, so tender with those who are with young, and so firm and so strong with those that are of full age. And so we make the declaration here and now, I am after the order of Melchisidek.

Prayer

What is scientific prayer? True prayer is not an instrument for altering or moving the heart of God. Our book shows that when Jesus prayed, he withdrew from the material senses to refresh his heart with brighter, more spiritual views. Christian Science shows us that there is no self apart from God to pray. We are not mortals praying to a vast God outside, worshipping a God, falling down, saying certain words that we think will appease this man-formulated God. Paul rebuked this kind of prayer. "Whom therefore ye ignorantly worship, him declare I unto you."

True prayer is the practice of God's presence — permitting the personal sense of self to fade into its native nothingness in the realization of the God presence, the God-power. In this divine presence, no finiteness can possibly remain.

Association Address of 1960

by

Clarence Steves

How gentle God's commands,
How kind His precepts are;
Come, cast your burdens on the Lord,
And trust His constant care.

Beneath His watchful eye
His saints securely dwell;
That hand which bears creation up
Shall guard His children well.

His goodness stands approved,
Unchanged from day to day;
I drop my burden at His feet,
And bear a song away.
(Christian Science Hymnal)

"*How gentle God's commands*" — God's law is in three words, "I am All" — so gentle, as it holds the universe in infinite oneness.

"*How kind His precepts are*" — God's law of kindness is, "Be ye therefore perfect for I am perfect."

"*Come, cast your burdens on the Lord*" — Come, cast aside the burdened sense of an I apart from God.

"*And trust His constant care.*" Man's conscious identity is forever cared for, for Love never loses sight of loveliness.

"*Beneath His watchful eye His saints securely dwell.*" Man is celestial.

"*That hand which bears creation up*" — that hand that is the power, the glory and supremacy of God, holds all. "*Shall guard His children well.*"

"*His goodness stands approved.*" Goodness is always proven.
"*Unchanged from day to day.*" Unchanged forever.

"*I drop my burden*" — the personal sense of self — "*at His feet,*"

"*And bear a song away.*" My song is, "I and my Father are one."

The Old Covenant of the Law

The old covenant defined and elaborated the doom of sin, and showed the inevitableness of death as its penalty. That was its truth, and hence its glory. And we read that the man appointed to serve this absolute covenant of sin's reward, was yet invested with divine glory. That doom was engraven, we read, in letters of stone tables, and it slew. That is the function of the letter of the law — it dooms to death whatever is not in exact accordance with its demands. Yet in receiving and administering to the people this covenant, a glory appeared on Moses' face.

How much more glorious then is the ministry of that Word which brings life! For the Spirit gives life. The glory on Moses' face died away after a while. It could not continue in the presence of the people. That was the reason, as is commonly interpreted, of the veil which Moses placed on his face. The children of Israel, because of that veil, never saw the light of the old covenant fade out and vanish into nothing. Had not the veil been there, they would have looked right on to the end of this covenant of finiteness and death, and so discerned its spiritual sense; but that veil represents the hardening of their hearts and the dimness of their eyes, whereby they cannot discern the spiritual sense of the Scriptures. When Moses is read in their synagogues, the veil is on their hearts still, for the real meaning of that ministry is a spiritual one.

The New Covenant of the Spirit

As the light of the old covenant which defines the doom of sin, fades and dwindles and at last dies away to nothing, the dawn of the new covenant rises and broadens — for the glory of the new (of righteousness) far exceeds the old (of death). It is the glory which we behold beyond the end of the finite and transitory — the eternal splendor of that which abides and never passes away. Then, like Moses, who in the divine presence removed the veil which he had worn in the presence of the people, so we behold the glory of the Lord, and looking, are changed — changed from the perishable and mortal into the image of His glory, ever deepening and broadening from glory to glory the image that is the eternal Spirit. The Bible says, ". . . when Moses went in before the Lord to speak with Him, he took the veil off." The "Lord" there means the Spirit — the Spirit which has reached us, the Spirit which has freed us from the law of sin and death.

So long as I am a minister of such a covenant as this, I will never fear. It is the love of God which has dissolved at last that old hardness and darkness which hid His truth; and in this love, we have forever bidden farewell to the sins that were hidden in the dark. The Word of God is ministered by me now in honesty and openness, with a conscience free and unfettered by sin — but shines forth in all its splendor. And what is this light? Is it not the light of God's own creation when He spake and said, "Let there be light"?

The old covenant had to fade. The new covenant came with the revelation of Christian Science. This revelation is Truth's day — the day in which Truth utters its eternal verities. Truth's conscious identity of itself constitutes this day, and gathers all ideas into perfect focus — not to be longed for, but to be seen here and now in all their grandeur.

This day, I AM is saying I AM to every incident, every event. It is the lawfulness of the one Mind commanding, "Be ye therefore perfect," for I AM perfect — lacking nothing, wanting nothing, needing nothing. "Man is the offspring and idea of the Supreme Being, whose law is perfect and infinite. In obedience to this law, man is forever unfolding the endless beatitudes of Being; for he is the image and likeness of infinite Life, Truth, and Love." (*Miscellaneous Writings*)

"Immortal Mind is God, immortal good; in whom the Scripture saith 'we live, and move, and have our being.' This Mind, then, is not subject to growth, change, or diminution, but is the divine intelligence, or Principle, of all real being; holding man forever in the rhythmic round of unfolding bliss, as a living witness to and perpetual idea of inexhaustible good." (*ibid*)

"As there is none beside Him, and He is all good, there can be no evil. Simply uttering this great thought is not enough! We must live it, until God becomes the All and Only of our being." (*No and Yes*)

Man as God's Reflection

In this day, man is not a person knowing Truth — man is the functioning presence of the law of God in operation, reflecting Mind's knowing.

The Ten Commandments were for the consciousness listening to the suggestion of the serpent declaring, "Ye shall be as gods." The Christ consciousness declares, "Dwelling in light, I can see only the brightness of My own glory." (*Unity of Good*) This Christ consciousness is the "Peace be still" to these suggestions for "It is your Father's good pleasure to give you the kingdom." Man is the kingdom of God.

It is the belief of being a mortal that needs the thunder of Sinai. Man in the image of God, needs no Commandments because he is the perpetual witness of good, not part infinite and part finite — not part Spirit and part flesh — not part incorporeal and part corporeal.

Our Leader warns us: "Divine Science is absolute, and permits no half-way position in learning its Principle and rule — establishing it by demonstration. The conventional firm, called matter and mind, God never formed. Science and understanding, governed by the unerring and eternal Mind, destroy the imaginary co-partnership, matter and mind, formed only to be destroyed in a manner and at a period as yet unknown. This suppositional partnership is already obsolete, for matter, examined in the light of divine metaphysics, disappears." (*Science and Health*)

"It is not wise to take a halting and half-way position or to expect to work equally with Spirit and matter, Truth and error. There is but one way — namely, God and His idea — which leads to spiritual being. The scientific government of the body must be attained through the divine Mind. It is impossible to gain control over the body in any other way. On this fundamental point, timid conservatism is absolutely inadmissible. Only through radical reliance on Truth can scientific healing power be realized." (*ibid*)

Man is God's being, God's reflection, God's knowing, God's seeing. Conservatism is defined as being disposed to preserve existing views; opposed to change; tending to preserve what is established. Radical means going to the root or origin; fundamental; thorough-going and extreme, especially in way of reform. Man is Principle's own functioning presence. We are not radical because we refuse to see a doctor, but radical because we insist that man is the compound idea of God.

We read in *Science and Health*, "The divine Principle of the First Commandment bases the Science of being . . ."

And the scientific statement of being declares: "All is infinite Mind and its infinite manifestation, for God is All-in-all." (*ibid*) This is declaring, "Thou shalt have no other gods before me." Are God and man separate or are they "coexistent and eternal"? Let us see the Ten Commandments from the standpoint of the inspired Word, and so make them practical. Usually they are discussed out of context. Let us put them back in their frame, and learn why Moses gave them as "Thou shalt not."

Who Was Moses?

Moses was "keeping the sheep" on the backside of the desert, meditating alone, seeking the verities of being. As he beheld the burning bush and saw that it was not consumed, he grasped the tremendous revelation that God, Spirit, was omnipresent, and so would necessarily have to be the substance of all. It was Moses' clear perception of God as Spirit that revealed this " . . . everlasting I AM, the Being who was and is and shall be, whom nothing can erase." (*Science and Health*)

Moses saw all identity "from a blade of grass to a star" as embraced in and constituted of the omnipresent substance of Spirit.

What was this that appeared to be going on? Was it a material bush burning or was it the substance of Spirit declaring itself, saying, "All is Spirit! The very ground on which you stand is holy." Moses had recognized the great fact of being — *God, Spirit, is All.*

Let us accept this fact, take off our shoes, put off all material impediments, all the tatters of material selfhood. God named Himself, I AM. When Moses said, "Here am I," did he not behold this I AM as the I of Abraham, the I of Isaac, the I of Jacob, called God? It was the same I that was called Jesus, Mary Baker Eddy, the I of each of us.

Persons don't have revelations. Revelation takes place in the absence of personal sense. Jesus and Mrs. Eddy were willing to let the personal sense of self fade, and *there* is revelation!

The great light that Moses beheld as the burning bush — that I AM is All — released the personal sense of little "i." The one ego is God. Personal sense keeps arguing, "But I am not eloquent!" But the reply is, "Who hath made man's mouth? . . . have not I the Lord? . . . I will be with thy mouth." Jesus said, "I can of mine own self do nothing."

Don't separate the Ten Commandments. Let them gently lead those that are with young. Let them feed and clothe the idea until the inner voice becomes the voice of God. Jesus spoke in parables, and Mrs. Eddy hid the revelation in a multitude of words. When the I goes to the Father, then the I that is God will express itself. Mrs. Eddy once said, "I am infallible now." The consciousness that knew man to be infallible *now* healed instantaneously. Mrs. Eddy knew that no process nor time would make man infallible. She held her ground — man *is* infallible.

Moses endeavored to show the people what God revealed to him, but they were not willing to lay aside personal sense, so they said, "You go and come and tell us!" So, Moses gently led them, fed them in the wilderness, protected them, and brought to them the Ten Commandments, the Law which governed and controlled them. Moses understood that "God's law is in three words, 'I AM ALL' . . ." (*No and Yes*), and endeavored to show the lawfulness of God even though he could not tell the Children of Israel.

Moses went to the Mount alone and prayed in secret. He saw the Commandments were necessary to regulate the people as long as they believed the Promised Land was outside of themselves, something to be attained. Christian Science does not teach that sonship is in the future. Moses said, "Thou shalt not." Christian Science is not something that gets the human consciousness ready for heaven. The human consciousness is basically rebellious; it is enmity against God. It can't receive the divine idea; it is not becoming a better mind. Mind is God only. Our present Mind is God. The human mind is basically dishonest and must have law to give it discipline.

Don't just follow the letter of Science for fear of punishment. The Psalmist said, "How I love thy law." Lawful living is requisite. The Pharisees chided Jesus' disciples for sitting down to eat without washing, but Jesus told them to make the whole platter clean. The Commandments are laws by which the human consciousness lives.

The "Thou shalt not" of the Commandments has been lived negatively. When we begin to see them and live them positively, the veil is removed — the veil of satanic suggestion that man is a person. Personal sense needs, "Thou shalt not." The disappearance of human sense *appears* as consciousness becoming more spiritual; but it is not the human becoming more spiritual. The human is disappearing, thus permitting the spiritual to become *more apparent*. Living the Christ will let the human fade. Mrs. Eddy brought this *living* spiritual understanding to Christianity. "It is your Father's good pleasure to give you the kingdom."

First Commandment

"Thou shalt have no other gods before me."

The First Commandment declares the universal oneness of God, the flawless, unlabored functioning of divine Principle. When the Pharisees brought the woman taken in adultery to Jesus, they said according to their law, she should be stoned. They wanted Jesus to deny the universal oneness of God. Living the Christ, he could know no accused and no accuser. The scribes could write the law, but they were not living it. Jesus stooped and wrote on the ground. Living the Christ, he saw only the immaculateness of being. "Jesus beheld in Science the perfect man who appeared to him where sinning mortal man appeared to mortals." (*Science and Health)* This was not Jesus seeing man, but "in Science" Jesus saw God. There was nothing *but* God to be seen. Hence he said, "Go and sin no more."

The First Commandment does not permit any personal sense of self. "The first demand of this Science is, 'Thou shalt have no other gods before me.' This *me* is Spirit. Therefore the command means this: Thou shalt have no intelligence, no life, no substance, no truth, no love, but that which is spiritual." (*Science and Health*) Thou shalt have no Ego separate from the divine. "When will the ages understand the Ego and realize only one God, one Mind or intelligence?" (*ibid*)

The First Commandment declares thou shalt have no personal sense of *me*, only God, the "only I or US." And, "As a drop of water is one with the ocean, a ray of light one with the sun, even so God and man, Father and son, are one in being." (*Science and Health*) In watching the raindrops fall into the ocean while in Florida, I noticed that they instantly became one with the ocean, instantly took on the qualities of the ocean. The drops became the surge of the wave, the power and cleanness of it. They instantly ceased to be mere drops and became the power in manifestation. The very moment the personal sense of I is immersed in the infinite ocean of Love, it takes on the essence of Love, the power and glory of God, and ceases to be a drop. There is no other substance but God, Spirit.

Thou shalt have no other presence but My presence, no other seeing but My seeing, no other action but the action of Mind, no other consciousness but the divine. Thou shalt have no other feeling but Soul, feeling its own well-being, no other taste but the love of good, no other embodiment but the embodiment of divine ideas, no other individuality but the indivisible oneness of infinite Love, immaculate and blessed. Thou shalt have no other breath but the deep-drawn breath, fresh from infinity, no other hearing but that which hears the still small voice, no other activity but the rhythm of Spirit, no other good but inexhaustible infinity, no other being but the one I AM. The First Commandment does not permit *anything* but God to say *I AM*.

Second Commandment
.

"Thou shalt not make unto thee any graven image . . ."

The truth of the First Commandment will not permit the personal ego to parade around and say, "I want, I need, I would like to have, etc." Satanic suggestion says, "I am your mind, your thinking." It would make us fall down and worship graven images. "Graven" means to carve in wood or stone, to make an idol. "Spirit knows that her impress makes harmony indelible." (*Science and Health*, third edition) The Christ-consciousness cannot be graven with the images of persons. The carnal mind holds its own false concepts, and would etch its own false beliefs upon its images.

"The harmony and immortality of man are intact. We should look away from the opposite supposition that man is created materially, and turn our gaze to the spiritual record of creation, to that which should be engraved on the understanding and heart 'with the point of a diamond' and the pen of an angel." (*ibid*)

Let us today know that the Christ consciousness is our only consciousness and no abortive ego can etch its false images on this Christ consciousness and call it our experience.

All the Commandments emanate from the First. "Jealous" means nothing outside. Life, Truth, Love, the one Mind, can countenance nothing but itself. Oxford dictionary defines jealous as "vigilant in guarding, careful in watching."

"Third and fourth generation" — Moses had to give a penalty because of the rebellious nature of the people. It was the best at the moment, but the later prophets lifted the veil when they declared that this proverb shall no longer be used, "The fathers have eaten sour grapes and the children's teeth are set on edge." Mrs. Eddy removed this teaching of false theology by declaring, "Man is the expression of God's being." (*Science and Health*) Jesus showed man was never born and never died. The seven synonyms reveal the wholeness and essence of God, and give man the dominion bestowed upon him in the first chapter of Genesis.

Third Commandment

"Thou shalt not take the name
of the Lord thy God in vain . . ."

Man is the name, nature and essence of God's being. The human consciousness takes this name in vain by accepting a finite, limited, corporeal "you" as man. The human sense takes God's name in vain when it limits good, which is inexhaustible; when it says someone has passed on, when Life is eternal; when it rejoices in what appears as birth, admitting even temporarily something human, when God is illimitable divinity. It takes God's name in vain by believing man is in need of being evangelized. God, being infinite Mind, leaves no world outside. God, being infinite Love, leaves no fear outside. Man is Love individualized. It is taking God's name in vain when habits assert themselves, for infinity never repeats itself. Knowing that God is universal and infinite never permits habits to assert themselves.

I once sat in the garden at twilight. It had never been just as it was at that moment. It was so new, so fresh! The water in the fountain, the song of the bird, the breeze — all new! No habit, no person sitting in the chair, but man *being* the breeze, knowing the birdsong. I AM, viewing the universe, never sees it twice the same, just forever new. Infinity is the name of God, and leaves nothing to take its name in vain.

Fourth Commandment

"Remember the Sabbath day, to keep it holy."

What is the Sabbath? The continuity of divine restfulness, the continuity of the royalty of being, right knowing, right living, the continuous reflection of Mind's knowing. The Jews believed the Sabbath was a day instead of what one knows. Jesus said, "The sabbath was made for man, and not man for the sabbath . . ." — in other words, it cannot be objectified. "The real Christ was unconscious of matter, of sin, disease, and death, and was conscious only of God, of good, of eternal Life, and harmony. Hence the human Jesus had a resort to his higher self and relation to the Father, and there could find rest from unreal trials in the conscious reality and royalty of his being, — holding the mortal as unreal, and the divine as real." (*No and Yes*)

Jesus found rest from the erroneous material senses in spiritual sense. "Keep it holy" is to keep the completeness of being, the conscious identity of being. Rest in divinity and escape from objectivity.

Fifth Commandment

"Honour thy father and thy mother . . ."

Keep Father and Mother forever free from "earth-born taint." Don't disown what appears as human father and mother, but recognize the universality of the Father-Mother God as the source of all. Be gentle with the human appearing as parents. Jesus revealed who his parents and his brethren were when he said, "Behold my mother and my brethren! For whosoever shall do the will of God, the same is my brother, and my sister, and mother." Loose from all parental belief of false responsibility. See God as the source of all ideas. Call no man father, for one is your Father, the Adorable One. Acknowledge, "before Abraham was, I am." Keep Father-Mother subjective. "From the infinite One in Christian Science comes one Principle and its infinite idea, and with this infinitude come spiritual rules, laws, and their demonstration, which, like the great Giver, are the 'same yesterday, and to-day, and forever;' for thus are the divine Principle of healing and the Christ-idea characterized in the epistle to the Hebrews." (*Science and Health*).

Sixth Commandment

"Thou shalt not kill."

Thou shalt not kill because Life is God, and so it is eternal. Never kill the inspiration of another or yourself, by believing him to be a person. Never kill the understanding of another, but know it is an infinite expression of the All-God, ALL ONE. Never kill by refusing to listen to another's point of view. Never kill *now* by recounting past error. Life lives and that living is man. Life is eternal noon. Never permit *now* to acknowledge yesterdays. Life is forever fresh, new, *now*, the evergreen of Soul. No private life is objectified in matter to be killed.

Once a soldier in battle realized Life was never in matter. He thought of a watch and realized there was no *time* in the watch, only wheels. So, also, there was no Life in body to be killed.

Seventh Commandment

"Thou shalt not commit adultery."

Never commit adultery by admitting you are an adult and thereby adulterate your childlikeness. Never commit adultery by trying to heal matter. Never permit Love to be adulterated. Love is Principle, God. Love is never in body. "Love never loses sight of loveliness." (*Science and Health*) It is never adulterated by being called sensation. Never see a child as less than man. Man is Mind's full expression, never immature, underdeveloped, and cannot be deflected by what the world calls a little child.

Eighth Commandment

"Thou shalt not steal."

When you gossip, you steal from your neighbor. You might not steal his money, but you assassinate his birthright. Believing we are persons living with persons, we steal our own spiritual sense. You steal if you call *now*, yesterday, or if you believe Mind is less than divine, or see man as less than perfect. Integrity is the essence of man because man is the infinite satisfaction of Soul. Integrity is the fact of being and demands manifestation.

A friend called me to report valuable papers stolen from her suitcase. I was surprised myself at what I said: "Do not work to know man is honest, but know that integrity is present and demands evidence of itself. If you work to know man is honest, you have the possibility of man appearing as dishonest. That would come from working in the second degree, the moral — instead of the third degree, the spiritual. (See *Science and Health*, page 115) Man is the being of integrity." The papers were returned in the mail the following day.

Ninth Commandment

"Thou shalt not bear false witness . . ."

You bear false witness if you look in the glass and say, "This is me." Look in the mirror of divine Science and see God and say, "How beautiful I AM!" See the evergreen of Soul. Never permit mortal mind to say it is *you*, because it is either egotism or the other end of the same stick.

When a patient calls with a tale of woe, be alert! He will try to make you think his claim is legitimate; but remember, it is not a man out there, just hypnotic suggestion. "Ye are my witnesses, saith the Lord." And, "If I bear witness of myself, my witness is not true." Mrs. Eddy calls man "the climax of creation . . ." (*No and Yes*) No matter what the material senses say, God is whole, and man is His ever-present witness. Never accept the suggestion of another.

Every country is the "land of Christian Science, where fetters fall and the rights of man are fully known and acknowledged." (*Science and Health*) Know that this land of Christian Science has not lost its integrity. This land gave birth to Christian Science. Pray for its President daily, not for a person, but for the office. Get rid of your "lavender kid zeal," your dainty statements that God will take care of it. Nothing but *true knowing* will take care of it — knowing I cannot be made to bear false witness against my universe, because all there is to it proceeds from the Father-Mother God.

"We, to-day, in this class-room, are enough to convert the world if we are of one Mind; for then the whole world will feel the influence of this Mind; as when the earth was without form, and Mind spake and form appeared." (*Miscellaneous Writings*) I *cannot* bear false witness against anyone because man is an *ever-present* of the Lord.

Tenth Commandment"

Thou shalt not covet . . ."

There is nothing to covet when we live from the standpoint of revelation and include all right ideas. All identity is my Father saying I AM. I AM not tempted to bear false witness, because all that is present as neighbor is my own consciousness. There is nothing outside to heal. Study "Love Your Enemies," in *Miscellaneous Writings,* and substitute neighbor for enemy. If my neighbor is objectified, I have something besides God.

Priestcraft

After the Commandments were given, the people were still not ready to see God face to face. They insisted on Moses acting as a medium for them. Thus, priestcraft was born, and a veil drawn over the Science. "And all the people saw the thunderings, and the lightnings, and the noise of the trumpet, and the mountain smoking: and when the people saw it, they removed, and stood afar off. And they said unto Moses, Speak thou with us, and we will hear: but let not God speak with us, lest we die.
"   The thunder of Sinai is heard when the human opposes the divine. A personal private ego hears the thunder and lightning. Revelation is thunder to personal sense. Man has no private ego. God is the only I AM. Moses could not lift the people to the mountain, so he had to translate the revelation to the people. The greatest danger in the organization today is priestcraft. The people don't want to come face to face with pure Science. They want a practitioner to "know the truth" for them. They will not give up their false sense of self and find the Christ as their own identity. Paul said, "Whom ye . . . ignorantly worship, him declare I unto you."

"For in him we live, and move, and have our being," but Moses could not say that. Moses was not talking to *man*, but to a rebellious people. Jeremiah asked if God was a God afar off and not a God at hand. "Ye are my witnesses, saith the Lord." The human mind is enmity against God and cannot understand God. The Christ says, "Come unto me . . . for my yoke is easy [no personal sense], and my burden is light." We are so afraid we must give up something. Let the I AM be the I of all. Bring all into obedience to Christ.

The *Church Manual* is discipline for the human mind which is enmity against God, and persists in believing itself a person. "Heaps upon heaps of praise confront me, and for what?" Mrs. Eddy asked. "That which I said in my heart would never be needed, — namely, laws of limitation for a Christian Scientist." (*Miscellany*)

There is too much *talk about* the absolute while continuing to *live* as a person — approving of *some* Christian Scientists, liking only the lecturer who says what *we think* is Christian Science, stopping our support of the church. *What is absolute Christian Science?* — to CONSISTENTLY LIVE THE CHRIST. To consistently *LIVE* the Christ would lift the movement into CHURCH. Absolute Truth is not something seen by a minority — it knows no intellectual snobbery. Living as the Christ never condemns nor damns.

We must support Mary Baker Eddy's demonstration of Church, a demonstration that goes far beyond what personal sense believes adequate support. The "Church Universal and Triumphant" (*Church Manual*), is already established. It is more than an institution of persons trying to demonstrate one Mind. Church *is* one Mind. The institution tries to prove truth. The Church embraces all with its divinity. The movement exists as the conscious knowing of the members. It is not a building on a corner; it has no priest, no laity, no practitioner, no patient, no priestcraft. Take an hour and ask yourself what church means to you. A church or Reading Room is not just an oasis in a world of sin, but Church is a universal fact declaring the omnipresence of harmony here and now, declaring that man's harmony cannot be invaded. *Know*, but be wise in what you say.

Veil

Jesus rent the veil — he was face to face with the Father. "He that hath seen me hath seen the Father." Never yield to the suggestion that a practitioner is like a priest — a go-between, or medium. Let the patient come face to face with his own Christ. God, Mind, identifies Himself. Identity is the persistency of Mind to identify itself. Man can only show forth what God is conscious of — God's conscious identity. There is no man *as* man — only man as reflection.

The veil is gone when the patient comes face to face with his own Christ, and refuses to chase shadows. The practitioner keeps his own Christ identity aglow until there is no more shadow. Keep the Christ so aglow that the patient cannot exist as a patient. This understanding is Melchizedek appearing with the brilliancy of the Christ itself.

"Hold perpetually this thought, — that it is the spiritual idea, the Holy Ghost and Christ, which enables you to demonstrate, with scientific certainty, the rule of healing, based upon its divine Principle, Love, underlying, overlying, and encompassing all true being." (*Science and Health*)

The I of God is present as the I of the practitioner, who has no pride of priesthood saying, "my patient." When the seventy returned and rejoiced, it was priesthood. Jesus showed them it wasn't anything *they* had done. Their names were written in heaven. Mind never heals — it only reveals!

"Hear, O Israel: The Lord our God is one Lord: And thou shalt love the Lord thy God with all thine heart, and with all thy soul, and with all thy might. And it shall be, when the Lord thy God shall have brought thee into the land which he sware unto thy fathers, to Abraham, to Isaac, and to Jacob, to give thee great and goodly cities, which thou buildest not, and houses full of all good things, which thou filledst not, and wells digged, which thou diggedst not, vineyards and olive trees, which thou plantedst not; when thou shalt have eaten and be full; Then beware lest thou forget the Lord, which brought thee forth out of the land of Egypt, from the house of bondage." (Deuteronomy)

The First Commandment means having God, All — seeing all is God saying I AM ALL, *all there is*. Moses' followers worshiped the letter instead of the Spirit. Church is not some place to go. It means to live Love and to embrace Church in your own divinity.

Is God near? Is our world divided into Roman Catholics, Protestants, Democrats, Republicans? Only God is present in the voting booth or anywhere. Roman Catholicism is a gruff, political organization, full of corruption. It is not a church or a religion. " . . . as in heaven, so on earth, — God is omnipotent, supreme." (*Science and Health*). Our defense is God. Don't resist — you'll lose. See the impossibility of evil — knowing God, Principle is present and in operation. Take off your shoes — human resistance — and *stand* on holy ground. The private hell of a Christian Scientist is to fight evil as real. "The Gabriel of His presence knows no contests." (*Science and Health*)

Only the power of God delivers. Moses maintained infinite patience all through the forty years, even though the people often wanted to turn back to their fleshpots in Egypt. Moses knew that Christian Science does not heal man — it *reveals* man. Turning to the golden calf was turning to matter. Would the Son of God fall down and worship a golden calf? The Son of God would take possession of the so-called human consciousness and delineate upon it the beauty of Soul until it disappeared into nothingness.

Put the Commandments back into their frame. Let the light of the Christ dispel the personal sense. Demand of personal sense, (Pharaoh), "Let my son go that he may serve *Me*." Refuse to bear false witness, to steal. Establish day with these Commandments, but keep them in the positive sense. See that they proceed from the divine Principle. See the impossibility of breaking them. "That man can break the forever-law of infinite Love, was, and is, the serpent's biggest lie!" (*Miscellaneous Writings*). See the impossibility of taking God's name, I AM, in vain. See the "stranger within thy gates" as your neighbor — your own conscious identity of being. "The Christian Scientist is alone with his own being and with the reality of things." (*Message for '01*) Our neighbor is never *there*, he is always *here*. We give him the qualities and character we see in him. Do not love him as your neighbor — love him as yourself. In the story of the Good Samaritan, the Jews hated the Samaritans because one of them married the daughter of Sanbalat. Jesus did not judge the Samaritan thus, but for what he did! He knew that Love is reflected in love.

Father, Son, and Holy Ghost mean God, man, and divine Science. God is self-existent, the essence and source of the two latter, and their office is that of eternal, infinite individuality. I see no other way under heaven and among men whereby to have one God, and man in His image and likeness, loving another as himself. *This is being the divine Science of divine Love*, which enables man to escape from idolatry of every kind, and to obey the First Commandment of the Decalogue: "Thou shalt have no other gods before me," and the command of Christ: "Love thy neighbor as thyself." On this rock Christian Science is built. It may be the rock which the builders reject for a season, but it is the Science of God and His universe, and it will become the head of the corner, the foundation of all systems of religion.

Witchcraft

Modern witchcraft is the belief of a personal mind which can be acted upon — a belief of a private mind. Witchcraft claims to take over by constant manipulation. Knowing man has no private mind, is your defense. Handle modern witchcraft. It appears as a husband disliking his wife or his children, or as dislike of many things in one's experience. Charge it with, "You are nothing but modern witchcraft, and I deny you." Get rid of it. A man with a growth on his neck was told that no such result occurs without mind to demand and produce it. Man is the expression of perfection. Mind demands perfection. *The belief of a human mind which can claim to produce an effect is modern witchcraft*. The man's neck was perfect the next morning. Work from the standpoint of the First Commandment, and you will be in obedience to the second. No argument is needed if the Christ is evident. The Christ evidence is not words, but power. It is the *knowing*, not the words — *knowing* that the only thing ever to be met is the claim of evil to be something when it is always *nothing*.

A doctor's verdict said that an immediate operation was necessary on a heart, or the patient would not live. But the answer came: Life is everlasting! The patient thought of how a mechanic removes a worn part of a car, but *puts back a new part*. She asked the doctor if he could put back a new part for what was worn out. When a practitioner came, the girl realized there was no heart but the Great Heart of Love — that it was all that was present and was functioning now. She saw that heart is a divine idea. Where the graven image of heart had claimed to be, there was seen the spiritual idea functioning perfectly. Never forget that man is reflection, not reflector. God is reflecting Himself and this reflection is *termed* man, but it is never anything separate. I AM declaring I AM is the spontaneous action of reflection. There is no corporeality in a mirrored form — there is not something reflecting on God. It is difficult to break the Satanic suggestion that the thing that sits in the chair thinking about God, is good. There is no right nor wrong thinker. Christian Science healing is not "right thinking," but knowing there is no mind to conceive "wrong thoughts."

Of Mrs. Eddy's ability and fitness to be the chief teacher of Christian Science, she furnished a notable proof in the 1880's when the public seemed to be in danger of accepting what was then propagated as "mental science," or mind cure, instead of Christian Science. Indeed, this propaganda persuaded more than a few avowed Christian Scientists to prefer a teaching that was mental in some sense, but was not purely spiritual. The situation was like the one related in John 6. When the Master declared, "It is the spirit that quickeneth; the flesh profiteth nothing [a purely spiritual teaching] . . . many of his disciples went back and walked no more with him."

Mrs. Eddy faced the danger in question firmly and resourcefully. In particular, she formulated and executed plans to provide more authorized teachers, and she did a great deal of writing — not in the least degree to modify Christian Science, but to make it more widely known, and to help the public comprehend its Principle and its purely spiritual practice.

"Searching your thought" is mental science, not Christian Science. Nothing in the problem will solve the problem. "The exterminator of error is the great truth that God, good, is the *only* Mind. . ." (*Science and Health*) There is no private mind. " . . . we must leave the mortal basis of belief and unite with the one Mind. . . "(*ibid*) This does not make us God, but makes us godlike. He that hath seen the humility of the Christ is freed of the arrogance of the human mind.

Reluctance

After Mrs. Eddy paid for publishing the textbook, she found she must write the chapter on animal magnetism. "My reluctance to give the public, in my first edition of Science and Health, the chapter on Animal Magnetism, and the divine purpose that this should be done, may have an interest for the reader, and will be seen in the following circumstances. I had finished that edition as far as that chapter, when the printer informed me that he could not go on with my work. I had already paid him seven hundred dollars, and yet he stopped my work. All efforts to persuade him to finish my book were in vain."

"After months had passed, I yielded to a constant conviction that I must insert in my last chapter a partial history of what I had already observed of mental malpractice. Accordingly, I set to work, contrary to my inclination, to fulfil this painful task, and finished my copy for the book. As it afterwards appeared, although I had no thought of such a result, my printer resumed his work at the same time, finished printing the copy he had on hand . . ." (*Retrospection and Introspection*)

This shows the reluctance of the human heart to give mental error the treatment it deserves, the disinclination to handle animal magnetism intelligently. Was Moses really addressing the people when he said, "Thou shalt not," or was he treating the *whole error*? Mrs. Eddy mastered her reluctance. Some students believe Christian Science is all sweetness and light, but the discriminating student is able to understand the difference between "Watching versus Watching Out." (*Miscellany*)

"An inquirer once said to the discoverer of Christian Science: 'I like your explanations of truth, but I do not comprehend what you say about error.' This is the nature of error. The mark of ignorance is on its forehead, for it neither understands nor can be understood." (*Science and Health*) In 1910, Mrs. Eddy added the word *unmasked* to the chapter title, Animal Magnetism, and we should never overlook that we are reading, not about animal magnetism, but about animal magnetism *unmasked*. The Lesson subject is on animal magnetism DENOUNCED — that is — *accused publicly*. It is accusing publicly the sum total of sin.

We should make no idol of body. Body is a tremendous word, embracing all that is beautiful and good. Body is not evolved from what is *eaten*, but what is *known*. *What I know is my body*. Joy, action, spontaneity — all constitute body. Hallow your name, Wonderful. Acknowledge your divinity. Hear through Christ — see through Christ. See what the words mean! Your body, your present environment, is the consciousness of Love's presence felt here and now.

Now is the accepted time. Let the letter fade out and know nothing is here but God manifesting His love. It isn't the words you say — it is what you *know!* A Sunday School child said "omnipleasant" and healed friction in the home. The First Commandment declares no other substance, no other cause. Never bear false witness against this day. Man never has been human. Being is God. There is no Mind but God, and no man to have a human consciousness. Hallow the name. Never gossip — that is the human mind acting as your mind. Ask, what is the Christ consciousness seeing? Judging another is an admission of your own inability to see the Son of God. What another thinks can't even find me. Defend yourself against the *belief* in another mind, not against another mind.

Resume

The Ten Commandments begin with universal, individual oneness functioning as flawless perfection unlabored in its own perfection — I AM saying I AM. Moses saw Spirit as All, indestructible in the burning bush, and took off his shoes. Jesus saw, "I and my Father are one." Mrs. Eddy saw, "Man is the expression of God's being." The oneness of Father and son is always a state of reflection.

A graven image is a personal, human concept of self — of man, family, or church. Take all things back to Mind.

Then the curse is removed. Man is the restfulness of Mind's knowing. Never kill beauty by separating it from its source. Feed it daily by the fullness of knowing — keep it alive in eternity and continuity. Never have habits — infinity never stops long enough to repeat itself. Let spiritual sense have newness of Life. Live the Third Degree and wipe out the depravity of the First Degree. (See *Science and Health*, page 115). Stay in the sanctuary, pitched inside and outside with the safety and purity of God's omnipresence. You can't divide presence into presences.

Now *LIVE* these Commandments. How gentle God's commands as seen in the definition of Christian Science "as the law of God, the law of good, interpreting and demonstrating the divine Principle and rule of universal harmony." (*Rudimental Divine Science*).

Association Address of 1963

by

Clarence Steves

Part I

When Mary Baker Eddy discovered God to be *Love,* and thus divine Principle, she wrote, "LOVE. What a word! I am in awe before it." *(Miscellaneous Writings)* Why does she say "in awe before it"? Is this a Promised Land, a universe of Love, which we look for, and hope with longing prayer some day to be able to experience? Mrs. Eddy also says, "I have a world of wisdom and Love to contemplate. . . " (Ibid) Where is this universe of Love before which our Leader stood in awe? Was it not her own conscious identification?

What does the word awe mean? It has the meaning of sublime, wonder, majesty and reverence. She saw that this universe was her own universal body and that man is this wonder of eternal Mind, — that man is the sublimity of Truth, the majesty of Principle, the freshness of Soul, the unalterable fact of perfect being. Then, cannot we too stand "in awe" before this word *Love?* Man is not something outside, contemplating Love. We can acknowledge here and now that man is the universe of Love. Man lives in and as divine Love. Man moves in and as divine Love. Man has being in and as divine Love. This is the oneness of Father and son, Mind and its infinite, indissoluble manifestation.

The "Scientific Statement of Being" as given in the Christian Science textbook, *Science and Health with Key to the Scriptures,* by Mary Baker Eddy, shows us that we never have been a part of a universe of time and personal sense, that only infinite Mind is infinitely manifesting itself, is All. So we are to acknowledge that this universe of Love is body, is home, is government, is church, is man, is All. Therefore, let us get used to being the universe of Love — not something that wants to be loved, not something that is trying to find something or someone to love — but that man is the loveliness of Love! Our Leader saw that this synonym *Love* also embraces the intrinsic value of the quality *Principle* within it. In this concept of the divine Principle, Love, we find the Love that never faileth, the Love that is impersonal, the Love that is universal. There is no personal sense to love or to be loved. If we refuse to accept the world belief that we are persons, then we will not be trying to love. God is Love, and man is the expression of God's loving. Man does not love; man is God loving, God being, Man is the embodiment of God, Principle, Love itself.

Someone once asked, "Please define the word *Love.*" And I answered, "You cannot define it intellectually. You can only live it!" Yes, Love must be lived. Love must be felt. This Love is living, and this Love is feeling, is conscious identity, and It centers on the very minutiae of our daily life. Love goes to every part of the body, universe, government, home, church, and makes it every whit whole. In her poem, "Satisfied," Mrs. Eddy writes, "It matters not what be thy lot, so Love doth guide. . ." And she continues, "And of these stones, and tyrants' thrones, God able is to raise up seed — in thought and deed — to faithful His." The "stones" are disposed of because Love knows nothing hard, nothing harsh. Love is the law of refinement. The law of Love is the law of purity. It is the law of gentleness. When someone asked Satchmo Armstrong, the Jazz artist to define Jazz, he replied, "When you have to define it, brother, you ain't got it!" So when we try to define Love, we do not have it.

Love cannot be defined. Words cannot define Love. Love is Soul, and Soul is indefinable. It is a feeling, Love is the term for God that must be felt. To feel and know that God is Love, and that this Love is present and felt, is to give the cup of cold water in Christ's name.

Now let us see that this day is proceeding from and resting upon Love. It has no objects of sense in it to love or be loved.

It is simply Love — immaculate, wholesome, pure Love, seeing nothing unlike itself. This is the message of today: that "Love never loses sight of loveliness." *(Science and Health)* Sometimes we are tempted to believe that we like someone, or that we dislike someone. But let us see that to like or dislike is personal; it is the evil, hypnotic suggestion that one is personal, local. Let us heal this suggestion today, and see that man is Love loving. It is the pure Love of God.

Why did Mrs. Eddy begin the chapter on "Christian Science Practice" with an illustration of pure impersonal Love? *(Science and Health)* Here was Mary Magdalene, a "strange woman," an outcast. Yet, Jesus knew that the Love that is God, is present in all its immaculateness, all its purity, to outshine any suggestion contrary to this Love. Mrs. Eddy says that if the Scientist reaches his patient through divine Love, the healing will be instantaneous. Then, in order to have instantaneous healing in our work, we must have the Love that is divine. It is not enough to be loving; it is not enough to be kind — this will not heal. But the Love that looks right straight through that which calls itself the patient, and sees Love that is God, this will outshine the patient, and then the patient will say, "I am well."

What is the patient? The patient is not a person, a place, or a thing. The patient is simply the suggestion that God is not all-present and not all-power. God is all-present, and God is all-power, and nothing apart from Him is present or has power. Therefore, the Christian Science treatment that knows itself to be Love, knows itself to be the Love that is Principle. It is always restful, peaceful. It never makes the mistake of taking in the picture and then trying to heal it. Christian Science heals scientifically. Christian Science heals metaphysically. Christian Science does *not* heal physically. It does *not* heal theologically. Christian Science is metaphysical healing, and this healing comes in the understanding that the only Mind there is, is present, and it alone is present to manifest or to express itself. So let us be obedient to our Leader and find this way of Love.

Our Leader was never interested in what someone thought of her or said about her. She did not live as a person. When she asked in one of her classes, "Do you love me?" they all replied, "Yes." Then she said, "Love, and include me, but don't love me [as a person]." The moment we have an object to love, our love ceases to be Principle. The Love that is Principle loves — it loves as the sun shines; it knows nothing unlike itself. Is not this the reason that our Leader says that the adamants of self-will, self-love, self-justification are against spirituality? The true sense of Love as Principle, being present and in manifestation, will not leave a self to be willful, a self that needs to be justified, or that could possibly love a false sense.

The Love that is Principle is present now, and is specifically felt, universally felt, and man is this feeling of Love's presence. Man has no other feeling because man's Soul is God, man's Mind is God, man's substance is God, man's seeing is God. Then all there is to man, is God being what God is — and what God is, man is, by reflection. Man gives back to God all that God gives. This is reflection.

Man has nothing as man. Man is simply the term, the scientific term for all that God is being. Hence this universal, generic man includes all identification. Is this not the reason that the Bible says, "My glory will I not give to another"? It must be, because there is no "another." The Bible also states, "Thou shalt have no gods before Me" — that is, thou shalt have no love before Me, thou shall have no identification before Me. This "Me" is Spirit, God. Our Leader tells us that Spirit constitutes its identification, man. Then is man something separate from God that must love? Or is man the Love that is Principle giving identity to itself? We know the answer is the latter.

Do not be afraid of what Christian Science teaches. We know Christian Science has lifted us out of the petty, personal love — the love that parades as person. The common popular use of this word love has been far removed from the true meaning — the Love that is Principle — and has taken on the connotation of lust. Let us know that animal magnetism cannot take this pure, unadulterated word *Love* and call it lust. Let us be sure that we see that Love never possesses its object. Love inspires, Love designates, Love illumines. It is therefore necessary for us today to be clear that the Love that is Principle, is alone present.

The Love, the Truth, the Life, the law that is God, constitutes its identity, and this identity is man. Man is Mind's way of making itself known as the operation of good. The indivisible I AM as cause, effect, present and identified, is the very function of his identity. Hence there is no man there, no man here. This man is everywhere. Even if it looks like another, it still is the indivisible I AM THAT I AM.

We are sometimes fooled by this false sense of a personal love, and then we seem to feel guilt-ridden, condemned, unwanted, unloved. Let us say to this evil hypnotic suggestion: There is no Truth in this picture that you are presenting, because to be truthful, it must be loving, kind, because God is Love. Love means freedom, Love means perfect action, Love means perfect functioning. There is, therefore, no Love in this picture of self-condemnation, and because there is no Love in it, then there is no

Truth in it, because Love alone is Life — God.

See that man's identity cannot be reached by any evil suggestion whatever no matter what form it seems to take, or in what form it seems to appear. God, Love, does not know it or see it, and God is all-knowing, and God is all-seeing. Then what is it that sees it and knows it and feels it? Is it not the opposite? Mrs. Eddy writes, "The exterminator of error is the great truth that God, good, is the *only* Mind." *(Science and Health)* Let us remember that this Mind is Love, the Love that is Principle, the Love that never loses sight of loveliness. Therefore, nothing can obscure this Love, nothing can *deflect* this Love and call its deflection a human being with flesh, living in personal sense, or time sense and space sense.

There is no space in the law of Love. God fills all space. Where then is the human being? God and man are co-existent. Then where is the personality? When all is Mind and Mind is infinite, All-in-all, there is no space left for error, personal sense, to occupy! All space is filled with God. There is no space. There is no space to conquer, there is no space to go into. God, real, tangible, solid, firm, is all-present. Thus, there is no space! Let us handle this argument that there is space to conquer, space to be explored. There is no space between God and man, and God and man is the one universal being — the being that is both cause and effect. Since God fills all space, where is the patient? Where is this demand that says, "Heal me, please."? Where is this personal body, when God is All-in-all? We must live this Christ attitude — that is, this pure, whole, perfect Love that Christian Science is demonstrating!

Christian Science, through the law of Love, elevates — it never condemns. That is why Mrs. Eddy begins the chapter on "Prayer" in the textbook, with unselfed love. An *unselfed love is* quite different from an *unselfish love,* An unselfed love is the love that has no self. With unselfish love, there are persons involved — someone feels so unselfish because he is doing what he calls loving acts, kind acts for others, wearing himself out, permitting animal magnetism to rob him. But unselfed love is the Love in which there is no self, there is just the Love that is Principle expressing itself

Jesus lived the *agape* love — the love of compassion, the love of pure redemption, the love of restoration, which looks through the offensive act and sees the pure Christ-man. Thus Jesus could say, "Thy sins are forgiven," because the sin was no part of man, the glory of God. When the *agape* love is being experienced, there is nothing to condemn.

This word, *agape,* is one of several Greek words, all of which are translated as "love" in the English version of the Bible. The Greek language has separate words: *philos* to express brotherly love, as the word *Philadelphia; eros* to express romantic love, and so on. But in the original Greek testaments, the word for "love" most often attributed to Jesus, is *agape.* Agape means the love that loves simply because it is love, without respect to persons. It is the love which needs no object, the love that is universal, the love that never loses sight of loveliness. Thus, it was the *agape* love with which Jesus beheld all. So when the *agape* love is being experienced, there is nothing to condemn. The Christ model is seen to be the only model. It is the model from the "Sermon on the Mount;" it is the model from which Jesus beheld the perfect man.

See with this Christ-vision with which Jesus saw constantly. If a sinning mortal appeared to Jesus, he looked through it and saw the model of Love, of God — that is, the Christliness of all being, intact, perfect. We are not seeing mortals. We are not sinning mortals trying to be immortal, or trying to make the old into the new. Nor are we made up of a congregation of persons called Christian Scientists who look at other Christian Scientists, and judge them as to whether or not they are acting up to what they feel is Christian Science. Why do we permit this adulteration? Anything is immoral or adulterous that sees less than pure being! In the Bible, we read, "Blessed are the pure in heart; for they shall see God." To see something less than God and call it man, is to adulterate. Man is God's action; man is God functioning. Jesus said, "Have I been so long time with you, and yet hast thou not known me, Philip? He that hath seen me hath seen the Father." We are alone with our own being and with the reality of things. Then we must never see man as effect. *See God,* cause in being. This "seeing" is man.

Are we elevating the membership of our churches? In the Glossary of the textbook under the definition of CHURCH, Mrs. Eddy writes, "The Church is that institution . . . found elevating the race." *(Science and Health)* Are we critical of one another? Do we permit self-condemnation to suggest itself? To elevate the race is joyful exaltation, joyful acknowledgment and acceptance of the Science of being as present identification. This is elevation. It constitutes self-immolation, unselfed love. In this elevation, we must learn to go unto the mountain, the "Mount of Transfiguration" so to speak. From the mountain, the pettiness of personal sense begins to disappear. We begin to lose all sense of persons, because from the mountain, the light of ever-present Love exalts us, but not emotionally, nor in a mental intoxication.

It exalts us beyond the use of words, beyond phraseology, beyond stereotyped, borrowed speeches. It exalts us into singing. It is the quietness which comes when sense is dumb, and the still, small voice of calm becomes the voice of God, the inward voice saying, "I AM THAT I AM."

As long as we stay on the level of condemnation or personal sense, we have forfeited the Christ-vision which is the only healer. Condemnation is to accept evil on its own basis. It says, "Give me a man," Christian Science does not give evil a man because Christian Science recognizes the only man there is, the expression of God's being, God's own self-reflection. In Christian Science, we are not dealing with material personalities possessing separate, private minds which must be educated in order to have salvation.

In Christian Science, we find that there is but one infinite Mind identifying itself as all the Mind there is. All the man there is, is conscious identity. Nothing is present as personality. What is present is divine Mind expressing itself. Christian Science shows us how to stay on the Mount and look out from the perfect vision that is God. Looking through the eyes of God, spiritual discernment, we see nothing unlike the risen Christ.

In the story of Jacob, we meet the claim of animality and jealousy, plus the attempt to steal the birthright of another. Then the fear comes, and the fear says, "Run!" So Jacob runs into a foreign country. He soon begins to accumulate what are called "goods." But he wants to return home eventually. How can he return home when his brother has threatened to kill him? Perhaps it was necessary for Jacob to have that struggle in order to see that man was never born, that man never dies, and that man's birthright as the son of God is forever intact. When Jacob began to see that he was not a person who had wronged another, that he was not a person to be condemned, that he was not a person to hide; when he saw himself to be the Christ nature of God, then he could say, "The day breaketh."

Yes, "The day breaketh" the moment we acknowledge that man is the son of God, and that man never was a prodigal, never lost his eternal birthright, never fell from the heaven of God's presence. This is to be the *agape* love to oneself. It is not enough to be this *agape* love to what is called "another;" but we must be this Love that is God to ourselves! We are willing to forgive another, and yet too often we are not willing to forgive ourselves. It was necessary in the case of Jacob, that he see his brother's face as if it were the face of God. It was also necessary for Jacob to lift up his own face without spot, to see his own face as the face of God.

Indeed, "The day breaketh," the day of Truth, the day of Love. It will keep breaking until we have the full Noon, the glory of the fullness of God's presence. Let not the evangel go — that is, hold as Jacob held, and declare, "I will not let you go until you have blessed me" — until you see yourself as the Love that is God, as the self-expressing I AM. Stand in awe before your true identification. Then the day no longer breaketh because it is the fullness of light itself. It is the eternal Noon — It knows no sunrise. It knows no sunset. It is the charity that never faileth. "Greater love hath no man than this," to lay down all sense of self so that he might see and be the Love that is God. This is the baptism of Spirit that Mrs. Eddy referred to in "Pond and Purpose" as the "omnipotent act" that "drops the curtain on material man and mortality." *(Miscellaneous Writings)*

When we start out from the standpoint of divine Science, (and there is no other standpoint), our Leader reminds us that we must know the starting point is that God, Spirit, is All-in-all, and there is no other might nor Mind. God is Love, and therefore He is divine Principle—then we know our starting point is correct. Thus what appears to be "another" is really not "another;" it is the Love that is God saying I AM — I AM ALL.

Jesus said, "A new commandment I give unto you, That ye love one another; as I have loved you, that ye also love one another."

Sometimes the Love that is Principle appears stern to personal sense, as in the case of Peter, when Jesus rebuked him. "But when he had turned about and looked on his disciples, he rebuked Peter, saying, Get thee behind me, Satan: for thou savorest not the things that be of God, but the things that be of men." Yet it was this Love that is Principle that was needed in Peter's experience. When this Love met the mob about to stone the woman, what did Jesus do? What did Mary Baker Eddy do with the same woman in the chapter on "Christian Science Practice"? Did they not both speak with the penetrating Christ-Love when they said, "Thy sins are forgiven"? Why? Because *agape* love knows no sin, knows no sinner. We must be this impartial, universal Love. We must abide in that spiritual state that does not fight error as a reality, but confidently allows Love to resolve it. In doing so, we live Christian Science. "Understanding is the line of demarcation between the real and unreal. Spiritual understanding unfolds Mind, — Life, Truth, and Love, — and demonstrates the divine sense, giving the spiritual proof of the universe in Christian Science." *(Science and Health)*

Are we aware that we have this spiritual understanding that is the line of demarcation, or separation, between the Love that is Principle, and the love that is personal? When this spiritual understanding is seen to be the identity of the one and only being — God, man, being one — then the line between reality and unreality is established. Then one is never fooled by appearances, and makes no attempt to treat the unreal, to make it conform to reality, or to make the unreal, real. Unreality cannot be treated to make it a better unreality. The "Scientific Statement of Being" has shown us that matter is unreal and temporal. Then anything that matter presents must be unreal and untrue.

The work of the metaphysician is to see what is reality, and to identify the world with, and as, this reality. As this Truth of being, or reality, is accepted, God and man *one* being, we must turn on the so-called mental assassin that would impose itself as the ego. We must dismiss it as unreal, and not try to treat it. We must see it as the murderer from the beginning — that is, we must see it as that which would deny the infinity of our being, that would deny the eternality of our being. Let us be certain that man has never been less than God being Love itself. We must dismiss the unreal with an abiding conviction that it is unreal.

God does not need a treatment; man exists as God being, so man needs no treatment either. Then this whole picture is nothing, and must be seen as nothing, for there is no God in it, and therefore there is no man in it. The one harmonious being — God, man, one — must be seen as all. Never see man as separated from God even for an instant. See man as God *being*, God in action, God loving, God knowing. This is the only possible way reflection can be experienced.

Let us know we cannot be made to forget that spiritual sense alone testifies to the Truth of our being; that corporeal sense lies and cheats. It cannot tell us the truth, because there is no truth in it. Why listen then to that which would defraud and is wholly dishonest? We cannot be made to believe that there is something present besides God, man, for where man is, God is. So God is all that is, and this is Love, this is Principle.

We know that the starting point of divine Science is that God, Spirit, is All-in-all and there is no other Mind, and this God is Principle, Love. Therefore, man is both lovely and lovable, because man is God being Love. Thus, we must never try to be loving; this denotes personal sense. We must see that the Love that is God is present and cannot be interrupted, cannot be interfered with. Never, under any circumstances, try to make yourself loving, or try to make yourself love someone. Instead, acknowledge that the Love that is divine Principle, the Love that alone is Life, the Love that is Truth, the Love that is Soul — with all of its feeling, with all of its action — this Love is present, and is identifying itself as the only self. This leaves nothing but Love to be experienced.

To have the feeling of Love itself, is to be relaxed, free, noble, grand. To feel happy and comfortable in the presence of what appears as others, is to be the Love that is alone present. Love is always comfortable, peaceful, balanced, calm. Love never tries to heal. Love never loses sight of loveliness, for the Love that is incorporeal, divine, supreme, infinite, sees nothing that cannot be loved. I have seen the most stubborn cases healed when all argument was laid aside.

Reality knows nothing of a personal nature, does not respond to it and does not record it. The procession of false mental pictures — birth, growth, maturity, decay, death — these false mental pictures leave no impression on fundamental consciousness, "The divine understanding reigns, is all, and there is no other consciousness." *(Science and Health)* This procession of false mental pictures, calling themselves waking dreams, sleeping dreams, must be seen as having no identity — not a person, a place, nor a thing. It is simply the way the one negative, carnal, so-called mind is appearing, or suggesting itself. It says 'I' when it is not 'I' at all. The Ego is divine and is constantly identifying itself, its nature, its essence, its wholeness; and this identification is given the term man. See that man is the scientific term for all that God is knowing, being, seeing. Man is not something separate from God. Man is God's consciousness of what God is. God is All, and the consciousness is man.

Nothing exists but God and God's idea. Be certain that you see that this consciousness knows only its present perfection. We must watch gossip. Yes, many of us are wise and alert not to gossip about what we call "another." We know the deadliness *of* having "another." To have another is to have the devil, and it will act like the devil. Mrs. Eddy has said, "Have but one God, and you will have no devil." Let us see that we must not gossip with ourselves, either. We must not gossip with ourselves concerning what we said, what we did, or what we didn't say or didn't do. It is all a form *of* egotism, self-importance, sympathetic mesmerism, all attempting to get us out into the procession.

It was related that Mrs. Eddy once said to her students that we get up in the morning, wash our garments clean, and then go forth into the day, and enter the procession of many. We enter the procession *of* people doing, people not doing. We see ourselves as personal Christian Scientists approving and disapproving, liking those who like what we like, and vote as we vote, but disliking those who do not do things our way. We see people smoking and let false personal sense come in with its self-righteousness. We see people drinking. We see ads on the television telling us to take this or to take that. Then, in a form *of* self-righteousness, we condemn it. But do we really see that it isn't going on at all? No electrical contrivance calling itself television, radio, and the like, can make it real, nor can it leave an impression on us. See that there is only the Soul that is God present, and the Soul that is God is identifying itself in its purity.

LET US STOP MALPRACTICING UPON OUR WORLD. Let us today, wash our garments clean! Wash them clean, and keep them clean. Why this senseless parading? Is it because we do not accept the "Scientific Statement of Being"? It must be. Do we see that we are not persons doing or not doing? Do we understand that the Mind that is infinite, the Mind that is divine, the Mind that is All, is present and expressing itself lawfully, joyously and intelligently?

The human mind claims to be expressing itself through personalities. The divine Mind, reality, is expressing itself through its ever-present Christ. This is the law of refinement, the law of perfection; it is the law of recovery to that which seems to be lost; it is the law of annihilation to that which should be annihilated. It is the law to all — one and all. Let us be sure we see that right where the human so-called mind is depicting us as humans needing to solve problems, right there the divine Mind is expressing itself in its indivisible, universal nature. This is most important because it is the Christ restoration.

In *Science and Health,* we read, "Divine Love always has met and always will meet every human need." *(Science and Health)* We sometimes believe that any seeming need will be met simply by declaring this truth. But the statement says it is divine Love that will meet the need. Then ask yourself — Where is my divine Love? It is divine Love that wipes out the human need. It is this great Love, divine Love, that is so needed today. If we start out from the standpoint of divine Love, not the human need, then the standpoint is correct. Seek ye first divine Love, the kingdom of God, and all shall be added unto you. A human need is simply the absence of Love — that is, the *suggested* absence of Love. So in order to meet the human need, we must see that the Love that is Principle is present, in operation, and that it is specifically felt. This leaves no absence called the human need. But let us see clearly that it is divine Love that meets the need — the Love that is impartial, universal, all-inclusive, not a selfish sense, but all-inclusive. This is what meets the need — Love that is divine Principle,

It is the true sense of *agape* love that is so needed by the world today. This love is not persons trying to be loving, but it is the absence of that which is called personality; it is the absence of that which is called personal sense, that lets the Love that is divine outshine the offensive people around us, outshine that which would be offensive to all. Then we no longer will throw "stones" so-to-speak, at others; but like Jesus, we too can say, "He that is without sin among you, let him first cast a stone," But all are with sin when they see their brother as a personality, or see their brother as something less than God being. The only "stone" there is, is the hardness of heart which refuses to see our brother's face as if it were the face of God.

On page 412 of *Science and Health,* a marginal note says; "Eloquent silence." Beginning at line 13, we read, "The power of Christian Science and divine Love is omnipotent. It is indeed adequate to unclasp the hold and to destroy disease, sin, and death." Then what is this "eloquent silence"? It is the Love that needs no words to say, "I love." The Love that is Principle needs no words. It is expressed in thought and action. The Love that is Principle is so all-inclusive, so universal, it leaves nothing unloved. This pure, divine, all-inclusive Love is light; when it is turned on in the world, the darkness, the personal sense, cannot cling. Darkness does not cling to the things in a room when we turn on the light. So when we turn on the Love that is divine, darkness, hate, resentment, harsh feelings — the stones of personal sense — are dissolved, and leave only the Love that is God, present. Let us see that the Love that is Principle, with its infinite penetration, is all that is present anywhere. And this is universal.

We need to claim our birthright of freedom and our birthright of loveliness. To claim means to demand on the grounds of right; to hold; to be true against implied denial or doubt. We must demand with the birthright of the son of God, with divine authority, that the Love that is Principle is present to be experienced. As long as one is experiencing Life — and that is forever — one must experience Love, because Life and Love are synonymous. Life and Love that is Principle, are inherent in our birthright under divine authority.

In our textbook, Mrs. Eddy gives us this "testimony of Spirit." "I am Spirit. Man, whose senses are spiritual, is my likeness. He reflects the infinite understanding, for I am Infinity. The beauty of holiness, the perfection of being, imperishable glory, — all are Mine, for I am God. I give immortality to man, for I am Truth. I include and impart all bliss, for I am Love. I give life, without beginning and without end, for I am Life. I am supreme and give all, for I am Mind. I am the substance of all, because I AM THAT I AM." It is this infinite understanding, this beauty of holiness, this perfection of being, this impartial, glowing, flowing Love that leaves no dam called "Adam." It leaves no Adam-man called "me" or "you;" only the flowing, loving, knowing straight from Principle. It becomes the substance of all, the action of all, and this is the inheritance that belongs to the son of God.

Acknowledge your birthright here and now, and know that nothing can interfere with that birthright, the birthright of dominion, the birthright of inclusiveness. We must not only claim every quality of God as constituting identity, but we must live these qualities against any attempted denial or doubt. The force of Love that is Principle, Love — here and now — repels every suggestion of the carnal, negative, evil one, and we can say, "Thy will be done," because the will of God is the will of Love. That Love is all that is present to be experienced here, now, everywhere — and always. Let us never be fooled, even for a moment, into believing that there is something present that needs to be eliminated.

LOVE! Love! This is the word that best describes our dear Father-Mother God, and it is the word that best describes man, God's love made manifest. Be this Love! Sing this Love! Rejoice in this Love, because it is the substance of your being. It is your action, it is your blood, it is your digestion, it is your assimilation, it is your very heart-beat, it is the pressure, it is the circulation, it is the temperature! It is everything that means *health,* that means wholeness, that means completeness! In short, as our Leader wrote in the last verse of her poem *LOVE* — "For Love alone is Life; And life most sweet, as heart to heart Speaks kindly when we meet and part." Let us thank God that we are living the Love that is Principle — this undeviating Love, this continuous Love, that is All!

Part II

Students of Christian Science should be obedient to the *Manual of The Mother Church -The First Church* of *Christ,*

Scientist, and learn how to defend themselves against aggressive mental suggestion. Let us declare to aggressive mental suggestion: You, malicious animal magnetism, in the guise of thought, you cannot use this concept called *me or another* to lust with, to fear with, to die with, nor can you discredit Christian Science, its teachings, the office of the Christ. You, malicious animal magnetism, cannot kill this concept through any claim of natural law. This human concept can only be translated with the ideal Christ, reality, and then the misconception disappears naturally, as darkness gives place to light. This translation carries all back into Mind as Mind. This is the Christ man, constituted of Godliness, and purity.

You, animal magnetism in the guise of religion, calling yourself Roman Catholicism, you cannot damn this concept nor keep it in hell, when heaven is the normal experience of man. You, animal magnetism, in the guise of government called "communism" et cetera, cannot manipulate, control, or brain-wash this concept, nor any concept, or interfere with the mental processes called "reasoning;" you cannot use electricity to impart suggestions to brain cells and have them carry out your diabolical schemes. Man has no brain made up of millions of electrical cells. There is no intelligence in matter, and so-called "brain" is just so much non-intelligent matter within the skull! Man, divine idea, functions as the presence of the Christ Mind. It is Mind expressing itself, for Mind is God.

This Christ treatment here and now absolves man, completely and absolutely, from every aggressive mental suggestion. This Christ likeness dispels the silly moths whose flimsy and gaudy pretensions singe their own wings. In this Christ light, this understanding translates the concept called "me", "you", "him", "her", into the ideal man, and can say, "Before Abraham was, I am." Nothing then is left to sin, to suffer, to die. The curtain goes up, and reveals man of the vast forever, man coexisting, man co-eternal, man coextensive with the infinite God that is All; man, never born, never aging; man the glory and the perfection that is being, giving evidence of its own perfection, freedom, and blessing.

You, animal magnetism, cannot pull this curtain down, and upon your screen called human consciousness show a finite me, damned, afraid. You, animal magnetism, cannot argue that there is a physical body calling itself me; you cannot suggest urgency, saying, "Heal me quickly, or I die." Because there is no "me" here but God. This "me" is all right, because it is God being the only me there is; it is Principle being its own idea — this one, universal being, God and man. Nor can you delay healing through the suggestion that this condition is difficult, or that it can not be healed, or that it is incurable. Christian Science healing is metaphysical, not physical. Christian Science heals divinely. Christian Science heals scientifically, not theologically. Christian Science healing is the operation of divine Principle, light, before which darkness is seen to be nothing.

Christian Science treatment does not create health, but Christian Science treatment removes the fear and the misconception, which appear to objectify themselves as false mental pictures, or error. From the starting point of divine Principle, Love, there is no fear. This is more important than to know there is no disease. In *Science and Health,* Mrs. Eddy writes, "If Spirit or the power of divine Love bear witness to the truth, this is the ultimatum, the scientific way, and the healing is instantaneous." On the same page she says, "Always begin your treatment by allaying the fear of patients." In the presence of the Love that is divine, all that fear can do is dissolve. That which seems to have objectified itself is dissolved with it. Then all will conform to the flawless, indestructible spiritual reality. This flawless, functioning presence is the cause of all identity. Man, effect, body, home, business, government, employment — these are all the flawless functioning presence of God, Love. All is Love's immaculate conception, wholly established in its wholeness and completeness; thus nothing is left but heaven being experienced.

It is important to know that there is no fear, because without fear, disease cannot even suggest itself. It is fear that claims to prolong it, that claims to feed it. But when Love is seen to be the only Life there is, the only Mind there is, there is nothing to feed fear. All that is unlawful is fearful. To see that fear is constituted of unlawfulness makes it take on a different meaning. We see then more clearly that it is suggestion, animal magnetism, without presence, without reality. The all-powerful goodness of God, all-inclusive, and man the effect of God's knowing this is the all-power and all-presence. Then there is nothing present to fear nor to be afraid. Man is never a condition of fearing. When animal magnetism suggests fear, simply know that *it is* afraid. *It* has always been afraid — afraid from its beginning, because from the standpoint of Truth, or reality, there is no beginning to be afraid, and there is no ending to be afraid. For all is infinite Mind and its infinite, loving, universal manifestation. Indeed, God is All-in-all.

Sometimes we accept the suggestion that the condition is physical, and this is so subtly malicious that it claims to perpetuate itself through this belief. The suggestion is that the so-called appearance is physical. But it is not physical. It is malicious, vicious animal magnetism. We cannot compromise with this apparent physical belief, that is wholly mental in its maliciousness, because any compromise indicates that we are accepting the suggestion that it is physical, material, and then we are on the level of *materia medica*. If we are on the level of *materia medica*, we come under all the doubt and the fear, as well as the so-called incurability. But the Christian Scientist must understand the scientific fact that so-called disease is not physical; it is malicious animal magnetism. It has no substance. Only in the presence of the glory of Love itself will it disappear into its native nothingness.

You sometimes hear it said that "mortal mind is having a difficult time with its heart." Mortal mind doesn't have a heart. If it had a heart, it would be kind and gentle and loving. So always know it doesn't have a heart to give it so-called "heart trouble." The only heart is the heart of Love, the heart of divinity, the heart of kindness, the heart of Truth. This is man's present heart, and it is always beating with the rhythm of the universe. Let us see that mortal mind, saying "heart," is a liar. It cannot tell the truth about heart, for heart is not a muscle — heart is love, heart is kindness, heart is gentleness. So man has the most perfect heart there is, — the heart of divinity. It is the Father's heart, and man really is this heart of God, being what heart always is — normal, kind, gentle, perfect in its function, perfect in its action.

Mortal mind has no body, because body is infinite. Body is the temple of the living God. So body is your loving, and loving is your body. Then ask yourself, "What kind of body do I have?" The body of Love. Not a body brought about through lust. Not a body that had to be educated, that had to be fed. Body proceeds from principle; it has the blood of innocency, the blood of immaculateness, the blood of infallibility. This is body, and this is heart. Love is the liberator. Love is the law. Love alone is Life. Therefore we are not healing physical, material conditions. We are healing the malicious suggestion that there is a so-called mind apart from God, a mind that knows something besides Love, a mind that is something besides Love. The Mind that is God, is the Mind that is Love, and this Mind is the Mind of man, and man has no mind but God, and therefore man's Mind is Love. So what is called mortal, human, carnal mind is not Mind; it is nothing but evil hypnotic suggestion; it has no body because it is nobody. Then never permit it to say "I", because it is *not "I."*

We must receive the Holy Ghost. What is the Holy Ghost? Is it not light, illumination? We speak of revelation. What is revelation? It is light, illumination. Could we not say that Love means light? For where Love is, there is light, glory, illumination. A face aglow with Love is always a face aglow with light. So let your light, glory, love, so shine that men may see this love, this glory, and glorify the Father, because this glory that cometh from heaven is beyond human countenance, beyond human so-called love. This love, proceeding from and resting upon divine Principle, outshines anything unlike itself. A real Christian Science treatment should not be mere words; it should not be argument. It should be simply the living Love, the glory, the light from this living Love outshining sin, disease and death.

If you must argue in treatment, be sure it is seen that you are arguing with what you call "yourself," and not with a patient. The patient is not somebody over there who thinks he has a disease, or that he is unhappy or uncomfortable. There never has been a patient. There is no patient here, over there, anywhere. The "patient" is evil, hypnotic suggestion, mortal mind, mesmerism. It is neither cause nor effect. There is no patient, no practitioner, no mortal mind to have a private body. God is All, and the allness and oneness of the ever-present God that is Love, eliminates the possibility that there is a patient. All is God *being* All!

Oh, let this Love that is aglow with light outshine what is called objectivity! In your home, in your business, wherever you are, be so unselfed as to let the Love that is Principle shine right straight through what looks like oneself. This was Jesus' great success. He knew that of himself he could do nothing. Mrs. Eddy knew that of herself she could do nothing. It was their ability to *unself* self that enabled them to do their great works!

In I John, we read, "Beloved, now are we the sons of God." That is to say, *now is* all there is to be experienced. Don't defile your being by having a yesterday, and don't adulterate your being by accepting the suggestion that tomorrow something might happen better than today. *Now* infinity is infinite. *Now* Life is eternal. *Now* Mind is all. *Now* Truth is true. *Now* perfection is identifying itself as man. We live in the *now*.

John wrote, *"Now* are we the sons of God . . . and it doth not yet appear. . . ."* That is, to personal sense, now never appears, because personal sense cannot live now. Personal sense must live in its dead past, or it must live in its unborn tomorrow. It has no now in which to live. So to it, it "doth not appear." But to that which knows itself to be the son of God, Love itself, it doth now appear. To live in this NOW is to experience the dominion of which Paul spoke to the Romans. "In all these things we are more than conquerors through him that loved us. For I am persuaded that neither death, nor life, nor angels, nor principalities, nor powers, nor things present, nor things to come, nor height, nor depth, nor any other creature, shall be able to separate us from the love of God."

Nothing can separate us from the eternal Noon. Let us be careful that we do not permit aggressive mental suggestion to rob us of *now*. Love is always now. Love can only live its nowness; and in the presence of this nowness, there is no accuser. The accuser can only stand in the past to accuse us that something happened out there, or to make us afraid that something will happen in the future. The accuser cannot stand in the presence of now. The Red Dragon cannot fight with the Gabriel of His presence, because the Gabriel of His presence is the *nowness* of His ever-presence.

In the Bible, we have the word *now* almost four hundred times. "Now is the day of salvation." Now! Maintain this *now*. It is so easy to get lost in a yesterday, or to anticipate the forest of tomorrow. But now is eternal Noon. NOW is man both lovely and lovable. To maintain the *now will* wipe out the suggestion of delayed healing. There is no matter to be healed. What is called matter is not a substance; it is not a condition. Matter is malicious animal magnetism. Matter is mortal error. Matter is not cause to have an effect. Healing cannot be delayed by the suggestion of tomorrow. There is no material condition. It is pure hypnotic suggestion, and it is handled by picking up the serpent called "yesterday" by its tail and picking up this serpent called "tomorrow," and seeing the nothingness of yesterday and tomorrow. We must so live the *now of* our eternal Noon that the nothingness of the suggestion will appear to us in the light of the ever-present *now* of Love.

There is only *here* and *now.* This Christ understanding makes all conform to the law of perfect action, perfect functioning. Mind is divine, and is the only action. Mind is the action here and now. Therefore Mind is not human, limited, finite, fluctuating. Mind is Principle. There is coexistence of Father and son; there is coincidence of Principle and idea. Then what is called a tumor cannot exist in coincidence. A tumor cannot exist in oneness. The one fact is here and now; and whatever is present called body must remain perfect, free, harmonious. Whatever is unlike it must get out now and forever. Likewise, what is called heart must conform to this *knowing:* that action is divine, and in this coincidence the only fact is the divine action, perfect and glorious. This redeems the human from whatever is offensive. This concept of body must remain until the ascension. Our textbook says that it was the self-same Jesus that appeared. That is, Jesus appeared until the ascension. We must see the utter impossibility of a so-called problem. We must see the infinite possibility of Mind's infinite allness. "Man is the expression of God's being." *(Science and Health)* Therefore *man is God being Love.* Then All is God saying I AM.

Handle the curse of Roman Catholicism daily. But it must be handled with the Love that is Principle. When this is done, there is no fear. It must be handled with such a sense of its nothingness that the knowing nullifies even the claim that there is Roman Catholicism. It is only the Love that is Principle that can really handle this heinous suggestion. Christian Science is the light of ever-present Love, and this light leaves no dark shadows of night. When the sunlight comes into the room in the morning, no shadow of night clings to the plants, the furniture, and the like. So it is with the light of the Christ. It leaves no shadow of fear, ignorance, superstition, black magic, et cetera. Christ leaves only the light of Love, outshining any claim of sin or ignorance.

Roman Catholicism has no head, because the God-head is the only head. Roman Catholicism has no Pope, because the only Pope is the infallibility of the Principle that is Love. Roman Catholicism has no priest, because the only priest is the spiritualized man. It has no church, because church proceeds from and rests upon Principle, Love, and is founded on Truth itself. Romanism has no foundation, because Christ is the foundation of the church. Jesus said, "Upon this rock I will build my church." He was referring to the Rock, the Christ, the Truth concerning all. Roman Catholicism has no medium through which it can operate, because its personality is unmasked in Christian Science, and man's individuality is brought to light. Roman Catholicism has no work to accomplish, because all is already accomplished. God is infinitely satisfied with His own universe. There is no miserable sinner for Roman Catholicism to save. Man is saved. Romanism cannot maintain itself on the fear of hell, because Christian Science shows clearly and definitely that heaven is an ever-present fact of being, and man is the heaven of Love's presence.

Roman Catholicism cannot, through any claim of curse, hypnotic suggestion, or mesmerism, appear on the body as disease, for there is only perfect ease, wholeness, and holiness. It cannot appear as a husband and wife who disagree, for the only husband, the only wife, the only bride, the only bridegroom, is the one universal I AM, saying I AM ALL. Roman Catholicism cannot through suggestion appear as dormant understanding, when man is the Christ-light, the understanding of divine Mind. It cannot appear as disobedient children who have no interest in spiritual light. Nor can it appear to operate through the suggestion of self, because there is no self apart from God! Be alert to the claim that Roman Catholicism can interfere with marriages. Protect your marriage. Protect your marriage by handling Roman Catholicism's curse that we were not married the way Roman Catholicism says it should be done. Handle this! See that your children were not born in sin, but that the only creator is God, and the only son is the son of God. Handle this curse daily, to see that what appears as children cannot be cursed, cannot be made mentally deficient. They cannot be made spiritually dull, nor can they be made disobedient! Romanism can not appear as an unsolvable problem in your experience, nor can it operate through hypnotic suggestion. Christian Science is the operation of the divine Principle, Love, and permits no problem to assert itself

Know that this treatment, given from the basis of divine Love, can only appear as great enlightenment, wisdom, love, refreshment. This treatment cannot be reversed by any suggestion. This treatment is not person-to-person. This treatment is the Holy Ghost, and it appears at this moment as the light of the world. Romanism cannot appear as doubt or fear, to mortally assassinate this treatment, or this spiritual *knowing*. When fear or doubt seems to appear, instantly declare: "I know thee for what thou art; now go back to your father, the devil, and tell him that you are a liar and the father of your own lies!"

Thus Roman Catholicism is seen to be only a corrupt political organization, and not something to fear, and not something to be prayed over. It must be seen for what it is—NOTHING! It has no organization, it has no adhesion, it has no cohesion. Be alert to its claim that it can interfere with your metaphysical work. See that it cannot project its delusions. See that its so-called blessings are all worthless and cannot be projected, because of the omnipresence and the omnipotence of divine Love. It is the understanding of Love's Allness, Love's indivisibility, Love's oneness, that wipes out any claim of a curse. What is called body should appear pure, wholesome, and clean.

Understand, we do not fear Roman Catholicism. We know it for what it is, and it cannot dominate, it cannot control. It cannot act as the President of these United States, because the presidency is established by the Constitution and the President is not a person. The President is not a place. The President is the consciousness, the whole knowing, the combined knowing, of the United States, the States united in one, and one in all. Therefore the light of this treatment eliminates, and completely obliterates, any claim that Roman Catholicism could be a President, or that it could in any way get us into difficulty or bring crises to us. Roman Catholicism cannot act. It cannot project itself. The President of these United States is really the Christ-consciousness, and it is this Christ-consciousness that cannot be invaded. It cannot be manipulated. It cannot be made to make an unwise decision. The Christ-consciousness, the only consciousness there is, is Principle's own self in operation. This is our President, this is our Congress, this is our Supreme Court, and this is the Government of every state in these United States! It is all-inclusive. It takes in every country; it takes in every hamlet. It leaves nothing out. It takes the cup of Christ to all!

Mrs. Eddy once said, "God told Moses to handle the serpent. But Moses said, 'There isn't any serpent. Where is the serpent?... Then Mrs. Eddy continued, "Handle it." Aren't some of us, as Moses, saying, "There isn't any serpent"? But God commanded Moses to handle error, and when he had handled it, he could say there wasn't any. Why? Because he had translated it into spiritual reality, making the seeming into the being.

Now be certain *you see* what you handle. You handle it as nothing. Then keep it nothing. Daily handle its claim of curse. You handle it by living the Love that is light. You handle it completely. You nullify it by Love. Therefore, when any suggestion of hate or resentment or fear or uncertainty comes, instantly say to it, "I know you for what you are; go back from whence you came; you are the devil, the liar, NOTHING!! And the light of ever-present Love obliterates you, and leaves only the functioning Christ, the light of the world!" This is giving the cup of cold water to all!

This treatment is scientific knowing. It is the spiritual understanding, the healing power, the power of the Word felt. It is Love living and knowing. It knows: I AM wonderful, the Father's daily delight.

The question is often asked, "Why are we not healing the cases we should?" To this question Mrs. Eddy replied, "It is because you do not understand how to handle animal magnetism." Mrs. Eddy says the specific term for error or mortal mind is animal magnetism. The specific term for all evil, whether it claims to be personal or impersonal, is animal magnetism. We have a chapter in our textbook that unmasks animal magnetism. It shows that it is not a person, a place or a thing, but is hypnotism or mesmerism. Hypnotism or mesmerism needs a personal mind through which to operate. So animal magnetism has no basis when it is seen that the "I" is God, and that man has no "I" but God!

Mr. Edward Kimball told of a woman who came into his office needing help because she believed she had feathers on her arms. He knew there were no feathers, but the aggressive mental suggestion had her see and feel feathers where there were no feathers. So we do not treat the feathers. We treat the patient for the belief that there is a private ego or mind that can have such delusions.

It is very important for us to see that there is no personal mind to hypnotize, or to be hypnotized. Mind is God, and there is no separation between Mind and what Mind knows, between Mind and what Mind sees. Therefore we must learn how to handle animal magnetism. To handle animal magnetism means, in everyday language, to *realize* that divine Love is all-presence and all-power, the only activity. To see divine Love, right where animal magnetism seems to be, brings the deflection into proper view. Love is the only presence, the only power, the only Mind or Life there is. Then we are to look through the mask that animal magnetism presents, and see divine Love. It is then that we feel the immensity and the ever-presence of Love, filling all space. What you have called animal magnetism thus vanishes, and all that is left to be experienced is the Love, that is divine Principle.

Mary Baker Eddy writes of angels entertained unawares. However, the treatment makes us entertain the angels *aware,* for we find in our Leader's *Message for* 1902, "A danger besets thy path? — a spiritual behest, in reversion, awaits you." This deflection, rightly viewed, will make every experience a Mind experience. Mass mesmerism or malpractice claims to be our experience until we handle animal magnetism from the divine standpoint, and then we have peace, because we have disarmed it. We see that if any action is going on at all, the action is God's Love-action. If it is going on at all, it is Mind, Love, identifying itself. The substance is Love. It then ceases to be delusion or illusion. As Jacob said, "I will not let thee go, except thou bless me." Divine Mind is All-in-all, and we must make every experience, every situation, every happening declare for God, divine Love. When we look it straight in the face, we can say to any happening, "If you are real, if you are true, then you have the magnificence of Love; if you have any action, then it is Love-action; if you have any life, then it is Love-Life." In other words, make every experience declare God, Love — divine Principle!

Where man is, God is. Then all that is present is God being Father-Mother, All-harmonious! What God is being Father to, is the son or man. We must not deal with animal magnetism as an entity having identity. When we make every situation reveal Love, then the offensive act ceases to be offensive, but becomes loving and kind. The dying man ceases to die, because Love alone is Life. The disease seems to lose its destructive activity, and Love is all that is present, saying; I am hale, whole, and hearty." Love then becomes our All-in-all, and we are lost in the eminence of this one divine presence. In this Christ-knowing, every case will be healed, no matter what the claim, no matter what the name or label. Our Leader says, "The use of a lie is that it unwittingly confirms Truth." (*Unity of Good*) Therefore, animal magnetism must be made to bring forth Love, all-power, all-presence, spontaneously expressing itself. See that this Love is all-penetrating, is all-inclusive, and leaves nothing out. Thus it is present in all its purity, to be experienced as conscious identity, or man.

Love is impartial in its adaptations and bestowals. It is unselfish, because it includes all. By making everything declare Love because Love is All, we find All is infinite Love and its infinite manifestation. We find Love indeed is All-in-all. What is called "oneself" is divine Mind expressing its own infinite identification, not a person with a mind. No! God is infinite Mind. Man has no mind but that of God. There is no personal, or private so-called mind.

Daniel did not look at lions and change them into divine ideas. Daniel did not consider himself to be a person. Daniel knew himself to be the functioning of the presence of the Love that is God. He knew all that could appear as his experience was Love loving. Let the King believe there were ferocious lions. That did not change the basic fact as Daniel saw it — Love was all there is or was to the King, and Love is all there is or was to the lions, This is why Daniel could say to the King, "Oh King, live forever." Because Love is All. Was not this what happened to the boys in the fiery furnace? They made the fire bring forth the presence of Love. So, in this purifying Love, there was no flesh to be dissolved; there was no flesh to be burned; there was nothing carnal to objectify itself, there was simply Love experiencing its own loveliness.

Is this not what Joseph did? Certainly Joseph had every reason to permit carnality or animal magnetism to seem real. But Joseph saw only the Love that is God present to be experienced, whether he was sold into slavery, imprisoned, or maligned by Potiphar's wife — it was of no importance. He had but one thing to do, and that was to witness to the presence of the Love that is Principle. That is what Jacob finally did also. He saw his brother's face as if it were the face of God, and the evangel said, "Love is all."

On the cross, Jesus said, "Father, forgive them, for they know not what they do." Jesus, living the Christ — that is, witnessing to the Love that is God — knew no crucifixion; he knew no death. He didn't rise from the dead, because he had never been born to die. He said, "Before Abraham was, I am." Yes, this seemed to restore what is called life, but Life had never died to be restored. Jesus knew himself to be the Principle that is Love. Jesus was not a person forgiving persons; Jesus was not a person living the Christ. Jesus *lived* the Christ, and there was no personal Jesus. There was no Jesus to limit him. There was no Jesus to act or react. There was simply the Love that is Principle being experienced and identified as the being of all. That is why Jesus could say with such certainty that they may be one, even as "we are one." He knew the oneness of all being. He had nothing out there to forgive. He had nothing out there to hate, because he knew the motivating power of Life to be Love, God.

Thus it is, that this Love must wrap all, embrace all. Put the garment of Love upon everything you see or meet or hear. Then we can experience what Mrs. Eddy tells us, "Man is the climax of creation; and God is not without an ever-present witness, testifying of Himself." (*No and Yes*) Man is the climax of Love in being. Man is the floodtide of Love. Love is divine Principle.

What about Mary Baker Eddy? Did Mrs. Eddy live as a person telling the Truth to the world? Or did she say, "Of myself I can do nothing?" When Mrs. Eddy asked those in her class if they loved her and they said "yes!", she said- "No, love and include me, but don't love me." She meant don't love the personal sense. Make what looks like the person bring forth Love's presence. She was not fooled by animal magnetism. She knew it, she unmasked it. In other words, she unmasked that which was called Mary Baker Eddy. She did not permit Mary Baker Eddy to be the avenue through which God worked, but she saw the nothingness of the flesh. She saw the nothingness of incarnate error. Living the Christ identity, Mrs. Eddy could say to the world (not as Mary Baker Eddy but as the Christ nature of God):" Follow your Leader only so far as she follows Christ." (*Message of 1901*) It was this precious Leader, Mary Baker Eddy, who was prepared to lay her earthly all on the altar of Divine Science, and who could later write of Christ Jesus, "To carry out his holy purpose, he must be oblivious of human self." (*Miscellaneous Writings*)

Thus it is with us. We must be oblivious of any personal self that wants to love or be loved. All must see that the Love that is Principle is present and identifying itself. This Love brings comfort, it brings peace, it brings home, it brings companionship, it brings abundance, and it brings food. Never leave it in the appearance. Always take it back, clothe it in Love, and see that right here is the Love that is God, saying I Am. Then one sees that all there is to what is called oneself is I AM THAT I AM.

Let this Love that is impartial, this Love that is universal, so flood our homes, or government, that the Love that is Principle, is seen to be All-in-all. Let us feel this Love. Let us feel it permanently, consciously, eternally, infinitely. For this Love that is Principle, leaves no personal ego to say "I." It leaves only the I that is Principle—present to say I AM.

A group of us were talking about the Bible story concerning the Shepherd who left the ninety and nine, and went after the one lost sheep. Someone asked the question, "What were the ninety and nine doing? Were they gossiping about the one that had left the fold?" The Master Shepherd went after the one. Now what were the ninety-nine doing? The ninety-nine were knowing that *one* had never been divided into a hundred parts. The ninety-nine were knowing that there is no ninety-nine, that there is only one, indivisible, adorable One, and this One identifying itself multifariously, and that there had never been a lost sheep. This parable is given to us to show us the One always remains One!

Make every experience reveal God, Love, because there can be only God, Love. Man is what God is loving, what God is being, what God is knowing. Watch carefully on this point, because suggestion would tempt you to believe that there is something operating as your experience besides the Mind that is Principle. Man has no mind but God. The Mind of Love is the Mind of man. Insist on this "in season and out of season." Let nothing else abide with you as Mind but this one divine Love, filling all space, leaving no room for aught but itself. Only God, infinite Love, is All, and this governs, controls, identifies, because it is All. The grandest, safest, wisest way is to make everything reveal the love of God, and then it ceases to be afflictive, it ceases to be frightening, because it is God saying I AM. The action is God, the functioning is God, the movement is God. All is God — circulation, temperature, everything is God — pressure is God, everything concerning the body is God, because it is all going on in Mind, as Mind, and nothing else is present to function, to act, or to be acted upon.

This is the law to your experience. It is the law to every happening. Be the law, so that nothing can misinterpret what is going on. Let the divine Principle interpret itself. This true interpretation is the Father saying, "This is my beloved son, in whom I am well pleased." The Love that is all-penetrating, all-inclusive, this Love becomes the Love that is you and me. Rest in this. Live in it. Rejoice in it. Make everything reveal God. God is All, declaring Himself to be the God of All. This is what I AM, this is what I have always been — the delightfulness of my Father-Mother God. This is the only day there ever has been — the day in which Love alone is Life.

Part III

All there is to what you call "yourself" is God being Himself, or cause being effect. This is the I that is God being I AM. Therefore, I cannot give my glory to another because there is no "another." The glory that is God as cause is the glory that is man as effect. Man is the effect of God's glory, so all there is to yourself is the glory of God. This glory cannot age, because this glory knows no time. This glory cannot fear, because this glory is Love's substance. This glory cannot be born, because this glory is Life's eternality. This glory cannot sin because this glory is the immaculateness, the infallibility of Principle. This glory cannot err because it has the substance of truthfulness. The glory of God can only love and be loved, because *Love is* All.

Acknowledge this to be your one and only self, the glory of God. Live this glory of God. Radiate this glory of God, and this is to be the temple of the living God. Acknowledge yourself to be now, here, the glory of God, and nothing inglorious can touch it. Nothing, therefore, that could make a lie could attach itself to the glory of God. See man, divine idea, as the presence, the very functioning, the activity of the glory of God. Seeing thus, is to have the experience of generic, preexistent, eternal nature. "Dwelling in light, I can see only the brightness of my own glory." Acknowledge and live this glory, for it is conscious identity.

Mrs. Eddy is quoted as having said, "There is one way through, and only one, and this is to become unselfed." It is interesting, too, that the very first sentence of our textbook, in the chapter on "Prayer", says this, "The prayer that reforms the sinner and heals the sick is an absolute faith that all things are possible to God, — a spiritual understanding of Him, an unselfed love." An unselfed love starts out from the divine Principle, Love itself. It is impartial in its adaptations and bestowals. Therefore unselfed love is the need of everyone. To be unselfed love, we must always start out from Principle, Love itself. See that effect, man, cannot testify of himself. Effect is always testifying to God. Effect, reflection, is not loving. Effect is simply testifying to the great spiritual fact that God is Love, and therefore Principle.

To be truly unselfed is never to be the patient, but to be always the Christ-consciousness or practitioner. Frequently we become the malpractitioner to ourselves, by accepting the satanic suggestion that it is our own condition, Then we treat it as if it were part of us, or on us, or in us, or in some way connected to us — that is, that we are involved with it. But be the practitioner, the Christ-consciousness, the Holy Ghost, and every effect will immediately declare: I AM THAT I AM. This is the one way of being unselfed.

To unself oneself is the whole purpose of Christian Science. Every idea that appears in the line of creation is unselfed love. The Bible says, "In the beginning God . . ." Every thought begins with God, the All-in-all. It emanates from Him as His glory, His perfection, His freedom. All is God being, because effect, to be oneself, must have nothing of itself, but must be the self that is God being itself. This is to be unselfed. The drop of water becomes one with the ocean the moment it touches the ocean. It ceases to be the drop, and becomes the surge and the power of the ocean. So when we drop the personal sense of ego into the infinite ocean of Love, all the characteristics, the qualities, the attributes that constitute Deity, constitute man. This is to unself self. In our textbook, we read, "The starting-point of divine Science is that God, Spirit, is All-in-all, and that there is no other might nor Mind, — that God is Love, and therefore He is divine Principle." Admitting that God, Principle, is alone present and operating, permits one to solve what appears to be the problem.

Let us never personalize evil. To personalize it is to make it difficult to handle. Watch unceasingly on this point. Satanic suggestion tries to get us to give it a name, to make it a place, or even a thing, or to say it is a person. It calls itself sickness, or accident, or a hurricane, whereas it is nothing but the claim of malicious animal magnetism, hypnotism or mesmerism. Evil is always saying, "Give me a man." It has no man, because all man is divine, all man is eternal, incorporeal, universal. Man is as impersonal as God, Principle itself, because man is the activity of the Principle that is Love. Watch carefully to see that evil is not person. It is not over there, not a group of people over there. It is not an organization over there, or a government over there. It is always right here, claiming to operate as our current mind. Suggestion claims to operate as our own consciousness and have us see it as person, place or thing. It even claims to be multiplied. But we must refuse to have many, — many patients, many problems, many races. It is always the one evil suggestion itself. That is where "alertness to duty" comes in. We must not be made to forget nor to neglect our duty to God, to our Leader and to mankind, but know there are not many patients waiting to be healed. There is but *one* patient, and that is the one evil, hypnotic suggestion, appearing in many guises, many races, many forms or bodies, and so on.

In order to heal with the Christ power, we must see evil for what it is not, no thing, no body — because of the indivisibility and the allness and the oneness of God. Our duty to our Leader is to see the revelation in its absolute clarity, Mrs. Eddy writes in *Retrospection and Introspection,* "Whatever. . . divides Being into beings, — is a misstatement of the unerring divine Principle of Science, which interrupts the meaning of the omnipotence, omniscience, and omnipresence of Spirit, and is of human instead of divine origin." So it is not scientific to divide what is called evil, mortal mind, into "many." If we accept the concept of "many", multitudes, and try then to heal them, we momentarily will have left our Science of being for shadow chasing.

Mrs. Eddy tells us in *Miscellaneous Writings,* "The noblest work of God is man in the image of his Maker; the last infirmity of evil is so-called man, swayed by the maelstrom of human passions, elbowing the concepts of his own creating." Here our Leader says that we "elbow" our own concepts. But never be made to forget that the oneness and allness of the Christ is the healer to the satanic suggestion of "many." There are not many. Even as there is but one God, one man, so there is but one claim of evil and its claim of a mortal man.

We know well the By-law in *The Mother Church Manual,* Article VIII, Section 6; "Alertness to Duty. It shall be the duty of every member of this Church to defend himself daily against aggressive mental suggestion, and not be made to forget nor to neglect his duty to God, to his Leader, and to mankind. By his works he shall be judged, — and justified or condemned."

Every student must be obedient to this By-law. It takes unselfed love to be alert to handle apparent evil in the guise of laziness, fear, superstition, apathy, inanity. As long as we can be made to believe that evil is person, place or thing, we are not able to help, to heal or be healed. The moment we see that tuberculosis is not disease, see that cancer is not rebellious cells, that diabetes is not organic, that heart trouble is not muscles, that the drunkard is not personality, that the hurricane is not wind and rain, that the earthquake is not a troubled earth, the thief is not a person, *then* we can heal instantly, because we have impersonalized suggestion and have seen that it is nothing more than the so-called activity of mortal mind — hypnotism or mesmerism. As Mrs. Eddy has stated, animal magnetism has been *unmasked.* Some students use the term "mortal mind" as if it were a mind apart from God. But our Leader says *mortal mind, hypnotism or mesmerism!* Then mesmerism is not mind; mesmerism is the absence of mind. Let us therefore, see that there is no mind to hypnotize, to mesmerize or to be mesmerized. We must know there is only *one* Mind, God!

The practitioner loses his ability to heal or to help when he or she personalizes the suggestion, wonders what it is, what its name is, or what a doctor would say about it. This is all there is to the so-called activity of malicious animal magnetism. It is Jesuitic deviltry, claiming to operate through manipulation, brainwashing, and the like. The alert student cannot be made to forget that the only Mind present to operate is divine, and this divine Mind is the present Mind of man. Love is the way. The greatest love is to see the impersonality of the claim, and the impossibility of it from the standpoint of revelation.

Many students, if not alert, are made apathetic. They say the Lesson Sermon is dull; they seem to get nothing from it. But do they see that animal magnetism is trying to preserve itself, trying to maintain itself by such arguments? Do they really see that at this point they are being made to forget? The Bible Lessons, of the *Christian Science Quarterly,* are especially significant on the subjects of: "Ancient and Modem Necromancy, alias Mesmerism and Hypnotism, Denounced", "Everlasting Punishment", "Probation After Death", and others. These Lessons must be carefully studied because they are exposing Romanism, Communism, and the general belief that claims to act as mentality.

When you find yourself apathetic or dull, *declare* instantly: You, animal magnetism in the guise of thought, cannot dull the apprehension of Christliness; you cannot dull the brilliance of what I AM; you cannot interfere with the clarity of the Christ power that I AM. Handle this apathy. As our Leader says, if necessary "insist vehemently upon the great fact. . ." (*Science and Health*)

When students permit this dullness, this apathy, to come in, it seems to be the first step toward separating us, or bringing apostasy. Watch this carefully. See that Mind is unerringly present to express its own directness, controlling all, seeing all. We see clearly the impossibility of matter, from the standpoint of the first sentence of the "Scientific Statement of Being." This leaves only the divine Mind in its unerring direction to be the experience, to be the Life, the intelligence, the substance, the Truth of All. It leaves only God present, Love in all its power, glory, freedom and being. Let us acknowledge and see our one and only identification from this standpoint of Love itself. Love that is Principle does not permit us to have "another." There is no "another" anywhere. It is all God experiencing what God is. *Unselfed* love does not have another. Unselfish love does "seem" to have another, with which it is unselfish. *Unselfed* love permits nothing but Love, Principle, Life, Soul to say *I* AM THAT I AM.

As Paul once said, "By Thy grace, I am what I am." True love for the Cause of Christian Science will not permit us to be made to forget nor to neglect our duty. We cannot be made to commit an act foreign to the natural inclinations. The Christ is the remedy here, and let us, with this great Love that is Principle, include all mankind. Then there is no malicious mind to operate as malpractice. Love for what Christian Science is doing and has done for all, will make students ever more alert. Our daily defense is our alertness to see that there is no private mind to manipulate or to be manipulated, to mesmerize or to be mesmerized, no private mind to be made to forget. Your work will show forth your alertness. Love is the way and Love is the liberator. Love gives us this daily defense. We must make the most of it by being alert.

Never be fooled into handling effect in your daily work and practice, but always see that there is but *one* Mind, even God, present to manifest itself lovingly. We are not dealing with a patient. We are dealing with the hypnotic suggestion that Mind is not all, and that there is something besides the goodness and love of Mind to be experienced as identity. This is a lie, a fraud. There is nothing present but God, good, the all-power and the all-presence. All there is to be experienced is this Godliness. Then let us leave the basis of belief of a practitioner here, a patient there, and let's unite with the one Mind, and bring out God's unerring direction. This is to have unselfed love, which is true prayer.

The false sense of the human seems to have us try to become the sons of God, rather than to simply live the revelation that man is the son of God. Don't try to pull yourself up by your own bootstraps — that is, don't try to make yourself loving, to try to make yourself kind. It is impossible, for man is Love in being. Man doesn't need to be made loving; man is loving. As long as we seem to accept the suggestion that we are mortals, we seem to grapple with spiritual facts. Let us not grapple any more. Let us not fight. But let us relax into what man divinely is. Drop the tenseness of trying for the relaxation of acknowledgment. Your environment is the infinite God-consciousness, and this is present to your sight and sense here and now. All there is to what I call "myself" is God being Himself, and He is all right, therefore I am all right. There is no doubt concerning it, because man is divine Mind's identification.

Let's look now, for a moment, at this statement from *Science and Health*. It says, "Jesus aided in reconciling man to God by giving man a truer sense of Love, the divine Principle of Jesus' teachings, and this truer sense of Love redeems man from the law of matter, sin, and death by the law of Spirit, — the law of divine Love." The true sense of Love — that is, this unselfed Love—redeems man from the suggestion of being person or personal, and permits man to function as divine idea, the direct functioning presence of Love, Principle itself. This truer sense of Love, the divine Principle of Jesus' teaching, is the law of Spirit, the law of divine Love.

When something is in the pawnshop, we pay the necessary amount to get the article out. This is called redeeming — that is, the article is freed. The Christ redeems us from the personal sense of self. We have paid the price for this redemption by giving up the personal sense — that is, the sense of a personal self with its restrictions and limitations. This redemption through divine Love frees every action, movement, function, and faculty from the satanic suggestion of material organs. When we believe that organs have anything to do with life, we have put ourselves in the pawnshop, and the Judaic concept of an eye for an eye will demand the utmost farthing. But let us keep our concept of self out of the pawnshop of personal sense, so that we do not have to keep going back to redeem it day after day. Let us redeem it once and for all by seeing that it is nothing but satanic suggestion that says we are material persons, that we did or we didn't do, that we said or we didn't say, or that we loved or we didn't love. Let us redeem ourselves here and now and forever by acknowledging that the Christ is the identity of all. Then when the "prince of this world" comes and says "I", we immediately see that we have been redeemed by the Christ. Therefore we do not act or react to the so-called "prince" of this world, and it finds nothing in us, because we are not in the pawnshop any longer. So we do not have to pay the price. For the true sense of Love, the true sense of I AM has redeemed us from the personal sense of "I." This redemption, as Love, never loses sight of loveliness. Hence, it sees nothing to redeem or to be redeemed. When the full redemption has taken place, only Love is present, reflecting Love. This is to have that unselfed love that heals instantly. Human morality, human will, human so-called right thinking cannot act to help in this law of redemption. Jesus gave us the true sense of love, and it is this true sense of love from Jesus' teachings, and Mary Baker Eddy's revelation, that redeems us. This marvelous redemption redeems all. This is *scientific* redemption.

We must be careful not to use Christian Science to change darkness into light, or to change what is called a bad physical condition into a good one. We must see that Christian Science is the revelation of that which is true now. Christian Science must be lived; it must be loved. Christian Science is not a poultice to be applied. Christian Science is to be practiced and lived. This living, this practice, this loving, is the Christ activity. We must be sure that we are not in the realm of physical healing. To accept the suggestion that we are in the realm of physical healing is to have the inept, incurability of medical mesmerism come upon us. Christian Science heals *metaphysically*. It shows that there is no mind but God. Man's being is, was, and ever will be in this Mind. There is no mortal mind to have a mortal body.

Christian Science is the most glorious thing that ever happened to what is called the human being. It shows us what God is and what man is. This is heaven here and now. Man is simply the term for all that God is being, the expression of God's being, the reflection of God. The reflection gives back everything that the original has, is, or can be. Nothing is withheld. There is no personal man. Man is generic. Get used to being generic man. Whenever something knowable, something grand, something glorious, is being done, or said, or heard, or seen, it is always the one I. It is the one I, God, being what I AM, doing it all.

Generic man does not permit identity to be here, and not there. Man is the infinite expression of infinite Mind. Acknowledging and living generic man permits one to live unlocalized. It permits one to experience infinity, without going or coming. This is to experience the universe of Love. See that man has never been present as personality. When alleged crimes seem to happen, always think: Not guilty! — for man is never guilty, for man is God's expression of His own purity, His own innocence. Always maintain your innocence to be generic, universal, everywhere present. This is to be the Father's full reflection. Acknowledge your generic nature. This brings with it such a sense of Love, universal Love, that we need not stand in awe of it, because identity is the loving of the Love that is God.

We should look deep into realism, and see even deeper into the "Scientific Statement of Being." If we accept the first sentence of this statement of being as the revelation of Truth here and now, there is no personal sense to contend with. There is no myth mind to have a myth body, because right where the human concept seems to be, the Life that is divine, the intelligence, the primal quality of Mind, the substance, the very being of God, is present; and this feeling, this knowing, this being, is identification. Now can we not see why Jesus could say, "He that hath seen me hath seen the Father"? It is always I seeing what I AM, being what I AM, knowing what I AM. Then everything concerning this myth mind must be mythological, deceptive. There is no such mind. There is no such body. The revelation of the "Scientific Statement of Being" is that there is no objectified identity, no objectified man — all is subjective being. This simply means that all exists in and of Mind itself. There is nothing outside of Mind that Mind can take cognizance of. Mind knows all, and this knowing *reflected, is* man.

Why does it seem so difficult to let go the personal sense of self? Is it not because we have become accustomed to thinking of it as identity? Yes, this is the reason. It is only as we have the unselfed Love that is God that we wipe out the selfishness that wants to pray all the time for itself — afraid that it might die, afraid that it is alone. To have the unselfed love that is God, divine Principle, is to have no self, no sense of self apart from God. It is where the drop of water ceases to be the drop and becomes the power and the glory of Love itself! It is where the pane of glass is dissolved, and no medium, no avenue, no channel is permitted. It is Love directly expressing and experiencing itself. Man has never been separated from God. If someone believes himself to be a sinner, show him the immaculateness of his true being. If someone believes himself to be old and unwanted, show him that he has never left heaven for a mess of pottage. We can rejoice because of this message of Christian Science. It is radiant with light. It is so tender, and so gentle it excludes nothing. It takes all in from the blade of grass to a star.

Never be self-centered. Never permit your love not to see the seeming anguish of another, and supply the need by knowing that right where it stands is holy ground. This is love. This is the Love that Jesus knew so well — the Love that is divine Principle. This is the Love that Mary Baker

Eddy knew so well. It is the universal Love. It is the Love that is "looking deep" into reality. Look deeper into reality all the time. Think, "Father, Love, All," for nothing else is here but the Love of God being felt. Love, Life, Truth, are ever-present to be experienced as identity. This Love, this feeling, this Love flowing from the throne of God, leaves nothing unlovely. It goes to every part of the body, making it every whit whole, as body means universe, body means infinity, body means consciousness.

In *Miscellany,* our Leader has written, "The little that I have accomplished has all been done through love, — self-forgetful, patient, unfaltering tenderness." All there is to what you call yourself is God being — God or cause being effect. This is why I can of mine own self do nothing, and this is why I cannot give my glory to another. The glory that is God, is the glory that is man. Man is the effect of God's glory in being. Man is the effect of Soul attributing. Man is the effect of Life and its vitality. Man is the effect of God being — God!

Sometimes we are not clear on the words *know* and *think.* The dictionary says that *know* is, "In possession of information; to identify; to acquaint with; to be skilled in; to understand." Now God is All-knowing. Therefore man has no need to think. Reflection cannot think. Reflection is *knowing.* The word *think* is defined in the dictionary as, "To think about; to ponder over; to take into consideration; to recollect." Man cannot think with the Mind of God. Man is the functioning of the Mind that is God. As long as we think we are persons, we must think, because it is natural to that state of thought. Once one finds oneself to be divine idea, at that point one stops thinking — one is no longer required to think — one is no longer permitted to think, because *knowing* is the natural state of man. Then let us leave the basis of belief that we are thinkers, and let us unite with the one Mind, and let Mind express itself, reveal itself.

Ask yourself many times during the day, Am I thinking? Or is Mind expressing itself? If you find yourself thinking, correct it, and know that nothing sitting in a chair can think. Mind is present and expressing itself, and this might seem to appear as what the world calls thinking, but the alert student is never fooled. He knows it is not thinking. He knows Mind is intelligently self-expressing, and this is knowing!

In Christian Science, we are not followers of anyone. In Christian Science, we live the Christ. In Christian Science, we do not follow persons because we are not persons to follow persons! When we speak of following our Leader, Mary Baker Eddy, we do not mean we follow her person. We follow the Christ teachings that she has so clearly given us. Mrs. Eddy says, "The Christian Scientist is alone with his own being and with the reality of things." (*Message of 1901*) If someone sees us as person, corporeal and finite, we are not responsible for what he or she sees. But we are responsible to "see" that we have never followed any person. This teaching cannot be compared; it is incomparable, because it is proceeding straight from divine Principle, Love. Paul said, "Now this I say, that every one of you saith, I am of Paul; and I of Apollos; and I of Cephas; and I of Christ. Is Christ divided?" If we accept that there are different kinds of teaching in Christian Science, with which we agree or disagree, we sap the movement of its vitality! Let us never do this ignorantly or maliciously. We should embrace the Christian Science movement in the only *one* true teaching, the one Teacher, and feel so keenly that this teaching embraces all, that the movement is this teaching made manifest! This love of the teaching will dissolve any misinterpretation or misconception. We must be certain that we never add fuel to the argument that there are different kinds of teaching. Christian Science is absolute. It is final. It cannot be diluted by whatever false theology would say. Christian Science must be practiced from the standpoint of its absoluteness. Never forget that Christian Science is the Science of Love, and this Love must be felt as conscious identity. The Love that is Principle is never cold or harsh. This Love is exact. Love is final. Love is orderly, always sparkling, shining, scintillating, kind, and gentle.

Thus we must drench everything that appears as consciousness with this Love, and remember that there is nothing objectified here in our universe. All is subjectivity. It is Love that is Principle saying I AM, and being this generic Love, is all that constitutes church, family, neighbor, friend, and so on. Sometimes it seems too difficult for some students to see that what appears as home, friend, church, work, is one's own conscious identity. It is not outside. If it is seen that the tree, the flower, the bird, the earth, the church, the universe, the friend, the teacher, are all subjective, then we are experiencing our generic nature. Then we love spontaneously everything that appears.

Mrs. Eddy has given the world a great example of how to lay aside the human sense of self. She has said of Jesus, "To carry out his holy purpose, he must be oblivious of human self." (*Miscellaneous Writings*) Throughout all her writings, she shows us how to get the human self out of the way, in order that the divine reality might express itself effortlessly and without any mediumship. It was our Leader's great ability to get personal sense out of the way that made her the great Discoverer to the world. This was her gift to humanity.

In the First Series of *We Knew Mary Baker Eddy*, we read, "The verse on page 39 of this poem, 'Christ and Christmas,' shows our Leader's utter realization that the human self was not a factor in her writing, but, rather, that it was set aside that the revealed Science of Christianity might freely flow. This stanza reads as follows:

> As in blest Palestina 's hour,
> > So in our age,
> 'Tis the same hand unfolds His power,
> > And writes the page.

Again, in this same First Series, we find a student asking Mrs. Eddy about a metaphysical statement that had been made by a Christian Science worker of some prominence at the time. The student told Mrs. Eddy, "I could not reconcile the thought to my own understanding of metaphysics... was I right in refusing to accept it?" Mrs. Eddy replied, "Your own interpretation is entirely correct, and in this connection I want to impress upon you one fact: no matter how exalted a position a Christian Scientist may occupy in the movement, never accept what he may say as valid unless you can verify the statement in our textbook, *Science and Health with Key to the Scriptures.*" Of course this is true. The textbook is our authority for teaching. The textbook says that, "The woman in the Apocalypse symbolizes generic man." Now generic man means the universality of man, the infinity of man, the indivisibility of man — man the full, infinite manifestation of infinite Mind. Therefore all is generic man. This then would symbolize the woman in the Apocalypse.

When the Bible speaks of "the woman", does it not mean that the *Motherhood* of God had to be revealed at some time? Jesus revealed the Fatherhood of God. Because of this, the Christian world has ever been grateful to be able to say, "Our Father, which art in heaven." Jesus knew that the world, (there was no Christian world at that time — it was mostly Judaic, Roman, etc.), was not willing to accept a feminine sense of God. So he predicted that at some future time "the Comforter" would come and bring us the Motherhood of God. The Bible records it as the "woman appearing." Thus it is that Mrs. Eddy revealed the Womanhood, the Motherhood, of God — that is, the feminine aspect or qualities of God thereby completing the revelation of our Father-Mother God.

In one of the early editions of *Science and Health,* author Mary Baker Eddy used the terms, "Mother", "She", and "Her", when referring to God. However, she changed this in the very next edition, because she realized the Christian world, including the students of Christian Science, would not accept this sense of a feminine God. Nevertheless, Mrs. Eddy has revealed to the world the Motherhood, the tenderness, the gentleness, the forever protective nature of our Mother-God who is Love. The revelation was completed with this truth — our Father-Mother God!

There should be no confusion on this point. Mrs. Eddy was and is the Discoverer, Founder and Leader of Christian Science. We are not chosen children of God. God does not choose. God is divine Principle, and everything in the universe is God saying I AM THAT I AM. It is Soul identifying itself. It is Love gently caring for its own self-expression. Let us be clear on this point, for then we see the completeness of the divine revelation known to the world as Christian Science.

In the First Series of We *Knew Mary Baker Eddy,* one of Mrs. Eddy's students made the statement that she felt that the secret of Mrs. Eddy's great achievements could be explained on no other basis than her at-one-ment with God, and her boundless spirit of universal love for all mankind. She writes, "Prior to my taking class instruction with Mrs. Eddy, this was beautifully expressed to me once by our Leader in conversation, in the words she used to describe her healing work, which, as near as I can recall, were as follows: 'I saw the love of God encircling the universe and man, filling all space, and that divine Love so permeated my own consciousness that I loved with Christlike compassion everything I saw. This realization of divine Love called into expression "the beauty of holiness, the perfection of being" *(Science and Health),* which healed, and regenerated, and saved all who turned to me for help.' The way Mrs. Eddy said the word "Love" made me feel that she must have loved even a blade of grass under her feet."

Love is instilling all. Love is penetrating all. But the moment we permit Love to have a personal sense, we cease to have the Love that is God, the Love that fills all space, the Love that encircles the universe, the Love that is manifest. The moment we have a personal sense of love, all we have is what is called human love and that has no tint of reality.

Mrs. Eddy saw unselfed love. The Eddy concept had been laid on the altar of divine Science. She says she saw that the human had none of the divine hues. She knew that the human had neither presence nor existence, because there is no human mind to have a human body to torment, to kill, or to murder. Mrs. Eddy saw the Love that is God, the Love that is Principle, the Love that knows nothing unlike its own Love, that sees nothing but its own Love. The Love that knows nothing to punish, knows nothing to have a hell for. The Love that is Principle operates as conscious identity, or man.

This is the Love that is the Christlike compassion. It is the Love that Jesus felt when he was confronted by the "strange woman." As is recorded in the beginning of the chapter on "Christian Science Practice" in our textbook, "If the Scientist reaches his patient through divine Love, the healing work will be accomplished at one visit, and the disease will vanish into its native nothingness like dew before the morning sunshine." *(Science and Health)* Pray for this Love. This Love can come only as we get rid of personal sense — the suggestion that we have a personal sense of self that acts and reacts, that likes and dislikes, that loves and hates, that has courage or can be afraid. Oh, understand, there is no personal concept of man. All man is divine, all man is infinite, all man is eternal. See the Love that is God penetrating all, instilling all, healing all. Then we will be seen only as incorporeal Love itself.

In *Miscellaneous Writings*, we read, "The. . . final immersion of human consciousness in the infinite ocean of Love, is the last scene in corporeal sense. This omnipotent act drops the curtain on material man and mortality." In our textbook, we read, "Divine Science. . . lifts the curtain on man as never born and as never dying, but as coexistent with his creator." This omnipotent act of acknowledging the infinite ocean of Love, including man — man that is the power of this Love in being, man that is the surge of this infinite ocean of Love, man that is the light of this divine Love — this potent act drops the curtain on material, personal sense. Christian Science lifts the curtain on man and drops the curtain on personal sense.

Now, when we are at the theatre and the final curtain drops, we know the show is over, and so we leave. Thus it is in Christian Science. The show is over—the show of personal sense is over. The curtain has dropped, and let us refrain from going back to see what is going on. The play is finished. The characters were only dreams — pure fiction. There is no substance, no identity in the show. We have dropped the curtain, and then man's identity or consciousness reflects only the light of ever-present Love. This is the Spirit, the substance, the consciousness termed in Christian metaphysics the ideal man, permeated with eternal Life, holiness, and heaven. We do not have to go any place to go home after the show is over. Man is home, man is heaven. We read in *Miscellaneous Writings*, "The encumbering mortal molecules, called man, vanish as a dream." If it is a dream, then tell it as a dream.

Man was never healed in Christian Science; man has been revealed as being perfect, even as God is perfect. Christian Science is not on the level of healing. We leave that basis of belief, unite with the one Mind, and bring out God's unerring direction. This lifts the curtain on man, and drops the curtain on personal sense; and then man, born of the great forever, lives on, God-crowned and blessed.

Now let us keep the curtain down on the dream. Never go into it; see it as a play, a farce. See it for what it is. The masquerade is over. Keep the curtain up on man, the glory of our Father-Mother God!

We must acknowledge the coincidence of Principle and idea, Father and son. When the human and divine coincidence is clearly seen, then nothing is present humanly; everything is present divinely. Divine action, divine circulation, divine rhythm called heart action, divine breathing — the deep drawn breath fresh from God, divine, sustaining infinite. Circulation, pressure, temperature, all are present in and as Mind. In this coincidence, then, we see there is no human, restricted sense of man. The coincidence recognized, is Principle and idea *one*. But right where the human seems to be, the divine saves us from this limitation and restriction that we are calling the human personality. We thus rise higher and higher from an unlimited basis.

We must never wait for what is called material sense to substantiate spiritual reality. Divine ever-present facts are always present and in manifestation. The carnal suggestion is that we must wait for the evidence to appear through what is called the treatment, or through the operation of the law of nature. Let us stop this suggestion of carnality by steadfastly identifying ourselves as the Truth of being which is always present to spiritual sense. The knower, the knowing, and the known, are all one being; and there is no possibility of lapsing from or returning to. Christian Science not only lifts the curtain on man — that is, the coincidence of Principle and idea — but Christian Science also drops the curtain on the personal sense of self in this true realization of coincidence. Love demands of us that we see the coincidence of Principle and its idea. In this true coincidence, the idea is seen to be the functioning presence of Principle itself, cause being effect, God being His own manifestation.

The "Scientific Statement of Being" gives us the true sense of coincidence, and it is necessary to see that this true sense leaves no humanity. It leaves only divinity. Mrs. Eddy stated that to carry out his holy purpose, Jesus had to be oblivious of the human self. We too must be oblivious of the human self whether it is called oneself or another. The human self is so impertinent; it is saying, "I — I am — I want — I did." Yet, all the time, there is only the "I" that is God, the I AM THAT I AM. So let us see that in this coincidence only the Ego that is God is left to say I AM, and nothing else has presence to say I am.

Cause and effect are one being, Principle and idea one, coincidental. The understanding that Love is present as Principle, and that man is Love's own self-expression — this understanding brings with it the coincidence of Father and son. For we have seen once and for all, that All is infinite Mind, infinitely manifesting itself as All.

Part IV

In the Bible, we read, "The Lord said unto Samuel, Look not on his countenance, or on the height of his stature; because I have refused him; for the LORD seeth not as man seeth; for man looketh on the outward appearance, but the Lord looketh on the heart."

"Love never loses sight of loveliness." (*Science and Health*) From the standpoint of the world, physique may be beautiful, perfectly formed, and so forth. But it can be a picture of beautiful evil — as our Leader says, "sometimes beautiful, always erroneous."

We read in the Scriptures, "Judge not according to the appearance, but judge righteous judgment."

"Having eyes, see ye not? and having ears, hear ye not?"

"But as it is written, Eye hath not seen, nor ear heard, neither have entered into the heart of man, the things which God hath prepared for them that love him. But God hath revealed them unto us by his Spirit: for the Spirit searcheth all things, yea, the deep things of God. But the natural man receiveth not the things of the Spirit of God: for they are foolishness unto him: neither can he know them, because they are spiritually discerned."

Mind is perfect Principle. Therefore its faultlessness is the faultlessness of its idea. We can never be fooled by the deception called personality, whether called oneself or another, because it has been proven to be pure deception. Know God as faultless Principle, forever conceiving faultless idea — idea constituted of the substance of Love. As we see this, we will never see the distorted picture called personality and thus criticize it, and come down to the level of the lie. Stay up on the wall of Love — the Love that is Principle — and look deep into reality. Looking through the eyes of Love, we can see only the loveliness and the brightness of our own being.

Body is the harmonious functioning of Love. Fear, hate, rebellion, dissatisfaction, resentment, are not cause — to cause corruption or interruption, or to interfere with the harmonious functioning of Mind. This harmonious functioning is the law of God, governing and controlling the functions of the body, wholly spiritual, matterless. Even what is called the human concept of body must conform to the perfect law of liberty, for all functioning, action, motion, is Love. It is Love that does the oiling, the lubricating, because body is frictionless. Love is the source of all movement, action, function, and this Love is Principle.

When the slightest suggestion comes, no matter how insignificant, let us be alert and deny it admittance. The Bible says that "He saw his brother's face as if it were the face of God," Love. All right then, what about seeing our own face the same way? Can we accept the suggestion that we are persons, and yet see the true spiritual individuality of our brother? It is impossible. Love never "loses sight of loveliness."

Many times during the day, remind yourself that the Principle that is Love is the source of all being, and that it is present, expressing itself as the action, the knowing, the movement, the seeing of all. Love is not only the source of all, but it is the condition of all. It is even the temperature of the body. It is the circulation of the body. This leaves no little "me" to try to function. Love is the liberator from every kind of suggestion. Suggestion, no matter how aggressive, how malicious, how vicious, cannot sustain itself in the presence of Love realized and felt as the identity of all.

Love gives one the feeling of infinite satisfaction. Mind's infinite manifestation is infinite completeness, infinite wholeness, infinite well-being, infinite satisfaction, because Deity is satisfied with His work. Why? Because it is the emanation of His own infinite self-containment, and self-containment is divine satisfaction or fulfillment. Man is the breath of the Almighty, the breath of the Holy Ghost. What is called matter can never condition man. Man is in good condition, because man is God-conditioned, Love-conditioned. Therefore man is in lovely condition always.

Matter is mortal mind, hypnotism, mesmerism. Mesmerism is not cause to have an effect. Therefore it can make no conditions for man. Matter is a harmless illusion of material sense.

Mind, divine Love, cares for and tenderly nourishes its own idea, man, because man is Love's self-completeness, Love's unassailable nature. Man is the beloved of the Father, in whom the Father-Mother is well-pleased. Therefore when a suggestion of guilt comes, *know* your innocence. You are innocent of ever having been a person, doing or not doing. Remind yourself constantly that there is nothing personally present, but just *Mind*, intelligence, Love, Life, expressing itself in all its identity called home, friend, work, or church.

The kingdom of Love will never be found by looking for it. You will never be able to say, "Lo here, or Lo there is the Kingdom." The kingdom of Love is within. Whoever shall know himself shall find it. Strive to know yourself, and you shall be aware that you are the son or daughter of the Father-Mother. It is by Love that men pass out of death into life. He who does not love has never been alive. David sang in Psalms, "Thy gentleness hath made me great." The understanding that the Love that is God is present, cannot be obscured, cannot be masked. This Love is present and is felt as conscious identity. This Love hath made us gentle. Love has created man in flawless perfection, and maintains man in unlabored self-perpetuation. How joyous, how relaxing it is, how liberating it is to know this fact, and to accept it as our present experience — Love ever expressing itself in flawless perfection for all.

A friend wrote that in teaching a Sunday School class one day, she told the class the story of Noah's Ark. After explaining it, she asked the children how it was that Noah and all in the Ark felt so safe during the long, long flood. No one answered. Then a very small five-year-old child looked up and said, "Because they were all cosied up with Love." Another time, it was the story of Daniel in the lion's den, and many of the children were wide-eyed as they thought of Daniel's plight. But the smallest child was not in doubt about Daniel's welfare because she knew that he, too, was cosied in Love. She knew the same about the three Hebrew boys in the fiery furnace. Some time later that little girl was in what seemed to be a very severe accident, where a part of a building gave way and fell on her. The men working to free her had feared she was mutilated. But she was all right. When her mother asked her later if she had been afraid while they worked to free her, the dear child said, "No, 'cause I was all cosied with Love." Do we have such childlike trust — are we "cosied" in Love?

"Cosy" to this child meant comfortable, loved, secure; and she applied it here with the word Love. Man cosied in Love, is warmed, protected, loved. Man is, and always has been, completely enfolded in God's love, inseparable, indivisible, eternal. Let us stop trying to bring this about. Let us relax and enjoy that man is cosied in the love of God, perpetual freedom. As the Hymn says, "He holds us perfect in His love, And we His image bear." Many healings are brought about through the childlike acceptance that this fact is true.

Let us be like the child and accept with joyous, relaxed freedom that it is already so — that Love is present and being experienced as identity.

It is said that Mary Baker Eddy once remarked, "Man walks the earth enveloped in atmosphere of Life, Truth and Love, which holds him in spiritual gravitation. And the force of Love, which man reflects, repels all the illusions of the carnal mind. Man is the son of God and knows his sonship."

We need to see that even what are called "infinitesimals" all belong to the Mind that is Love. The carnal mind claims that infinitesimals are its agents for subversive activity. It asserts that a germ can destroy the health of man, that a clot of blood can rob him of his intelligence, that a touch of electricity can consume him, that a bullet can take his life, and so on. But Jesus once said that the very hairs on the head are numbered, are cared for, and that the lilies of the field were and are clothed by divine Love, and the least of all seeds, the mustard, could become a tree for birds to rest in. Does this not show us that Love takes care of the infinitesimals as well as the infinite? There is nothing too small or too great that the Father cannot care for. See that everything that concerns your identification home, church, work, all is cared for by the love of the Father.

Sometimes intellectuality fools us. Mrs. Eddy wrote, "'Tis the Spirit that makes pure, That exalts Thee, and will cure." So it is the spirit of Love, the spirit of Truth that relaxes and brings joyous, childlike acceptance. We can be obedient to what our Leader says, "Willingness to become as a little child, and to leave the old for the new, renders thought receptive of the advanced idea." (*Science and Health*) Man is forever in the Love that is God. The very atmosphere is Love, the presence is Love, the substance is Love, the Life is Love, Mind is Love; seeing is Love, feeling is Love, hearing is Love. It all comes down to the one eternal fact: that God is Love and man is all that God is being. What God is being, is man — universal, eternal, forever warm, forever loved, forever tenderly watched over. Without man, Love would be unexpressed. Principle and idea is one, and in this coincidence, in this oneness of the Father and son, in this eternal coincidence, nothing unlike Love can remain, because in the coincidence, all that can possibly have presence, reality, substance, is Love.

'Tis Love, always Love. Say the word quietly. Love. Rest in it. Love. Feel it. All-penetrating, going to every part of the body — and body is universal — body is church, body is government. Feel this Love, and then nothing is left to respond to the personal sense. Truly, it is unselfed love. It was this unselfed nature that Jesus knew so well — this *agape* love, love that never loses sight of its own pure being. Our Leader, Mary Baker Eddy, saw this Love, and was willing to lay aside every suggestion of personal sense, and let the Love that is Principle, be the only presence. We can now go forth as the very living of this divine, ever-present Love, "For Love alone is Life." (Poem: *Love* by Mary Baker Eddy)

The Sermon On The Mount

Association Address

by

Clarence Steves

In the writings of Mary Baker Eddy, we find the Sermon on the Mount referred to as the "Essence of Christian Science" and also as the "diamond sermon." Essence is derived from the word *esse* or to be. The essence is the being. So the Sermon on the Mount is the living of Christian Science. Man is the essence of God, I AM THAT I AM. "Son, all that I have is thine."

In *Retrospection and Introspection*, Mrs. Eddy writes, ". . . our Master's greatest utterance may well be called the diamond sermon. No purer and more exalted teachings ever fell upon human ears than those contained in what is commonly known as the Sermon on the Mount — though this name has been given it by compilers and translators of the Bible, and not by the Master himself or by the Scripture authors. Indeed, this title really indicates more the Master's mood, than the material locality.

"Where did Jesus deliver this great lesson — or, rather, this series of great lessons — on humanity and divinity? On a hillside, near the sloping shores of the Lake of Galilee, where he spake primarily to his immediate disciples.

"In this simplicity, and with such fidelity, we see Jesus ministering to the spiritual needs of all who placed themselves under his care, always leading them into the divine order, under the sway of his own perfect understanding. His power over others was spiritual, not corporeal. To the students whom he had chosen, his immortal teaching was the bread of Life. When *he* was with them, a fishing boat became a sanctuary, and the solitude was peopled with holy messages from the All-Father. The grove became his class room, and nature's haunts were the Messiah's university.

"What has this hillside priest, this seaside teacher, done for the human race? Ask, rather, what has he *not* done. His holy humility, unworldliness, and self-abandonment wrought infinite results. The method of his religion was not too simple to be sublime, nor was his power so exalted as to be unavailable for the needs of suffering mortals, whose wounds he healed by Truth and Love.

"His order of ministration was 'first the blade, then the ear, after that the full corn in the ear.' May we unloose the latchets of his Christliness, inherit his legacy of love, and reach the fruition of his promise 'If ye abide in me, and my words abide in you, ye shall ask what ye will, and it shall be done unto you.'"

The diamond sermon would be that which is brilliant, pure, glittering, glowing, sparkling, colorful, scintillating. Dedicated students are proceeding from and resting upon divine Principle; therefore they will have all the facets of the diamond and have the essence of true being.

To have essence is to have the simplicity of the Christ, the fidelity of the Christ, leading into the divine order called heaven. It is to be under the sway of the perfect understanding that is the Christ — not the understanding of a person called Jesus, for this understanding is not personal. It is the result of all things brought to light. This sermon is to be the very bread of Life. Under the sway of the Christ and having the experience of the Christ, the fishing boat becomes a sanctuary and the solitude is peopled with holy messages. It is not peopled with people trying to understand, people trying to know the truth, not with people at all, but with holy messages, or divine ideas, illuminating the universe with light. It is the All-Mind stating itself in its integrating power of Love. This is the essence of the Sermon on the Mount. Even the grove becomes the class room; "natures's haunts were the Messiah's university," the university of true being. And here all are given the degree of "this is my beloved Son in whom I am well pleased."

In this university, there are no degrees of understanding — only the one Mind infinitely expressing itself. In this Christ university, there are no favored, certain ones endowed with certain qualities, for the only teacher is the divine Principle, Love, embracing all with its warmth and loving. Nothing is unloved. Nothing is unwanted. In this university of Christ, the oneness of all being is known and rejoiced in. In this university, only one thing is demanded — the complete abandonment of any sense of a personal ego. The whole Sermon on the Mount, from the opening words to the closing ones, is based on the oneness and indivisibility of all being. It is the complete abandonment of the personal sense of I that permits the Christ to show forth our normal, natural being.

Never believe that Jesus held a special position in this university because of the way he was born. It was not the way he was born that made him the Christ. It was what he knew of the Father — the divine I — that made him exceptional. Suggestion will say that you can not do this or that because of the way that you were born — that is, you were born in a human way. Mrs. Eddy says it was Jesus' knowledge of pre-existence that made him mighty. So you can say that it is your understanding of pre-existence that made you, not the belief in birth. Man was never born into a finite, corporeal sense of being. Man is not person, nor is man personal. He cannot say, lo here or lo there is man. Man is like the wind — personless presence. Man is the term used to show forth the completeness, essence, and wholeness of divine Mind. It is understanding that the I or Ego never came into being. But the only I is self-existence, and the manifestation of the Ego called the Son is ever one with the Father. Understanding this true Christ-method makes for simplicity and yet sublimity. It is this oneness that upsets all that suggests division.

This Sermon on the Mount is to show the order of the ministration of the Christ. "First the blade, then the ear, and after that the full corn in the ear." First, the students of this universal truth — the university of oneness — are to have the blade. They are to see that there is something divine about themselves, that there is something beyond the three dimensional sense of self.

Second, the ear — seeing and knowing oneself as a divine idea governed and controlled by the Mind that is Principle. It is still thinking of oneself as living with others, acting and reacting to their moods, but knowing the Truth that there is one Mind present to adjust, etc. But finally the full corn in the ear must come and see that idea is the very functioning on the part of Mind itself. In this full corn in the ear, the 'mortal molecules called man' have disappeared, and man of the vast forever has appeared. It is to be one with your own being and the reality of things.

This fullness of the corn in the ear, is to look out from Mind and see it is very good. There are not many students who take this last step. And yet, if this precious Christian Science is to remain and do the greater works spoken of by Jesus, we must be willing to leave all for the Christ. One of our lecturers once said, "It is our business to look out from God, Mind, as Mind, not up to it." There is a greater step to be taken in this direction — few are willing to take it. I know there is great work to be done by those who see far and are not dismayed by the reality of being.

Mary Baker Eddy writes in the textbook, *Science and Health with Key to the Scriptures*, "The time cometh when the spiritual origin of man, the divine Science which ushered Jesus into human presence, will be understood and demonstrated." Also, "That is, he who perceives the true idea of Life loses his belief in death. He who has the true idea of good loses all sense of evil, and by reason of this is being ushered into the undying realities of Spirit. Such a one abideth in Life — life obtained not of the body incapable of supporting life, but of Truth, unfolding its own immortal idea. Jesus gave the true idea of being, which results in infinite blessings to mortals."

And again she states, "Jesus waited until the mortal or fleshly sense had relinquished the belief of substance-matter, and spiritual sense had quenched all earthly yearnings. Thus he found the eternal Ego, and proved that he and the Father were inseparable as God and His reflection, or spiritual man. . . . That saying of our Master, 'I and my Father are one' separated him from the scholastic theology of the rabbis. His better understanding of God was a rebuke to them. . . The opposite and false views of the people hid from their sense Christ's sonship with God." So why be anything less than the full corn in the ear?

Then, in order to have the full understanding of this Sermon on the Mount, we must be willing to unloose the latchets of our own Christliness and inherit the legacy of Love. To accept fully and completely "if ye abide in me," you must abide in this true sense of I AM, seeing that there is no personal ego, but only the divine I present saying I AM, and this is the scientific statement of true being. Leaving our earthly all on the altar of divine Science is the starting point of divine Science — drinking deep of the Christ cup, drinking *all* of it, accepting fully and completely one's own Christliness. Then "I will abide in you and ye shall ask what ye will and I shall give it." God gives fully of Himself to His own self-expression. Nothing is withheld. "All that I have is thine." This true knowing is the saviour from the suggestion that one has been a person good or bad, loving or unloving, young or old. Suddenly you find that the full corn in the ear is experienced. As the compound idea including all right ideas, you are no longer dwelling in the land of dry bones, but you are in the land of Christian Science, the land of fetterless being, the land of conception unconfined, the land of fullness called the heaven of His presence. To have the full corn in the ear, you see that you are not *in* the kingdom of the Father, that man *is* the kingdom of the Father. The Christian Scientist is alone with his own being and the reality of things. The reality of things is to experience the heaven of His presence here and now.

Drinking deep of these draughts, drinking deep in this university, we have the directness of the expressing on the part of Mind, Love, itself. Truly this is My servant in whom I am well pleased. This is the oneness of Principle and idea. This is the marriage. The essence of the Sermon begins to appear. Now we will have the newness and freshness of the diamond itself when all is brought into sharp, clear focus. We see ourselves as we are seen, not through the dark glass of the human mind, but through the Mind that is God. A thousand years of knowing that God is Mind — over there, outside what we seem to be — is worthless and emits no light; but when we bring the idea into focus, that idea is the functioning of the Mind that is God. This brings light instantaneously. This is to experience the Sermon on the Mount, looking out from the mount of revelation. There is no "lo here" or "lo there" to this mount of revelation. It is not a climbing up to great heights and then descending to tell others of this tremendous revelation. No, this mount of revelation is a continuous withinness.

In *Unity of Good*, Mrs. Eddy records, "God is All-in-all. Hence He is in Himself only, in His own nature and character, and is perfect being, or consciousness. He is all the Life and Mind there is or can be. Within Himself is every embodiment of Life and Mind."

Let us now look at this Sermon which is the essence of Christian Science, this sermon which is the diamond.

"The whole picture facing us today is the suppositional opposite having its convulsions and revolutions," That is from *Miscellany*. This is the convulsion going on in the world today, even in our own movement. Mrs. Eddy also says, "Christian Science is revolutionary and upsets all that is not right." The Bible records: "I will overturn and overturn until he come whose right it is." This revolution is beyond the seeming actors called persons, or even beyond what are called nations, religions, economies, etc. Issues today are too great to personalize them, and think of people as right or wrong. It is a revolution that started when Mary Baker Eddy discovered the allness of Spirit and the nothingness of matter. And this revolution is causing the convulsion as mortal mind, and its supposed substance called matter, is seen as illusion, and the illusion is being dispelled. Does not our Leader warn us not to be disturbed when the breaking up comes, but to stand by until we see the raindrops of divinity refresh the earth?

What are the raindrops of divinity? Truly, it must be the warm, gentle, refreshing rain from heaven putting substance on the dry bones, making the desert bloom even as the valley, lifting all out of the diabolical suggestion that persons have egos, into the glorious realization that *there is but one Ego present and self-expressing*. What greater refreshment could come than to know that one is not a person trying to know his God, but that one is the very performing presence of that which he has been calling God? What peace on earth! Truly, it is "be still, and know that I am God."

For years, this movement has demonstrated the great revelation of Christian Science, healing every known disease; indeed, every problem of the human mind has been adjusted. Christian Science has proved beyond all doubt that "there is no life, truth, intelligence nor substance in matter;" that matter is nothing more than objectified mortal mind; and that mortal mind is nothing more than an improper focus, looking through a glass darkly. The movement generally sees that we are not dealing with sick matter, well matter, old matter, young matter, unemployed matter, etc.; but what the movement does not see as a whole, is that *there is but one supposititious opposite, claiming to iden-tify itself in multitudes of bodies, and that all these bodies carry out its beliefs, delusions, myths.*

Patients are not people with a mind to be enlight-ened; patients are nothing but the one evil, or wicked one, claiming to have identified itself. Treatment should always be impersonal; and the more impersonal the treatment, the more specific it appears to be. Why? Because healing oc-curs the moment it is seen that the patient is not something over there needing help, but that the only patient is here as suggestion denying the allness and everywhereness of the I AM THAT I AM. *A patient is a universal false belief claiming to have identified itself.* We must awaken to the fact that there is but one human mind, and it is wholly dishonest.

The greatness of the discovery of Mrs. Eddy is the impersonal nature of good and evil. Through all the edu-cational processes, one is taught that he has a private ego or mind, and that this ego must become aware of certain facts, etc. But in *Science and Health*, we read that the human mind is not to be a factor in healing, and that it is enmity against God, the only Mind. Of course, the belief that one has a personal, private mind with which to agree or disagree with others, is enmity to the one Mind self-expressing and self-understanding its own declarations. Over and over throughout her writings, Mrs. Eddy warns her students of attempting to study Christian Science with the belief of a private mind. In this great Sermon on the Mount, Jesus warned his followers that they cannot serve God and mammon. You can not accept the fact that the only I is God, and then believe the devil, or animal magnetism, also has an I or ego There is but one Ego, and this one I, or God, is all-seeing, all-acting, all-performing, all-know-ing, all-presence, all-intelligence, all-identifying, all-living, all-loving. This divine Ego identifies itself infinitely and universally, and does not leave a presence, power or know-ing for another ego to say I. *All I is God.* When Mrs. Eddy wrote the textbook, she wrote it from the standpoint of the beginner, from the standpoint of the student, and from the standpoint of the one who knew himself to be the divine manifestation itself. When reading articles and listening to lectures, see from what standpoint the Science is being expressed. All these articles and lectures, are legitimate from the standpoint from which they are given, but never permit anyone to say that you cannot live divine revelation here and now.

"There is but one way to heaven, harmony, and Christ in divine Science shows us this way," Mrs. Eddy tells us. In the marginal note we read, "The one only way." What is this one only way? "It is to know no other reality — to have no other consciousness of Life, — than good, God and His reflection and to rise superior to the so-called pain and pleasure of the senses." Then this one only way is to see that the only I or Ego is God. Did not Jesus, speaking from the standpoint of the Christ, say, "I am the Way"? Is there any other way than to speak from the standpoint of the Christ, which is the divine manifestation of Mind itself? *Mind declaring its own perfection is the Christ.* Then the one only way is to know no other I or Ego than God.

This way is straight and narrow because it permits not the slightest deviation. It does not permit living as a human person with a personal ego knowing something of this one and only Ego. Mrs. Eddy says, "Mortals are egotists. They believe themselves to be independent workers, personal authors, and even privileged originators of something which Deity would not or could not create." That is from *Science and Health.* Also she tells us, "A slight divergence is fatal in Christian Science."

The straight and narrow way does not permit the slightest divergence. It is either the I that is God or the I of the suppositional opposite, called the whispering serpent, Lucifer, devil, Red Dragon, animal magnetism, or hypnotism. It is the most hypocritical thing that one can do to believe that he is something that he is not — namely a human person, knowing, doing, loving. The textbook says, "Through repentance, spiritual baptism, and regeneration, mortals put off their material beliefs and false individuality." Mortals put off their false individuality. But what has this to do with the one only way? Absolutely nothing. For "entirely separate from the belief and dream of material living is the Life divine." This Life divine is the only I or Ego being what I AM — "My beloved Son in whom I am well pleased."

Putting off the false individuality is simply allowing the personal sense of I to fade out for lack of identification. Never permitting it to say "I" in any manner or degree. When it tries to assert itself, instantly "be still, and know that I am God." Continuing the above quotation, we read, "It is only a question of time when they shall all know Me (God, the only I or Ego) from the least of them unto the greatest." It says "only a question of time." Then if it is only a question of time, why not be done with time now and have eternity? Eternity is not a continuation of time. Eternity is the infinite *now* always being *now* without any past sense or future sense. "Eternity, not time, expresses the thought of Life, and time is no part of eternity. One ceases in proportion as the other is recognized. Time is finite; eternity is forever infinite," we read in *Science and Health*. Permitting the mortal molecules to disappear, man of the vast forever appears. The foreverness of I AM is now. So if it is only a question of time when all shall know the I AM, then let us be done with time here and now, and see that I AM THAT I AM. Truly God is the way, the Truth and the Life, and no man can come unto the Father any other way.

Jesus, knowing this to be true and living from the mount of revelation, said, "Verily, verily, I say unto you, He that entereth not by the door into the sheepfold, but climbeth up some other way, the same is a thief and a robber. But he that entereth in by the door is the shepherd of the sheep." Does not the personal sense of I rob and steal? Jesus continuing said, "The thief cometh not, but for to steal, and to kill, and to destroy; I am come that they might have life and have it more abundantly." Paul later said, "Let this mind be in you which was also in Christ Jesus: Who, being in the form of God, thought it not robbery to be equal with God." And our Leader later gave as a Tenet of The First Church of Christ, Scientist: "And we solemnly promise to watch, and pray for that Mind to be in us which was also in Christ Jesus." We are to watch what? — to see that it is recognized that there is but one only way, the way of the I that is God, the Ego-God and the Ego-man, the I-God and the I-man; to watch that no personal sense of I intrudes to mar the beauty and purity of one's own being.

What is prayer? *The deep inner knowing that man is the knowing of the Mind that is Christ.* Man is not the knower; man is the known. To have the I that is the Christ, is to know no other reality than the reality of perfect being, to rise superior to the suggestion that one is a person living with other persons, to rise superior to the suggestion that one is in a mess, to rise superior to the suggestion that one is sitting in a chair listening to the divine reality itself.

Christ Jesus said we must do unto others as we would have them do unto us. In the Science of being and in the vast forever, there are no others to do unto; but what appear as others is the way the I of all being is appearing in its multifarious forms. To be merciful is to have the true sense of mercy, and to clothe all in Christliness, never to see what is called our brother as person or personal, but to keep the Christ robe "woven into one web of consistency without tear or rent." The I of our being has never been divided into others. Does not *Retrospection and Introspection* say, "Whatever . . . divides Being into beings is a misstatement of the unerring divine Principle of Science"? To continue in the one only way, it must be seen that the I of

Being can appear only as *one* and never as another. The Bible states, "My glory will I not give to another." Jacob "saw his brother's face as if it were the face of God."

To be just, is to see that the I that is Principle can never be masked by another. To be just is never to see your brother as another, but to see your brother as the very functioning of the I AM that is Principle, Love.

"Blessed are the pure in heart: for they shall see God." See only from the one and only standpoint of I itself. There is no other seeing, no other knowing. To be pure is to permit no motes of personal sense to intrude. "If Jesus awakened Lazarus from the dream, illusion, of death, this proved that the Christ could improve on a false sense. Who dares to doubt this consummate test of the power and willingness of divine Mind to hold man forever intact in his perfect state . . .?" Also in the textbook, we read, "Jesus demonstrated the inability of corporeality, [the personal sense of ego] as well as the infinite ability of Spirit, [the true sense of I] thus helping erring human sense [that which believes in persons, places and things] to flee from its own convictions and seek safety in divine Science." It is only the purity of divine Ego itself that permits this. In this one only way, what happens to "an eye for an eye and a tooth for a tooth" of the Mosaic creed?

What does it mean, to give our brother our cloak also, and to walk the second mile? It is the joy of knowing that there is no private person with a private mind separated from the love and tenderness that is Love, the only Mind? *To give our brother our cloak, is to cloak him in his own divinity, to cloak him in the Love that is Principle.* To go the first mile is to free our brother from the belief of being person and having a personal mind with certain characteristics, qualities, etc. that need to be gotten rid of. But to go the second mile is to see that he has never had a prodigal experience, never had a mind separate from the one and only Ego; to see that he is begotten only of the

Father, forever one with Father-Mother all-harmonious; to see him as not having a body formed by lust, but as the body of Love, the very shrine of Love itself, immaculate and wholesome. To go the second mile is to see that there never has been a healing taken place, that perfect God and perfect man have always existed, indivisibly One. To go the second mile is never to repeat that you know Mrs. Smith was once a Roman Catholic, or that Mr. Jones was once a drunkard. Oh, go the whole second mile and see that there has never been a human concept of yourself or another; that there has never been a mind to have a finite localized concept carrying out its delusions and illusions. That the only man there has ever been is the man that is and ever has been Love's experience. Oh, rejoice and be glad that this second mile does not permit one to talk of himself in terms of humanity, but to think out from divinity. Let us stay with the one only way — *the Christ way.*

Jesus looked deep into realism, instead of accepting only the outward sense of things. Jesus left "the mortal basis of belief and united with the one Mind." He spoke of this Mind as His Father, and knew that idea could of itself do nothing; but his Father, the only I or Mind, worked this way, and he worked this way. Jesus knew that the personal Jesus had to be laid aside for the Christ, and he was willing to do this. At one time he said, "He that hath seen me hath seen the Father." Of course, he that sees the activity of intelligence, Life, Love, sees the Father in manifestation.

It is all so simple. The people see this tremendous occurrence happening before their very eyes, yet they see not the Christ of their own being, but rather a person called Jesus doing mighty works. The Bible records Isaiah as saying, "The people that sat in darkness have seen a great light" — the light of divine revelation. This true light wipes out any deflective sense called "divers diseases and torments," and only divine reflection is present. This is called healing.

Multitudes began to follow this wonder worker called Jesus. The Bible records it in Matthew, "There followed him great multitudes of people." Jesus, the highest human corporeal concept of the divine idea, saw that something had to be done or the whole purpose of his mission would be lost. Do you not remember when Jesus asked his disciples, "Whom do men say that I am?" They replied in substance that he was Elias, Moses or some other prophet come back to earth. How he instantly saw that the people were perverting the true appearing of the Christ and calling it a person? He wanted to know if his disciples had a better concept of the facts of being, and he asked them, "Whom do ye say that I am?" And Peter, with his great impetuosity, said, "Thou art the Christ, the Son of God." And Jesus knowing, even as Mrs. Eddy did later, that the human perverts whatever it touches, quickly turned to Peter and said, "Flesh and blood hath not revealed this unto you, but my Father." That is, Peter did not have the ability as a person to distinguish between Truth and error, between Spirit and flesh. It is "the divine Principle of the universe that must interpret the universe." Then a most profound revelation took place. It appeared as Jesus saying that upon this great truth the Church must be built. And when the Church that proceeds from divine Principle, rests on the understanding that man is the Christ of the living God, then this Church has the foundation of eternality and continuity, and the gates of hell, personal sense and its personalities, cannot prevail against it.

Jesus saw also that the multitudes were misinterpreting the healing works, for they were following him as a person, not for the Christ, but for the loaves and fishes. If his mission was simply to make sick matter healthy, lame matter walk, dead matter live again, blind matter see, then the second state of the man was worse than the first. To make one comfortable in a lie, is to make the second state worse than the first. Christian Science awakens one out of the belief that man is a person sick or well, blind or seeing, living or dead. Christian Science is to show that man is not person or personal, but idea, the very directness of Mind itself. "Have I been so long time with you," Jesus asked, "and haven't you seen the Father yet?" It was the great work of the Master to show that man has no existence as man, but has existence only as the Christ, which is the direct manifestation of I AM.

Man has no existence as man. Man cannot say, "I am the reflection of God." Reflection is nothing in and of itself. Reflection can make no remarks concerning itself. Even according to belief, if you were standing in front of a mirror, could the mirrored reflection say, "I am your reflection?" Reflection exists purely as reflection. Does not our textbook tell us that man is that which has not a quality underived from God? He has no mind but God. Man has nothing underived from Mind. So man never has existence as man. He has existence only as the I or Ego self-expressed. This Jesus knew, and also, in his infinite wisdom, he knew that he must prevent any perversion of this great fact. He must not leave his followers in the darkness of the belief that they were to become good persons, loving persons, but to show them that they were not persons at all, good or bad, moral or immoral, knowing or not knowing the Truth. His whole mission was to take away the sin of the world, and the only sin is the belief that man is something separated from God. Does not our Leader say, "Let us rid ourselves of the belief that man is separated from God. . . "? Science shows that existence separate from God is impossible.

The Bible continues, "Seeing the multitudes he went up into a mountain." We have already seen that it is not a place, but a mood. The human mind depicting bodies many and minds many — Jesus rose above the personal sense; and from the mount of revelation, of the indivisibility of all being, he saw, not as Jesus, but looking through the eyes of

Mind, spiritual discernment, he saw Mind's own indivisible Self.

Jesus never identified himself with the mass or multitude thought. He knew that he was not one of many, but was the divine *One* in evidence. He maintained the attitude and altitude of the Christ constantly. Here he was set upon the Rock against which the gates of hell could not prevail — the suggestion of many could make no impression. When he was set or firmly established, he called his disciples unto him. He did not call the mass unto him. Rather he called his disciples to instruct them further in spiritual facts. The disciples, believing themselves persons living in a dimensional universe, saw a person expounding the facts of being. It is, and was, the Truth uttering itself, a wholly within experience as Jesus resorted to his higher selfhood. He called his disciples unto him. If one is lifted up, the I of all being is lifted up, and this draws all men unto it. So the eternal wonder is that space is filled not with people ignorant of their birthright, prodigals trying to get back to the indivisible being; but the eternal wonder is that space is peopled with Mind's own self-expression. But the disciples, believing themselves one of many, saw a Jesus giving spiritual instruction. From the standpoint of the Christ Science, this is not the attitude nor altitude of the students of this Christian Science.

In *Miscellaneous Writings*, our Leader writes of personal sense, "I earnestly advise all Christian Scientists to remove from their observation or study the personal sense of any one, and not to dwell in thought upon their own or others' corporeality, either as good or evil. . . . He advances most in divine Science who meditates most on infinite spiritual substance and intelligence. Experience proves this true. Pondering on the finite personality of Jesus, the son of man, is not the channel through which we reach the Christ, or Son of God, the true idea of man's divine Principle. I warn students against falling into the error of anti-Christ. The consciousness of corporeality, and whatever is connected therewith, must be outgrown. Corporeal falsities include all obstacles to health, holiness, and heaven. Man's individual life is infinitely above a bodily form of existence, and the human concept antagonizes the divine. 'Science and Health with Key to the Scriptures,' on page 229, third and fourth paragraphs, elucidates this topic."

In the same book, she states "If one asks me, Is my concept of you right? I reply, The human concept is always imperfect; relinquish your human concept of me, or of any-one and find the divine, and you have gained the right one — and never until then. People give me too much attention of the misguided, fallible sort, and this misrepresents one through malice or ignorance."

She also wrote in *Miscellany*, "'In the beginning was the Word, and the Word was with God, and the Word was God' (St. John). This great truth of God's impersonality and individuality and of man in His image and likeness, individual, but not personal, is the foundation of Christian Science. There was never a religion or philosophy lost to the centuries except by sinking its divine Principle in per-sonality. May all Christian Scientists ponder this fact, and give their talents and loving hearts free scope only in the right direction! . . . Mary of old wept because she stooped down and looked into the sepulchre — looked for the per-son, instead of the Principle that reveals Christ. The Mary of to-day looks up for Christ, away from the supposedly crucified to the ascended Christ, to the Truth that 'healeth all thy diseases' and gives dominion over all the earth. The doubting disciple could not identify Christ spiritually, but he could materially. He turned to the person, to the prints of the nails, to prove Christ, whereas the discharged evi-dence of material sense gave the real proof of his Saviour, the veritable Christ, Truth, which destroys the false sense with the evidence of Soul, immortality, eternal Life without beginning or end of days. . . I have risen to look and wait and watch and pray for the spirit of Truth that leadeth away from person — from body to Soul, even to the true image and likeness of God. St. John found Christ, Truth, in the Word which is God. We look for the sainted Revelator in his writings, and there we find him. Those who look for me in person, or elsewhere than in my writings, lose me instead of find me."

Let us look at the well known Beatitudes. Obedient to Mrs. Eddy's admonition to take the inspired Word of the Bible, let us see just what the Sermon on the Mount is from this inspired Word. The disciples, believing themselves to be persons hearing another person, naturally would record what they thought they heard as well as their own inter-pretation of what is being said.

"Blessed are the poor in spirit: for their's is the kingdom of heaven." Why are the poor in spirit blessed? Blessed are they that see the nothingness of personality, and see its absolute poverty; that it really has no life, truth, or intelligence in it. Blessed are they that are poor in supersti-tion, poor in pride, poor in egotism, poor in human will, poor in personal sense, poor in hurt feelings, poor in the belief of being person knowing something of the only Mind. And blessed are they who see that man is not something separated from the only I or Ego, but that man is the rich-ness of the Mind that is God, the all-knowing Mind and the All-Mind. "Son, all that I have is thine." Yes, all that the I has *is* the son, the kingdom of the Father. The moment that one sees the poverty of human existence, at that moment their's is the kingdom of God. What does the kingdom of God mean? According to the Glossary, Kingdom of Heaven is defined as: "The reign of harmony in divine Science; the realm of unerring, eternal, and omnipotent Mind; the atmosphere of Spirit where Soul is supreme."

So blessed are the poor in personal ego, for their's is the realm or reign of the only I or US. Truly, it is the heaven of heavens to know that there is no personal ego.

No personal ego to combat with other egos. No personal ego to know or not to know the truth. No personal ego called self to put one into hell. What a blessed experience to know there is only one I to experience its own presence. This is the blessedness of being the functioning of the great and only I AM.

"Blessed are they that mourn: for they shall be comforted." The word *blessed* according to some authorities should be translated "Oh, the happiness of . . ." So here we have, Oh the happiness of being free of the personal ego and the heaven of accepting the divine I as the all I or Ego. The textbook states, "It should be thoroughly understood that all men have *one* Mind." Man has no mind but God. In this blessedness or happiness, there is no personal ego trying to find 'how' or 'why.' True happiness never comes through reasoning. It comes only through divine revelation — Mind expressing itself — and this expression is the son. Blessed are they that let the dead bury their dead. Never mourn over past mistakes. They that mourn shall be comforted, because in this precious Science they find that it never was the I of being. Nothing but a personal sense of I mourns over what is called the loss of something or someone. It calls such mourning love, but it is pure selfishness. The moment that we are willing to let the old go for the new, at that moment the mourning ceases and the blessedness appears, for the Christ-man in all the glory of the Father appears.

Why mourn over the sepulchre? Mary looked into the tomb of personal sense and mourned. But later, seeing the risen Saviour, she said, "Rabboni." Why not say "Rabboni" to what is your own Saviour? The Saviour from the belief that one is, or ever has been, a person knowing something of Christian Science, and trying rather desperately to change the stones into bread. You cannot make the human concept better. So never mourn over it. Never try to patch it up, and say it is good enough for today. It is nothing but a three dimensional sense of that which is dimensionless.

What appears to be another across the room or miles away, is not another, but is your own indivisible self saying I AM THAT I AM. Rejoice and be glad over the loss of personal sense.

In *Unity of Good*, we read : "Bruise the head of this serpent as Truth and 'the woman' are doing in Christian Science, and it stings your heel, rears its crest proudly, and goes on saying 'Am I not myself? Am I not mind and matter, person and thing?' We should answer: 'Yes, you are indeed yourself and need most of all to be rid of this self, for it is very far from God's likeness.' The egotist must come down and learn, in humility, that God never made evil. An evil ego and his assumed power, are falsities. These falsities need a denial. The evil ego has but the visionary substance of matter. It lacks the substance of Spirit, Mind, Life, Soul. Mortal mind is self-creative and self-sustained, until it becomes non-existent. It has no origin or existence in Spirit, immortal Mind, or good. Matter is not truly conscious; and mortal error, called mind, is not Godlike. These are the shadowy and false, which neither think nor speak. All Truth is from inspiration and revelation — from Spirit and not from flesh. We do not see much of the real man here, for he is God's man, while ours is man's man. I do not deny, I maintain, the individuality and reality of man; but I do so on a divine Principle, not based on a human conception and birth. The scientific man and his Maker are here; and you would be none other than this man, if you would subordinate the fleshly perceptions to the spiritual sense and source of being. Jesus said, 'I and my Father are one.' He taught no selfhood as existent in matter. This incensed the rabbins against Jesus, because it was an indignity to their personality; and this personality they regarded as both good and evil. This ego was in the earthquake, thunderbolt, and tempest. The Pharisees fought Jesus on this issue. The fight was an effort to enthrone evil. It furnished the battle-ground of the past, as it does of the present. Jesus assumed the burden of disproof by destroying sin, sickness, and death to sight and senses. Jesus acted boldly against the false evidence of the senses."

First, the mourning period is necessary — that is, to see the utter nothingness of the human concept, sometimes beautiful, but always erroneous. All is Mind and Mind's own glorious self-expressing. Blessed are they that mourn for the past — see its utter nothingness in the glorious *now* of eternity. *Man is the present revelation of Mind's knowing, not something having revelations.* Truly, there is only *now* in which to know and rejoice. The all-knowing, all-living Mind can express itself in the *now* only. There is no past *now* called yesterday and no future *now* called tomorrow, for *now* is. There is only the continuity of *now*. Our Leader writes that there is "not the fleeting freshness of youth but the evergreen of Soul." "Manhood is its eternal noon," — *now*, undimmed by a noon yesterday and a noon tomorrow.

It is the eternal noon that permits freshness and continuity. So that which says it was born, is an unreal concept of an unreal mind. How rich one is in the knowing that I AM THAT I AM. This is the Comforter. Jesus said, "Unless I go away, the Comforter cannot come." Unless the personal sense of I goes away, the Comforter, the true sense of I, cannot come. Isaiah wrote, "To appoint unto them that mourn in Zion, to give unto them beauty for ashes, the oil of joy for mourning; the garment of praise for the spirit of heaviness; that they might be called trees of righteousness, the planting of the Lord, that he might be glorified." Never mourn over personal sense, for the Comforter cannot come unless the false personal sense of I goes away. Unless the personal sense of teacher, practitioner, mother, father, son, daughter, etc., goes away, the true I cannot come. Oh, happy are ye when ye rejoice and are exceedingly glad for the I AM is come that you might have life and have it more abundantly.

"Blessed are the meek: for they shall inherit the earth." In *Retrospection and Introspection*, we read, "Meek-

ness and temperance are the jewels of Love, set in wisdom."
Gentleness, consideration, a most beautiful grace, are asso-
ciated with the lowly in heart, free of the egotism that goes
with personal sense. Jesus considered pride as a cardinal
sin because it is the opposite of meekness, which certainly
ushers one into the kingdom of the divine I or indivisible
Ego. It takes great meekness to see that all there is to oneself is the function of the Ego-God — the Ego-God and the
Ego-man. There are no comparisons in this true sense of
being. There are no degrees. The meek are not persons
with a false sense of humility. I and my Father are one, is a
blessed experience. There is mightiness in meekness. The
Nazarene was mighty as he was meek. Watch the false
sense of meekness which says, "Oh, you know I did not
do that." Of course, the personal sense of I does nothing,
but it is the I that worketh this way, for my Father worketh
this way. Have the assurance, not of a personal sense, but
the assurance that is born of living the Christ. Never think
in terms of two, in terms of being a person doing this or
that; but think of yourself as a divine idea doing everything
through reflection. There is only one I or Ego present to
express itself, and even when it looks like another, it is still
the only I or US. Be certain that the false sense of meekness
does not bring separateness and twoness. Oneness is the
whole theme of Christian Science. Some that are humanly
meek are nothing more than doormats. Meekness is not a
personal quality. Meekness is a divine attribute, for it knows
nothing outside of itself. Meekness inherits the earth, for
it is unopposing because it knows it includes all.

"Blessed are they which do hunger and thirst after
righteousness: for they shall be filled." Oh, happy are ye
when the hunger feeling and the thirst feeling is filled by
the recognition that Soul satisfies its identity, man. Oh,
happy are ye when all feeling proceeds from and rests
upon the divine I. All feeling belongs to Soul. It is the
sacred obligation of Soul to keep its self-expression, man,

at the point of perfect feeling and satisfaction. There is never a moment when personal sense can pervert this feeling and say, "I do not feel well. I am starved for love. How I crave for completeness. I so want to be happy." Oh, happy are ye when it is recognized that all feeling belongs to the I or Ego of one's being. False sense or personal sense, divisions, separation, always seems to pervert this feeling and suggest that something from the outside is needed. Perhaps a friend, a cocktail, a cigarette. The indulgence in this day is due to the general acceptance that feeling is in physicality or personality. To indulge in any feeling which seems to come from the personal concept of body, looking for thrills there, is to deny the Christ of your own being. Christian Science will not take away thrills, but it will give infinite, eternal thrills. What could be more thrilling and satisfying than to know oneself from the standpoint of divine revelation?

Think of including the universe! Not looking out at the blue sky, the warm sunshine, the rhythm of the universe, the beauty of the flowers, the music of the birds, etc., but including all right ideas. What joy and fullness of satisfaction comes in this acknowledgment that man is the infinite completeness of Mind itself. Mind completely satisfied! Mind that is Love itself! What feeling this is! Man does not have feeling. *Man is the feeling of Soul.* Man is the feeling of Spirit's might and tenderness; the feeling of the unalterableness of Truth; the feeling of the absolute stability of unchanging Principle; the feeling of Soul's graciousness; the feeling of Mind knowing all, and so infinitely satisfied in this all-knowing, with nothing else to know or be known; the feeling of Life's infinite, measureless being, not merely a sense of existence, but the feeling of an eternal spring, a conception that is unconfined, not only reaching to the divine glory, but feeling of the divine glory itself. True feeling is never shared with what is called another. True feeling does not come and go. Feeling is that unutterable intuitiveness that knows all is well because all *is* well. Living this Beatitude from the standpoint of completeness and true feeling, is a perfect Christian Science treatment.

Soul-feeling, Soul-being, wipes out the suggestion of thirst, the desire for more understanding, thirsting for more truth, hungering after righteousness. Man does not hunger after righteousness. Man is the satisfaction of Soul-being. Man is the expression of Soul-being. The feeling for color, the feeling for music, harmony, beauty, etc., the feeling for words — this is Soul-appreciation. Man is the feeling of Soul. Never permit personal sense to say, "I want." Never be a victim of personal feelings, liking this but not liking that. Principle feels and experiences its divine accuracy, equilibrium, balance. Love feels its own loveliness and dissolves the problem into its nothingness. Life feels its aliveness. Soul feels the joy of being. Truth feels the divine truthfulness of Christian Science. This true sense of feeling never lacks affection for what appears as another. This true feeling includes all and excludes nothing. This feeling is personless. Truly, this feeling is satisfaction, completeness. Blessed are ye with this true sense of feeling, for ye are filled — that is, the full representation of the all-feeling Soul.

"Blessed are they which do hunger and thirst after righteousness: for they shall be filled." Oh, happy are they that hunger and thirst for the true sense of I or Ego, for they shall be filled — that is, they shall recognize that man is the full representative of Mind, the I-God being I-man. The very recognition that there is something beyond what the senses are presenting begins to feed with the bread of Life, the bread that cometh down from heaven. This hungering and thirsting shall be filled with the joy of finding oneself not only in the kingdom, but as the very kingdom of the Father.

"Blessed are the merciful: for they shall obtain mercy." Oh, the depth and breadth and infinite nature of this I. Nothing static concerning it. To be truly merciful means to be fearless in the knowing. "Paganism and agnosticism may define God as the great unknowable; but Christian Science brings God much nearer to man, and makes Him known to the All-in-all, forever near." Seeing that the very I of one's being is God, then the very I of one's being is the all-knowing, and man is the known. The only way to be merciful in its true sense, is to rise above the petty personal into the realm of personless presence. Do not be afraid that you will lose your identity or end of Life. You will not lose family, friends, church, etc., but will find your life even as Job did — find it within. The only way to be merciful is not to permit suggestion to say "there is your husband" or "there is your wife" or "there is body;" but to handle the suggestion that says there is man apart from God, by knowing that "Love never loses sight of loveliness."

Oh, the freshness, newness and spontaneity in being truly merciful. True mercy is to see our brother's need and to supply it, and the only need the brother ever has for us is to see him from the standpoint of divine revelation, from the standpoint of I itself, for the Christian Scientist is always alone with his own being and the reality of things. Do not permit the senses to argue, "But my brother is over there."

Oh, be merciful to what appears as yourself. Do not permit suggestion to say that you were born out there and now look at what you are — a victim of time. Jesus called it a murderer, for it is suggesting that Life begins. "Organization and time have nothing to do with Life." Be the eternal noon, undimmed by a declining sun or declining time-sense. Oh, be merciful and permit no personal sense of self to say I. See that the divine I, incorporeal, infinite, and supreme, is all that is present to say I. Oh, be merciful to what is called yourself and never permit suggestion to say, "Yes, but I am human now and I must work out from here." Be truly merciful now. See this insidious whisperer for what it is. If

you permit it to say I for you, then you have the hell of what
it has to give — limitation, frustration, inadequacies — a
truly loveless experience. But permitting the I that is God to
identify itself as the very I of your being, brings with it the
very heaven of His presence. God-given dominion comes
when we subordinate the false testimony to the true facts of
Science. Thus dominion comes when we permit Christian
Science to dispel the misty personal sense and accept the
glowing reality of true being.

"Blessed are the pure in heart: for they shall see
God." The only purity is I beholding what I AM. There
can be no purity in the dualistic attitude of God and man
as separate. Equipollence means equal at every point. Impurity is the suggestion of more than one — for instance,
God-substance and man-substance. All substance is God.
You lose your sense of purity when you admit there is another kind of mind called mortal or human. To be pure in
heart, pure in consciousness, is as Mary Baker Eddy once
said to a student, "I will not blaspheme the holy name of
God by admitting an imperfection in His creation." In order
to have the purity that is Mind, it is necessary to see that
one is never a person knowing of the one Mind; but the
knowing is the one and only Mind knowing itself. Even
though it appears as the knowing of that which you are
calling yourself, "It is I, be not afraid." It is most necessary
to keep clear on this important point. In order to have the
purity that sees God, it is necessary to see as God — not
something looking out of two holes called eyes and trying
to see the goodness and purity of God, the I of all being.
But looking through the eyes of Mind — spiritual discernment — and seeing right through the only eyes. These eyes
are not organs, not optical — they are the blessed eyes of
your own Christ-discernment. It is not a person looking
at another person trying to see the man of Principle. But
Principle alone present, and with its all-seeing, seeing its
own self-expression, man. This singleness of I is the bless-

edness. Is this not casting the mote out of thine own I?

"Blessed are the peacemakers: for they shall be called the children of God." The only peacemaker is seeing from the standpoint of one. There is no peace in the belief of two. "Principle and idea is one and this one is God, omnipresent, omniscient, and omnipresent Being, and His reflection is man and the universe." And one's reflection is man. Here is the Adorable One. And man is the adorableness or blessedness. Peace or oneness is an ever-present fact of being. The world is well aware of the failures of trying to get nations together, peoples together, families together, churches together, etc. There is no two-getherness in Christian Science. All is infinite, indivisible Mind and its infinite indivisible manifestation. Mrs. Eddy writes in *Miscellany*, "The infinite is one, and this one is Spirit; Spirit is God, and this God is infinite good." Get rid of the dualistic attitude of Principle and idea as two. "Let us rid ourselves of the belief that man is separated from God, and obey only the divine Principle, Life and Love." Peace must be from within. That is why the world has never attained it. The student is in a state of war when he accepts the suggestion that he is something besides divine idea, the very performing of Mind itself. When he believes that he knows both good and evil, then there is war — a state of contraries. Handle this daily!

"Blessed are they which are persecuted for righteousness' sake: for their's is the kingdom of heaven." Christ Jesus was persecuted because he made himself the son of God. There will be persecution as long as statements of Truth are made from the dualistic attitude of one's being a person knowing the Truth, and making a statement of Truth to that which does not know. This brings resistance. It is casting your pearls before the swinish human thought. But from the standpoint of Truth itself, there is no resistance nor persecution. Only personal sense can offer resistance or give it. Let the Truth utter itself because it is true. It is not trying to convince something outside of itself that is true. If you accept the suggestion that idea is something separated from Mind, there will be constant conflict in thought. Idea is Mind manifesting itself. It is the direct-ness of Mind. The immediacy of Mind. There is no veil between Principle and idea. See that there is no personal sense of I to make a divine utterance. This is what Jesus rebuked with Peter. Flesh and blood did not reveal it to Peter; but the Father — that is, Mind has declared itself in all its majesty and grandeur and might and freedom, for it has infinite accomplishment. Never resist what appears as another. That is nothing but animal magnetism misin-terpreting what is truly going on.

"Rejoice, and be exceeding glad: for great is your reward in heaven." Government by divine Principle, Love, brings the reward of being the kingdom of heaven itself.

Jesus now presented another facet of the diamond sermon, giving the essence of true being by referring to salt. He said, "Ye are the salt of the earth." Why did he use salt? Because it was a most common commodity in the household, and it was one that was a great necessity. Here they were down-trodden, under the yoke of foreign government, being taxed heavily, and yet here was Jesus saying, "Ye are the salt of the earth." Let us look deep into realism. *See that what you humanly appear to be is not important; but to know yourself from divine revelation — this is the salt*. Why not recognize your divinity? See your true worth as the son of God here and now — not something to be gained in the future, but *now*. When a little salt is added to food, it gives zest, substance. So it is to the one who even slightly recognizes that there is something divine concerning himself, here and now. The more salt that is added, the more will the divine reality appear. To lose the savor is to lose the glorious view of oneness as the son of God. To think of oneself as a person blessing other persons, working with other persons, living with others, trying to use Christian Science to bring about harmony, etc., is to have lost the savor, and it is then good for nothing but to be trodden under foot. Stop accepting the suggestion that there are two universes — one that is all right and one that is all wrong.

The moment that you think from the standpoint of idea being with other ideas, you have lost the savor of the salt. The salt is the I or Esse being what I AM. You lose the savor or essence when you think from the standpoint of idea. The only relationship is between Principle and idea, and never between ideas. There is no interrelationship. Even though it may appear to be another, it is always that I of your own being. "Thou shalt have nothing beside Me." See your brother's face as if it were the face of God. Love your neighbor as yourself. You lose the savor when you think in terms of another. If you believe there is another, you are always trying to adjust something or other, to tell them something, to share something, to help them, trying to make them understand. You are denying your own Christ-being and losing the savor of your own salt. But when you see that all there is to what is called another is the way God is expressing Himself at that moment, this is the language of true being. Then there will be no attempt to give salt, but to recognize that true worth is never personal. It is the I that is Love appearing to itself as itself. This is truly loving one's neighbor as one's self.

We lose the full savor of love if we think of something or someone as being loving, when God is Love. If we think of someone as beautiful, then we lose the savor of the beauty that is Soul. Thinking of someone as young or old, we lose the savor of true Life. Believing someone knows more than another, is to lose the savor of the oneness of Mind. It is to be trodden under foot, if it is personal. Be the salt that loses not its savor — the salt that is impersonal being. It is I being what I AM. When the truth is declared without love, and there is no joy — the salt has lost its savor. Truth declaring itself is the very being of joy. The gladness, joy, happiness well-ing up from within — this is the salt retaining its savor.

Here is another facet of the diamond sermon — *light*. "Let there be light" is recorded as the first command of Mind. In *Unity of Good*, Mrs. Eddy has God saying "Dwelling in light, I can see only the brightness of My own glory." What a wonderful word is light! Light never permits the multitude thought, the misconception, deception, distortion. Without light, there would be no form, color, etc. This true light "lighteth every man that cometh into the world." This truth of light prevents even that which appears as a human person from being entirely hopeless, destitute. If some light appears, it will dispel that which one is not. Let your light shine. All is reflection of the one and only light. Let your light shine that men may see your good works and praise the Father, the source of light. Never praise reflection, but always the source, Mind. Putting light under a basket is to believe the light to be personal. There is no such thing as a loving person. It is *Love* loving, even though it appears as a person loving. If this were not true, there would be no Love. A person is absolutely incapable of loving. Personal love can turn to hate, therefore it was never love. "Love never loses sight of loveliness" — this is the doctrine of Christian Science.

"Divine Science rolls back the clouds of error with the light of Truth, and lifts the curtain on man as never born and as never dying, but as coexistent with his creator." (*Science and Health*)

Mrs. Eddy asked, "What chased the clouds away?" It was Love. Jesus said, "I am the light of the world." Light and Love are one. "The light of ever present Love illumines the universe. The perfection of being, the beauty of holiness, all are mine for I am God," light. Without light, there is no reflection. When Jesus said, "Let your light so shine before men, that they may see your good works, and glorify your Father which is in heaven," was he not telling all to let this light of ever-present Love shine forth, and let it be your one and only being? Let this Love that is light so shine that all darkened sense, deflected sense, personal sense, will fade into its nothingness, and all will be brought into the sharp focus of divine reflection. This light must never be put under the bushel basket of personal sense.

This light that is Love knows no mine and thine. It knows nothing of a shadow called past, nothing of a dim perception called future. It knows only the full glow of its eternal noontide. Radiant, beautiful, resplendent, it holds all in the now of beauty. Its light is never deflected into what is called another. What a feeling to come into the presence of that consciousness that knows its own radiant divinity. Not a striving presence trying to love, but the radiancy of divine reflection. Surely this light is never put under a bushel basket, and hidden, and brought out only for the favored few. No, it is being the Gabriel — having the quietness and peace and ever-presence of ministering Love. The Gabriel has no contests. Why? Because it is His presence. The presence of infinite, ever-present Love sees nothing but its own immaculateness. But thinking in terms of personal sense is the bushel, and it limits and restricts and blights whatever it touches. Bushel means a measure. Don't measure good, truth, life, love by believing it is personal, limited, localized, etc. True Love never loses sight of loveliness. Oh, let your light shine. That is, recognize that the light that is God in its pure shining outshines any suggestion of an I besides God. Throughout the Bible, it speaks of light appearing, angels, stars, etc. The full appearing of light is called Holy Ghost. Look out from your own star, the light of revelation, and see that this is what I AM.

Law is another facet of the diamond. Christian Science has not come to abolish law. Christian Science is the law of God, interpreting the divine presence of universal harmony. It is the law that demands perfection and furnishes its own demand. Christian Science fulfills law. Man is the result of law, and not chance. Man is law embodied. Law does not operate in man's behalf — man is the law in being. There is nothing that can be done about it. Speak as law. Go to the case as law. See that day is lawful, proceeds as law and rests upon law. This day is Life expressing itself in accordance with law. Be the law to the malpractice that this is another day. This *is* day. Scribes and Pharisees believed themselves to be righteous because they followed what is called law. Actually this made them *self-righteous*. Self-righteousness judges from its own acts and standards. Christian Science judges no man. It says the harlot thought can go into the kingdom of heaven before the Pharisees. Why? Because the harlot thought sees that which needs to be corrected and corrects it. The self-righteous thought sees nothing in itself to correct. It sees only the other fellow's mote. Is this not why Mrs. Eddy wrote, "Make self-righteousness be still, break earth's stupid rest"? What is more stupid than to believe one's self a human person who can judge the actions of another? This is pure animal magnetism. But seeing thy brother's face as if it were the face of God, is true judging.

There is yet another facet — love for our brother. To be angry with one's brother, is to say, "Thou fool," and is to deny one's own Christliness. Never permit anything to deny the adorableness of all being. Only personal sense loves this and hates that. And personal sense is always a wrong or false sense. Lay your gift on the altar. The greatest gift is to see all from the attitude of the altar of the Christ. Altar means the starting point. So the starting point is that God, good, is All-in-all. Lay your earthly all on the altar of the Christ. Lay everything on the starting point. All must rest upon and proceed from divine Principle. There is no other altar. Here you lay your gift by seeing that your brother is the way the Father-Mother Love is appearing. This is the blessedness. Never leave your brother as a brother. See that what appears to be another is the functioning Christ, Mind, in self-expression.

"Agree with thine adversary quickly, whiles thou art in the way with him." Agree to disagree. Glossary defines "Adversary. An adversary is one who opposes, denies, disputes, not one who constructs and sustains reality and Truth. Jesus said of the devil, 'He was a murderer from the beginning. . . He is a liar and the father of it.' This view of Satan is confirmed by the name often conferred upon him in Scripture, the 'adversary.' Jesus acted boldly against the accredited evidence of the senses."

Adultery means to believe that something outside of yourself gives pleasure, happiness, etc. This is adulterating true being. In Christian Science, you cannot weigh evil against good, disease against health, poverty against wealth. In order to have the joy that is spiritual, ever aglow with the facets of our diamond sermon, we must cease to identify ourselves and what appears as others from the limited restricted viewpoint. Let the divine Principle of the universe interpret what is going on, and from this mount of revelation the joy that no man taketh away is ours. The Bible says, "Therefore with joy shall ye draw water out of the wells of salvation." This is the sinless joy that constitutes man. Then refuse to see or think of yourself as a person with some understanding of Christian Science, using this understanding to judge another. This is not getting rid of the mote that is in the eye. The only mote is to have a personal sense of I or ego. Casting this out, we are no longer concerned with what are called persons — no, not even what has been called our own. In referring to her own personality, Mrs. Eddy says, "It cannot think of me and I will not think of it." Also she says, "Nothing is more fatal than to indulge a sinning sense or consciousness for even one moment. Knowing this, obey Christ's Sermon on the Mount, even if you suffer for it in the first instance, — are misjudged and maligned; in the second, you will reign with him."

Cast the mote out of your own eye. Mote is not seeing clearly. Therefore cast out anything that denies simplicity and oneness. Never evaluate the happenings of daily experience according to educated belief, personal sense, etc., and call this good and that evil. This is the mote, or incorrect seeing. To demonstrate the nothingness of matter, it must be seen that matter is simply a misstatement, and not substance. This is it, is matter misstatement and not matter substance. Who said this is good and this is evil? "Who told thee that thou wast naked?" Educated belief.

Mrs. Eddy gives us many motes in the textbook as examples of this. Here is one: "Therefore, the only reality of sin, sickness or death is the awful fact that unrealities seem real to human, erring belief, until God strips off their disguise."

Here is another mote, "It is ignorance and false belief, based on a material sense of things, which hide spiritual beauty and goodness." You cannot possibly pull the mote out of your brother's eye, because what you are tempted to believe to be the mote in your brother's eye, is the beam in your own eye, your own lack of clear seeing. Admitting there is a brother with a beam, is malpractice. "Mortal mind produces its own phenomena, and then charges them to something else, — like a kitten glancing into the mirror at itself and thinking it sees another kitten." We also find in *Science and Health*, "Mortal mind sees what it believes as certainly as it believes what it sees." Christ Jesus said, "But I say unto you which hear, Love your enemies, do good to them which hate you. Bless them that curse you, and pray for them which despitefully use you."

Another mote relating to healing: You cannot help a patient if you admit the belief that what you think you see is a patient with a disease. What mortal mind is aggressively suggesting as a patient, is a false sense of man. When we give up the mote or false sense of man, the patient is no longer a patient. The only reason you can help what seems to be another, is because of the understanding that the patient is nothing but a lying suggestion claiming to have personalized itself and calling itself me, you, him, her, etc. The patient is nothing more than an evil suggestion claiming to be where you are, but suggesting it is going on "over there." In Christian Science practice, healing never goes on "over there." It is always within that the evil suggestion is handled as nothing, and what looks like "over there" is all right also.

In *Miscellaneous Writings*, we read, "Christian Science never healed a patient without proving with mathematical certainty that error, when found out, is two-thirds destroyed, and the remaining third kills itself. Do men whine over a nest of serpents, and post around it placards warning people not to stir up these reptiles because they have stings? Christ said, 'They shall take up serpents;' and 'Be ye therefore wise as serpents and harmless as doves.' The wisdom of a serpent is to hide itself. The wisdom of God, as revealed in Christian Science, brings the serpent out of its hole, handles it, and takes away its sting. Good deeds are harmless. He who has faith in woman's special adaptability to lead on Christian Science, will not be shocked when she puts her foot on the head of the serpent, as it biteth at the heel."

Mote: Keep the Christ-consciousness so hallowed that there will be no attempt to criticize what appears to be another. When it is necessary to point out some error in a church worker, do it with great love and never with a sense of personality. Whatever seems offensive will disappear in the presence of the Christ-consciousness maintained by church members.

"Whoever challenges the errors of others and cherishes his own," Mrs. Eddy writes, "can neither help himself nor others; he will be called a moral nuisance, a fungus, a microbe, a mouse gnawing at the vitals of humanity. The darkness in one's self must first be cast out, in order rightly to discern darkness or to reflect light." (*Miscellaneous Writings*) Don't be called a mouse.

Mote: "Behold I make all things new." What is this I that is holding what appears to be another in the past? Do not I fill heaven and earth? Is not this judging your own inability to maintain your own Christ vision, to be the I that is God?

Mote: The distinction between you and me is merely in a mortal mind concept. I do not find the word *you* or the word *me* in divine Mind. "Mine and thine are obsolete terms in absolute Christian Science." There is no you in Mind, there is only I. There is no me in Mind; there is only the I that is God. Thou shalt have nothing besides Me.

Mote: Cast out the suggestion that practitioner is knowing the Truth for the patient. Knowing is universal, and it is Truth knowing Truth and not *for* something. There is no personal nor impersonal patient to know the truth for. You cannot know the truth for a point in space called patient. So all-knowing is the all-knowing Mind knowing, and what Mind knows is its beloved son. Specific cases are healed much more quickly in universal knowing. You are in a realm of duality when you have two, teacher and pupil, practitioner and patient.

Mote called lack. The greatest lack is to identify yourself as person. Even that which it seems to have, shall be taken away. But identifying yourself as Mind's own abundance, a living witness to inexhaustible good, this fulfills the verse in the Bible, "To him that hath, shall be given, and to him that hath not, even the little that he hath shall be taken away."

Mote called envy. There is no occasion for envy. What appears to be another's good is your own good, if you refuse to accept the suggestion that it is "over there." The very fact that you are conscious of it, shows that you include it; and you include all right ideas. If a yacht is needed, it will appear. A train, plane, whatever is needed, will appear in the language that can be understood. Oh, get rid of the mote that it is over there and belongs to this one or to that one.

Mote: Never use Christian Science to bring something about, or something into being that does not exist. This is Judaism, trying to hold Spirit in the grasp of matter; this is the attempt to change the stones into bread. There is but one universe. You have two universes as long as you are trying to demonstrate something in Christian Science. This will bring with it a basic frustration.

Mote: Never accept the suggestion that you are a loving person, or a good student. Love is never personal, nor are there good students. "Why callest thou me good? There is none good but one: that is, God." Love is divine Principle. It is the most profound meaning for the word *God*. Love is the essence of being. See that there is no personal sense clamoring to be loved, wanting to be loved. See that Love is Principle; and all there is to idea, is this Love being. Man is not something knowing that Love is present. Man is Love knowing that it is Love — Love reflected in love. See that Mind never repeats itself. But this repetitional belief called mankind is mortal mind claiming to express itself in multitudinous ways.

Miscellany states: "God is one, and His idea, image, or likeness, man, is one. But God is infinite and so includes all in one. Man is the generic term for men and women. Man, as the idea or image and likeness of the infinite God, is a compound, complete idea or likeness of the infinite one, or one infinite, whose image is the reflection of all that is real and eternal in infinite identity. Gender means a kind. Hence mankind — in other words, a kind of man who is identified by sex — is the material, so-called man born of the flesh, and is not the spiritual man, created by God, Spirit, who made all that was made. The millennium is a state and stage of mental advancement, going on since ever time was. It's impetus, accelerated by the advent of Christian Science, is marked, and will increase till all men shall know Him (divine Love) from the least to the greatest, and one God and the brotherhood of man shall be known and acknowledged throughout the earth."

Mote: Do not have political convictions. Have spiritual convictions.

Mote: The human picture is not to be saved. It is to be seen that it is nothing more than a perverted picture of that which is one and indivisible, and it fades into its nothingness in the acknowledgment of true being.

Mote: Refuse to be petty — solving what are called personal problems. Feel universal Love. Be Love's divine adventure to be *all*. Enlarge your concept of treatment. It increases its effectiveness when it includes all. True healing is the yielding of the human to the divine.

Mote: Guard against thinking of persons, or of being personal. Mrs. Eddy says, "It is more important to know there is no personality than to know there is no disease." When treatment is impersonal enough, you give it all the power there is. Know the impersonality of the patient. Error is nothing, and must be seen to be nothing. In knowing that both truth and error are impersonal, you are not only giving treatment, but you are the living treatment.

Mote: Cast the mote out of the eye that says you are Northerner, Southerner, even a citizen of the United States. See that this is the land of Christian Science, where fetters fall and the rights of man are fully known and acknowledged. We are citizens of the world. Acknowledge man as the compound idea. This is being a citizen in the widest sense. This is generic man aware of his universality. Never localize nor finitize yourself.

This point is made in this passage from *Miscellaneous Writings*, "All loyal Christian Scientists hail with joy this proposed type of universal Love; not so, however, with error, which hates the bonds and methods of Truth, and shudders at the freedom, might, and majesty of Spirit, — even the annihilating law of Love."

Mote: Get rid of the mote of being a practitioner knowing the truth for a patient. This is living in the realm of belief. Truth knows, and this knowing is man.

Mote: Students living the Christ do not babble the letter. "It is the spirit that quickeneth; the flesh profiteth nothing."

Mote: Man is a prodigal, and the practitioner goes out into the far country and gets hold of him and brings him back to his Father's house. The moment you permit what appears to be your "i" going out after other little "i"s' to save them, you have become in belief the prodigal. Paul wrote to the Corinthians: "For this cause have I sent unto you Timotheus, who is my beloved son, and faithful in the Lord, who shall bring you into remembrance of my ways which be in Christ, as I teach everywhere in every church."

Mote: Personal understanding. Understanding is vital, limitless, forever teeming with its own vitality.

Mote: Rising above the religious belief that there are Hebrews, Greeks, Catholics, Protestants, etc. to the glorious fact of being Christian Scientists. Christ Jesus said, "Give not that which is holy unto the dogs, neither cast ye your pearls before swine." Never make statements of truth from the standpoint of I or the only Ego, to that which believes itself to be a person and is listening to what appears to be another person. *Know it, but talk it never.* Making statements from the standpoint of I to the unprepared thought, rouses the seven thunders of hate. Thinking from the standpoint of I itself, and thinking it is persons hearing persons making statements, is to give it to the dogs. Hearing what appears to be another saying, "I AM THAT I AM" is to rouse the thunders of hell for it will say, "He makes himself equal to God." When the statement is made from I itself, then there is only peace and quiet, for it is I making a statement concerning itself, and not a person making it about the only I. If you believe that you are a person or personal, you will say, "Mr. So-and-so said this or that." But this is evil suggestion. Only Truth can utter truth. "Of myself, I can say nothing." The woman at the well said, "Come see a man that told me all things." Jesus had endeavored to awaken her to her own Christ within by talking to her of the well within. But the unenlightened thought saw something outside saying this. He was a wonder worker. Watch this carefully. *Never quote.* See that it is Truth declaring itself. The statement obtains no authority by saying, "Mr. So-and-so said this." If a person said it, it is worthless and is to be trodden under foot. But to see that the salt lose not its saltness, see that it is only I or Ego stating itself correctly and spontaneously. It is your own withinness. It may appear that something up here is saying this or that, but never permit the personal sense to pervert the true appearing of your own Christ. Never give that which is holy to dogs; never give the subjective sense of I to the objective or personal sense.

Christ Jesus admonished his followers: "Beware of false prophets, which come to you in sheep's clothing, but inwardly they are ravening wolves." The suggestion that other systems are as good as Christian Science and easier to understand, must be totally rejected. Christian Science demands complete self-surrender. All others permit you to patch up the old and say it is good enough — you can keep the personal ego and still have truth. This is the wolf, and truly "I never knew you." I can only know what I AM — my own brightness.

The Sermon on the Mount includes the parable of those who wisely build their houses on the rock, and those who foolishly build on the sand. In the Glossary' of *Science and Health*, we find this definition: "Rock. Spiritual foundation; Truth." When Jesus asked his disciples, "Whom do men say that I the Son of man am?" they answered, "Some say that thou art John the Baptist; some Elias; and others Jeremias, or one of the prophets." Our wise Leader says that this was a suggestion that Jesus was a medium. And she continues, "This ghostly fancy was repeated by Herod himself. That a wicked king and debauched husband should have no high appreciation of divine Science and the great work of the Master, was not surprising; for how could such a sinner comprehend what the disciples did not fully understand?" In the marginal note, Mrs. Eddy calls this "Ancient spiritualism." Are we, students of this precious divine Science, free of modern spiritualism? Do we accept or reject the suggestion that we have loved someone, but in return received no love? That we have been good to someone, but have received no good? Is this not building our movement upon the shifting sands of personal sense?

Jesus knew that if he permitted his works to be built upon a personal understanding of either himself or his disciples, that these same shifting sands would soon cover his foundational work, and it would be lost to the ages again. Our Leader, in her article "Principle and Practice," sees the same danger facing the Christian Science movement. Is the healing work based upon something personal called practitioners, or is it the absence of the personal ego, and the I that is God, being what the I or Ego is? And what the Ego-God is, has been called the Ego-man. This is the precious foundation of Christian Science, and no other foundation can be laid than is already laid. It is the cornerstone of all church building. Our textbook continues: "His students saw this power of Truth heal the sick, cast out evil, raise the dead; but the ultimate of this wonderful work was not spiritually discerned, even by them, until after the crucifixion, when their immaculate Teacher stood before them, the victor over selfishness, sin, disease, death, and the grave." And is there any other teacher than the "immaculate Teacher?" Truly it is the immaculate One, the divine Mind "unfettered and uncontaminated by human hypothesis and divinely authorized." This is the Teacher, the divine Mind, stating itself, and what Mind states is its beloved Son, in whom the Father is well pleased. The reference continues: "Yearning to be understood, the Master repeated, 'But whom say ye that I am?' This renewed inquiry meant: Who or what is it that is able to do the work, so mysterious to the popular mind? . . . With his usual impetuosity, Simon replied for his brethren, and his reply set forth a great fact: 'Thou art the Christ, the Son of the living God!' That is, The Messiah is what thou hast declared, — Christ, the spirit of God, of Truth, Life, and Love, which heals mentally. This assertion elicited from Jesus the benediction, 'Blessed art thou, Simon Barjona: for flesh and blood hath not revealed it unto thee, but my Father which is in heaven;' that is, Love hath shown thee the way of Life."

Here is the foundation against which the winds and waves can shock, oh, nevermore. It is the only safe foundation upon which to build. It is to acknowledge fully and completely that one is the Christ-man, the divine manifestation, the direct expression, the immediacy of Love itself. There must be no hesitancy in accepting fully and completely one's Christliness. Let no false theological teaching interfere here. Let us burn completely all bridges behind us, so that there will be no timidity in accepting the great spiritual fact that I AM THAT I AM. "Have I been so long time with you, and yet hast thou not known me, Philip? he that hath seen me hath seen the Father."

Do not be afraid of what Christian Science teaches. Let no argument of the carnal mind, in its effort to per-petuate its fabulous existence, say, "This is going too far." One of our earlier lecturers said, "One of the things which prevents people from demonstrating the divine Mind as their own Mind, is the feeling that it is going a bit too far to expect that God should dwell among men and be their intelligence." We declare the divine presence of God, the only Mind, it is true; but even as a class we, as Christian Scientists, do not admit it. We do not believe it. If you say to a person, "Right thinking is not the action of a distant Mind, but is the evidence of a present Mind," he will ask, "What do you mean by that?" Then he will say to you,

"Look out! You are going too far." But nevertheless, it is true. There is only one Mind. Even though to mortal sense I may be thinking erroneously, that does not change the fact that the divine Mind is the only Mind that exists. The revelation of Christian Science has come to correct this mistake of thinking erroneously.

When Christian Science was young, and Mrs. Eddy had just begun to establish this movement, she would say that Mind is the Mind of man more absolutely, unequivocally and dogmatically than she does now. Now, she explains its meaning more, because some students began to say, "I am God," hoping thereby to claim divine power in such a way as to exercise omnipotence for their selfish ends. Consequently, Mrs. Eddy took great pains to show the difference between God and man, and we must never confuse it. However, in making that distinction, students have made a separation, all the while desiring oneness. We must see that Mind and idea is one, and then, that this one is Mind.

So returning to the above reference, when Peter replied, "Thou art the Christ, the Son of the living God," we have Jesus saying to Peter, "Blessed art thou, Simon Barjona: for flesh and blood hath not revealed it unto thee, but my Father which is in heaven" — that is, Love hath shown thee the way of Life. Jesus knew, even as the Discoverer of Christian Science knew, and all students must know, that revelation is divine Mind expressing itself, revealing itself. Flesh and blood cannot reveal the Truth of being. God must reveal Himself, and upon this revelation rests the Science of being. In the marginal note, we read "Divine response" — for truly it was a divine response. Nothing called Peter could have known the Christ of Jesus. It was the Christ of Peter that recognized itself as the one and only Christ. But we know the human tries to pervert this, and say some person did this or said that. It is always I, the only Ego. Then Jesus came forth with the true and living Rock, and said, "And I say also unto thee, That thou art Peter; and upon this rock I will build my church; and the gates of hell shall not prevail against it." In other words, Jesus purposed founding his society not on the personal Peter as a mortal, but on the God-power which lay behind Peter's confession of the true Messiah.

The Glossary of *Science and Health* gives the definition of Church: "The structure of Truth and Love; whatever rests upon and proceeds from divine Principle." That which proceeds from Principle is built upon the rock of divine, unvarying, unchanging Life, Truth, and Love. The gates of hell cannot prevail against this Church. That is, the belief in persons or personal interpretations cannot prevail in the presence of the knowing that Church is not constituted of persons banded together to "fight the good fight with all their might." Nor is this church constituted of persons "going as to war." This holy Church comes down from heaven. It is God-ordained, and God-established. In this Church, there are no persons praying to a far-off God, worshipping a God as "if He needed anything when he giveth to all Life, breath and all things." No, in this one and only Church, let all the earth (personal sense) be still.

Our Leader gives us many admonitions as to the need to guard against malpractice that would cause us to indulge in personal sense. The first admonition for spiritual self-defense is found in the *Church Manual* Art 8: Section 6, "It shall be the duty of every member of this Church to defend himself daily against aggressive mental suggestion." Daily means in perfect continuity. It has nothing to do with twenty-four hours. The definition of Day in the Glossary is: "The irradiance of Life; light, the spiritual idea of Truth and Love. . . The objects of time and sense disappear in the illumination of spiritual understanding, and Mind measures time according to the good that is unfolded. This unfolding is God's day, and 'there shall be no night there.'" Night, darkness, doubt, fear, the objects of time and sense, the beliefs of birth, age, and personal sense, shall disappear in this light of Truth. The aggressive mental suggestion that we are persons trying to know more of the one Mind, persons trying to live harmoniously with other persons, persons trying to be loved or wanting to love, persons trying to find happiness outside of oneself — all these aggressive mental suggestions must go down in this true concept of Church. The suggestions are the gates of hell that cannot prevail in that consciousness that knows from the standpoint of Mind itself. Your only defense is from the standpoint of Christ.

The aggressive mental suggestion that we are one of many, one of millions, brings with it the multitude thought and a crowded sense of day. See that there is only the one I or Ego present to self-express. "We" do not have to express God, the only Mind. Mind expresses itself, and this expression of itself is man, your only self. It is truly the Adorable One saying, I AM THAT I AM. As long as there is a personal sense of I, it can be made to forget, for forgetting belongs to the mind of mortals, the popular mind. I can never be made to forget what I am. The human concept of man, no matter how earnest and sincere it is, can be made to forget. For accepting the belief of personal sense and having a private mind or ego, brings with it all the hell of the human mind. It has nothing but hell to give; but the heaven of the knowing that the I of one's being is God itself! What peace, what love, what Church! Remembering one's duty to God, is to know now and here that there is only one I or Ego, only one Mind present to express itself. Our Leader is the Christ, for Mrs. Eddy says, "Follow your Leader, only so far as she follows Christ." To acknowledge the Christliness of man is our duty; our duty to mankind, is to see that even what appears to be mankind is not another kind of creation, but is the human mind misinterpreting the divine indivisible One.

Obedience to this By-law is not a person being obedient to another person. It is the constant alertness to this admonition that brings with it great freedom — freedom from the aggressive mental suggestion that we are persons, encased in mortal, finite, destructible bodies; that we are in rooms, in atmosphere, in this or that. It is a constant alertness and joyous knowing that this is truly the Church against which the gates of hell — personal sense — cannot prevail.

The second admonition is Article 8, Section 1: Rule for Motives and Acts. "Neither animosity nor mere personal attachment should impel the motives or acts of the members of The Mother Church. In Science, divine Love alone governs man; and a Christian Scientist reflects the sweet amenities of Love, in rebuking sin, in true brotherliness, charitableness, and forgiveness. The members of this Church should daily watch and pray to be delivered from all evil, from prophesying, judging, condemning, counseling, influencing or being influenced erroneously." There must be no personal attachment even though it parades around and says 'me.' What is this me? This me is mortal mind. See that mortal mind and body are one, and this one a myth — myth-man, myth-body. Whatever the nature of the problem that suggests itself, see that it is myth-man talking about its myth-body, but not about I AM. Surely there must be no personal attachment to the belief that one has a personal sense of ego. Let there be no personal attachment to church, home, parents, husband, wife, or children.

See everything in its true depiction: divine idea, included in what one divinely is already now and here. The language of the appearing will appear in grander form, but never leave the idea in the language. For it is here that the moth and rust can corrupt, and thieves break through and steal. Store all in heaven — that is, see it as proceeding from and resting upon divine Principle, Love. Have no attachment to the problem. See that it is not my problem, his problem, their problem or this or that church's problem. See that it is nothing more than a belief of the human mind — belief without a believer. When you see it is not a personal believer, you have detached it and it is seen as nothing. "You must see error to be nothing, for then and only then can you handle it in Christian Science." The whole purpose of Christian Science is to be free from the personal concept. In Science, divine Love alone governs its concept, man. Divine Love not only conceives its concept, man, but constitutes its idea. Then man is the loving of Love, the very embodiment of loveliness. This knowing rebukes the sin, the personal sense of I called you; this knowing is charitable for it sees its own purity; it is forgiving, for Mrs. Eddy interprets "Forgive us our debts" as "Love is reflected in love."

"The members of this Church" — this Church proceeding from divine Principle, Love, newborn of Spirit, bringing forth the fruits of Love — "should daily watch and pray to be delivered from all evil" — daily, continuously, watch to see that one is alone with his own being and with the reality of things, and prays with the joyous acknowledgment of I and my Father are one in being. This prayer delivers from the suggestion that one is a person, one of a series, one of a multitude, and wipes out prophesying, for all is in the eternal now. That which is to be, is now, and that which was, is now. It is the eternal now. Because of this, Jesus could say of his own Christ, "Before Abraham was, I am." In oneness, there is nothing to judge. Believing oneself to be a person judging the acts of another, is being the hypocrite — and Jesus pronounced that the harlots go into heaven before this type of thought. Knowing the oneness of Mind, there is nothing to counsel or be counseled. Just I knowing what I am — all-intelligent, all-wise, all-knowing. In this true sense of being, there is nothing outside to influence or be influenced — just I being My expression.

The third admonition is found in the Daily Prayer: "'Thy kingdom come;' let the reign of divine Truth, Life, and Love be established in me, and rule out of me all sin; and may Thy Word enrich the affections of all mankind, and govern them!" Here is the acknowledgment of the indivisibility of Principle and idea. This prayer is true knowing and it is Church, for it proceeds from and rests upon Mind's own self-knowing.

"Thy kingdom come." Man is the kingdom that is come, the very manifestation of the I that is God-Love. "Let the reign of divine Truth, Life and Love be established in me." Truth, Life, and Love established, is Christian Science. This Truth, Life, and Love self-expressing itself as Science is man. Man is Christian Science in being. Our books ask the question "What is His name?" and answers it, "Christian Science." Then we are no longer named by what are called parents.

All malpractice is based upon the belief that one is a person with a personal name to distinguish one from all others. This is not Christian Science. In Christian Science, there is no "another." "The Christian Scientist is alone with his own being and with the reality of things." In this aloneness, there is only the one name to be hallowed forever — the Adorable One. Man's name then proceeds from and rests upon the divine Principle, Love. This is the new name promised in the Bible. This new name is independent of time, place, space or circumstance. In Philippians, we read, "God also hath highly exalted him, and given him a name which is above every name: That at the name of Jesus every knee should bow." In the presence of this new name, every named disease, even the names of fear, doubt, or envy, shall all bow down to the Christ-name. Truly, this is thy kingdom which is come. Students of this precious Science have left all for the Christ-name.

In *Miscellaneous Writings*, we read this: "Christian Scientists bring forth the fruits of Spirit, not flesh; and God giveth this 'new name' to no man who honors Him not by positive proof of trustworthiness." Bringing forth the fruits of Spirit or Love is given the name Church — as we find in the Hymnal, "O God, our Father-Mother, Thy name we see expressed by man, who in Thy Science is perfect, holy, blessed." Oh, may the student be worthy of the name — that is, the Science of Christ. Truly then your name is hallowed. Thus the reign of divine Life, Truth and Love is established and has ruled out of the personal sense of me all presence, identity or reality. All that is present to say I, is the Great I AM, that is all-seeing, all-knowing, all-acting, all-loving; and what this great and only I AM is doing, seeing, saying, loving, is called the beloved son. This knowing, seeing, and loving enriches even that which appears to be mankind. This daily knowing establishes the kingdom, the Church, upon the Rock of Christ, and from this Rock comes the living waters. Drinking deep of this water, quenches all longing, all desire, and leaves a deep and satisfying peace — no personal ego, but the I that is God being the I that is man. Truly this is the daily prayer.

The fourth admonition is found in the *Manual*, Article XVII, Section 2: "Gratitude and love should abide in every heart each day of all the years." Gratitude is the warm feeling that permeates all true being. This warmth of feeling, this gracious feeling, is Soul identifying itself, and this warmth and grace is man. It is your one and only Self. The heart of Christian Science is the uninterrupted now of eternal Life — Life uninterrupted by suggestions of separation called birth and death. This knowing that Life is never attained through birth, leads one deeper and deeper into the great heart of Love where all sense of persons, places, and things are forever dispelled. Truly, this is living the day where the objects of time and sense disappear. From this great heart of Love, this warmth and depth of feeling, one looks out on his universe and sees the loveliness of love is all around. One feels and is the love that never loses sight of loveliness; he is not something knowing that God is Love, but being the feeling of Love itself. This is the palpitating presence of the Christ-Love.

Then the admonition comes, "Let the dead bury their dead" — have no consciousness of a yesterday filled with success or failure; no consciousness of a yesterday from which stems all habits, routines, prejudices, etc. Let the dead yesterday bury itself, and it is buried forever — this is the presence of the consciousness that knows only *now*. There has never been a yesterday in which to be born, a tomorrow in which to die. There is only the uninterrupted consciousness of Life itself. No dead yesterdays nor unborn tomorrows, but the joyous consciousness of *now* — undimmed by a declining sun. The eternal aliveness of *now*. The freshness of *now*. In this, there is no unforgiven debt — only Love reflected in love. In obedience to this By-law, we leave all for the Christ and "follow thou me." This true sense of I exemplified the risen Lord, with all stones rolled away — the stones of the dead past, the stones of uncertain future. The true knowing of I AM turns all stones into bread — the bread that cometh down from Heaven. Even the stones of memory are dispelled in the presence of the risen Lord, in the presence of the knowing that I AM THAT I AM. Then one finds that man is the heart of Love, and truly gratitude fills this heart everyday in its unbroken continuity of now.

In *Science and Health*, we find the following: "Jesus beheld in Science the perfect man, who appeared to him where sinning mortal man appears to mortals. In this perfect man the Saviour saw God's own likeness, and this correct view of man healed the sick. Thus Jesus taught that the kingdom of God is intact, universal, and that man is pure and holy. Man is not a material habitation for Soul; he is himself spiritual. Soul, being Spirit, is seen in nothing imperfect nor material."

And in *Unity of Good*, Mrs. Eddy writes: "Good. All consciousness is Mind; and Mind is God, — an infinite, and not a finite consciousness. This consciousness is reflected in individual consciousness, or man, whose source is infinite Mind. . . "

"God is All-in-all. Hence He is in Himself only, in His own nature and character, and is perfect being, or consciousness. He is all the Life and Mind there is or can be."

"Through the eternal reality of existence I reach, in thought, a glorified consciousness of the only living God and the genuine man."

Our fifth admonition is found in *The First Church of Christ*, where we read, "To Christian Scientists: Take Notice. See Science and Health, page 442, line 30, and give daily attention thereto." What does page 442, line 30 say that is so important that our Leader admonishes us to give daily attention thereto? "Christian Scientists, be a law to yourselves that mental malpractice cannot harm you either when asleep or when awake." What is this mental malpractice that we are to be the law unto? Mrs. Eddy asks the question, "What is mental malpractice?" and answers it "A bland denial of Truth." What is this bland denial of Truth? Is it not the aggressive mental suggestion that we are persons with minds and souls rather than the divine, direct manifestation of Mind itself? This true understanding, or the Ego, is the law to the bland denial that there is a personal ego present. "Thou shalt have no other gods before Me." Thou shalt have no sense of a personal ego. There is but one I, even God, including both its cause and effect aspect. Be the law to the belief that one is trying, striving, to demonstrate Christian Science. Be the law by knowing that Love, by the nature of its infinitude, is present and is a law of annihilation to the suggestion that fear and hate are present.

If you look into a mirror and accept the suggestion that you are seeing yourself, this is mental malpractice. What is called the mental malpractice of what is called another is harmless. It is what is called your own malpractice that must be watched. How is the I used? Watch it and see.

Never permit the personal sense of I to make a statement. Let it always be from the I AM THAT I AM. Our Leader calls this personal sense of I a myth, and it must, of its own consent, yield to Truth. This personal sense of I, being a myth, can never be logical; it must always be mythological. The dictionary has this: "Logic. Reasoning correctly; follows as a reasonable inference." And "Myth: Purely fictitious narrative concerning natural phenomena." Nehemiah said to this myth I or ego, "There are no such things done as thou sayest, but thou feignest them out of thine own heart."

Someone once said, "In our mastering of the myth let us remember that our Leader gives us the pattern of conquest when she says that the myth-mind must by its own consent yield to Truth." Not should, or could, or might yield, but *must*. Through battle? Through argument? Through weight of numbers? No, for the Word of Revelation to this age says in the textbooks "by its own consent."

In our work let us realize that we do not have to outsmart, out-fight, out-argue a myth-mind. "The exterminator of error is the great Truth that God, good, is the only Mind, and that the supposititious opposite of infinite Mind — called devil or evil — is not Mind, is not Truth, but error, without intelligence or reality." This myth-I then fades into its nothingness in the presence of reality. All is in reality the manifestation of Mind, the only I. Then let us be the law to the malpractice that one is a superior person, an inferior person, a white person, or a black person, a student of this teacher or that teacher. Do not our books say under the heading of "Foundation stones," "Whatever divides Mind into minds misstates Christian Science"? Whatever says egos instead of I AM misstates, and it is this misstatement that we are to be the law unto. Malpractice is thinking in terms of persons rather than from the standpoint of I itself. It is being egotistical rather than egoistic, objective and exclusive rather than subjective and inclusive.

Believing that a practitioner here is knowing the Truth for a patient over there, is malpractice. Believing that one is a member of a branch church, working with many others, is malpractice or bad practice. For did not Jesus say that his Church was built on the Rock of Christ? Then being the law to the bad practice of seeing many, is seeing from the standpoint of Christ itself. This is truly living Church. This is being the City of God. Never practice incorrectly on yourself by believing that you have once been a human being, but now you are divine idea, the directness of Mind itself.

Some students are not handling malpractice. They are permitting it to handle them. They speak and talk from the standpoint of the I that is God, and live as good human beings, bad human beings. If you identify yourself with the personal ego, you are accepting the whole of the carnal mind and its myth-mindedness. If you seem to find this going on, instantly know that this is not the I of my being. It is nothing but Lucifer claiming to sit on the throne of God; it is nothing but the whispering serpent, the devil, nothing claiming to be something. It must be seen for what it is. It must not be ignored.

So be the law — not persons awake or asleep — not persons masking the divine, not persons at all — but Love's deep satisfaction that it is *all*. This is being the law.

The sixth admonition is found in *Miscellaneous Writings*: "One thing I have greatly desired, and again earnestly request, namely, that Christian Scientists, here and elsewhere, pray daily for themselves; not verbally, nor on bended knee, but mentally, meekly, and importunately. When a hungry heart petitions the divine Father-Mother God for bread, it is not given a stone — but more grace, obedience, and love. If this heart, humble and trustful, faithfully asks divine Love to feed it with the bread of heaven, health, holiness, it will be conformed to a fitness to receive the answer to its desire; then will flow into it the 'river of His pleasure,' the tributary of divine Love, and great growth in Christian Science will follow, — even that joy which finds one's own in another's good."

SEE OVER
FOR
ORDERING INFORMATION

TO ORDER

To acquire additional copies of *Selected Addresses of Clarence Steves, C.S.B.*, you may order from your local bookstore (have them check in "Books in Print"), Amazon.com, or contact the publisher:

Healing Unlimited
(800) 962-1464
email: *heal@ChristianScience.org*
www.ChristianScience.org

Price is $16.95US each or equivalent. Quantity discounts are available. Please check with each distributor for appropriate shipping charges. Contact the above organizations for a catalog of their offerings. Prices are as of January, 2006, and subject to change.

67829301R00202

Made in the USA
Charleston, SC
22 February 2017